The Written Suburb

University of Pennsylvania Press

Series in Contemporary Ethnography

Dan Rose and Paul Stoller, General Editors

Camille Bacon-Smith. *Enterprising Women: Television Fandom and the Creation of Popular Myth*. 1991

Robert Desjarlais. *The Aesthetics of Esperience: Emotions, Healing, and the Sentient Body in the Nepal Himalayas*. 1992

John D. Dorst. *The Written Suburb: An American Site, An Ethnographic Dilemma*. 1989

Douglas E. Foley. *Learning Capitalist Culture: Deep in the Heart of Tejas*. 1990

Kirin Narayan. *Storytellers, Saints, and Scoundrels: Folk Narrative in Hindu Religious Teaching*. 1989

Sally Ann Ness. *Body, Movement, and Culture: Kinesthetic and Visual Symbolism in a Philippine Community*. 1992

Dan Rose. *Patterns of American Culture: Ethnography and Estrangement*. 1989

Paul Stoller. *The Taste of Ethnographic Things: The Senses in Anthropology*. 1989

Edith Turner, with William Blodgett, Singleton Kahona, and Fideli Benwa. *Experiencing Ritual: A New Interpretation of African Healing*. 1992

Jim Wafer. *The Taste of Blood: Spirit Possession in Brazilian Candomblé*. 1991

THE WRITTEN SUBURB

An American Site, An Ethnographic Dilemma

John D. Dorst

UNIVERSITY OF
PENNSYLVANIA PRESS

Philadelphia

Permission is acknowledged for use of previously published material:

"An American Vision: Three Generations of Wyeth Art," advertisement in *Time Magazine*, March 11, 1987. Reprinted by permission of AT&T.

Quotations from publications copyrighted © Brandywine Conservancy. Reprinted by permission of the Conservancy.

Quotations from *Chris: A Biography of Christian C. Sanderson*, copyright © Thomas R. Thompson. Reprinted by permission of Thomas R. Thompson.

Postcard photographs (Chapter 1, Figures 14, 15) by Ernst Beadle. Reproduced by courtesy of *House and Garden*, copyright © 1973 by The Condé-Nast Publications, Inc.

Copyright © 1989 by the University of Pennsylvania Press
All rights reserved
Printed in the United States of America

Library of Congress Cataloging-in-Publication Data

Dorst, John Darwin.
   The written suburb : an American site, an ethnographic dilemma / John D. Dorst.
      p.   cm. – (University of Pennsylvania Press contemporary ethnography series)
   Bibliography: p.
   Includes index.
   ISBN 0-8122-8160-8. — ISBN 0-8122-1282-7 (pbk.)
   1. Chadds Ford (Pa.)—Social life and customs. 2. Suburban life—Pennsylvania—Chadds Ford. 3. Suburban life—United States—Case studies. 4. Postmodernism—Pennsylvania—Chadds Ford. 5. Postmodernism—United States—Case studies. 6. Tourist trade—Pennsylvania—Chadds Ford. 7. Tourist trade—United States—Case studies. 8. Ethnology—Pennsylvania—Chadds Ford. 9. Ethnology—United States—Case studies. I. Title. II. Series.
F159.C33D67   1989
974.8'14—dc19   88-37485
                                                            CIP

Third paperback printing 1994

For my parents

Contents

Illustrations

FIGURES

Chapter 1

Chapter 3

Chapter 4

Chapter 5

MAPS

Chapter 1

Chapter 4

Chapter 5

Acknowledgments

It is with real pleasure that I take this chance to name the institutions and individuals who contributed in various ways to the production of this study. I will no doubt overlook some who are worthy of mention. To them, my apologies.

The University of Wyoming's College of Arts and Sciences provided me a summer faculty development grant in 1985, which allowed an extended return trip to Chadds Ford. The College also provided a release from teaching for a semester, without which I could not have completed a first draft. The University of Wyoming American Studies Program, under the directorship of Eric Sandeen, defrayed expenses that would have prevented me from including some of the material published here. During the period of my original fieldwork, the Chadds Ford Historical Society provided indispensable assistance. Maps 3 through 5 in Chapter 1 were provided by that organization. All the maps in Chapter 1 were expertly drafted by Linda Marsden at the University of Wyoming Cartographic Services. The text of the print advertisement for the international exhibit of Wyeth art (Chapter 3) is quoted by permission of AT&T. The four postcard images of the Brandywine River Museum (Chapter 1, Figures 14 and 15) are courtesy of *House and Garden*, copyright © 1973 by The Condé-Nast Publications, Inc.

Of my Chadds Ford informants, several deserve special mention. These include Joseph Messersmith, Virginia Johnson, George Heebner, and above all Thomas R. Thompson. Mr. Thompson deserves my personal thanks for his consistent willingness to assist me in my work. But I would also like to acknowledge a more general debt of gratitude for his own work in keeping alive one of those idiosyncratic voices, Chris Sanderson's, that our current cultural order seems bent on suppressing.

I am most grateful to Susan Stewart, Dean MacCannell, and Paul Stoller, all of whom provided extensive comments on the first draft of this text. Their advice was sage and for the most part I have followed it. My thanks as well to Janice Radway, who read through the text. The staff at Penn Press, most notably Patricia Smith and Alison Anderson, also deserve my thanks for the combination of their prompt assistance when I needed it and their willingness to let me go my own way.

A number of friends, some of them my former teachers, others my colleagues, participated directly or indirectly in this text. My special thanks to Henry Glassie, John Szwed, Eric Sandeen, Mark Booth, Madonne Miner, John Warnock, Tilly Warnock, Cedric Reverand, and Susan G. Davis. Above all I want to acknowledge with affection my friends Robert Horan, Samuel Schrager, and Robert Torry. Many conversations with them over periods of years have influenced this study in ways that I'm sure neither they nor I suspect.

Finally, I reserve my deepest gratitude for two people, Dan Rose and Holly Combes Dorst. Dan aimed me in the direction of Chadds Ford in the first place and has sustained an interest in my work for going on a decade now. It is no longer possible for me to separate our shared scholarly interests from our friendship, which I cherish.

Holly's contribution to this book is so out of proportion to my ability to acknowledge it that to say more would only trivialize what she has meant to me. I hope she knows.

Introduction: Postmodernity as an Ethnographic Dilemma

A "POST-ETHNOGRAPHIC" SNAPSHOT

The scene is the rolling, wooded landscape along the back roads of the middle Brandywine River Valley in southeastern Pennsylvania. A car is parked at the entrance of the lane leading into Spring Meadows, one of the fancier housing developments in a region generally known as Chadds Ford. Spring Meadows is designed according to the deep-suburban principle of "cluster housing," with expensive spec and custom homes in various traditional/rustic styles gathered on one part of the development property, the rest left as open space to be shared by all the residents. The car's owner is there by the road. He aims a camera, photographing across the open space, across the pond and its surrounding marshy ground, toward the grassy hillside and the houses farther up.

He is, it turns out, Bob S———, president of the Spring Meadows community association, which among other things determines how the open space will be managed and what look will be cultivated there. He is interested in local history and has even informed himself about the farm from which Spring Meadows was carved (the original farmhouse and barn have been preserved). As far as he is concerned, Spring Meadows realizes a suburban ideal. It embodies the essence of the Chadds Ford look, "open, rolling, and green," and the spirit of rural community, typified by a general sociability among development residents and contrasting to the "cliqueishness" of some of the older developments in the area. He has driven out along the entrance road on his day off to photograph his own house, a "New England colonial with saltbox roofline." His snapshots will reproduce a conventional visual rhetoric found in countless postcards, amateur and professional paintings, tourist advertising, and real estate brochures.

Claude Lévi-Strauss seems to have believed that the modern western world defies ethnographic documentation, that it is simply too complex to grasp in this way (MacCannell 1976:1, Clifford 1988:237–246). One could argue that this complexity tends increasingly toward the formation of cultural/social enclaves—interest groups, lifestyles, leisure cohorts, recreational movements, etc.—that, although physically dispersed, resemble in many ways the insular entities that have always been ethnography's stock in trade. If our advanced consumer culture cannot be described as a totality, perhaps it can be documented piecemeal as an archipelago of lifestyle islands.

But there is another way, I believe more fundamental, by which the modern western world defies, or at least seriously complicates, the ethnographic enterprise. Lévi-Strauss's sense of the limitations of ethnography under current historical conditions is based on a quantitative principle. There is just too much stuff—forces, institutions, social relations and roles, and so on. The dilemma might be viewed more profitably in qualitative terms. A profound transformation has occurred in the very structure of cultural production over, say, the last three decades in the west, and this tectonic shift renders thoroughly problematic the ethnographic enterprise as professionally practiced. To put it in a formula, the culture of advanced consumer capitalism or, less acceptable but more fashionable, postmodernity, consists largely in the processes of self-inscription, indigenous self-documentation and endlessly reflexive simulation. Theorists of ethnographic representation have for some time now acknowledged that all cultures generate texts about themselves (taking "text" in an expanded sense),[1] but postmodernity virtually consists of this activity. It "spontaneously" does for itself, and massively so, the sort of thing ethnographers and other species of documentarist claim to do. In fact postmodernity is definable as a historical formation precisely by this activity. If the task of ethnography can be described as the inscription and interpretation of culture, then postmodernity seems to render the professional ethnographer superfluous. By its very nature postmodernity abolishes a conceptual distinction traditional ethnography relies upon, that is, the distinction between the site of ethnographic experience/observation and the site of ethnographic writing. Whole institutions central to the postmodern order, mass marketing and advertising for example, engage in ethnographic research and generate countless ethnographic texts. More modestly but perhaps in the end more profoundly, the impulse for self-documentation and the reproduction of images of the self pervade our everyday practice. The suburban photographer by the roadside is a postmodern paradigm.

The specific subject of the following chapters is Chadds Ford, Pennsylvania. For several decades, up until 1957, the Chadds Ford community was served by a mercantile establishment we would be likely to call a general store, though it was known to natives just as Work's store. Its site today is occupied by a Sunoco station. In the early 1980s a small building, little more than a shed, near the center of Chadds Ford village was refurbished with wooden plank siding and a shake roof. Outfitted as a gift/souvenir shop, a sign went up announcing it as The General Store. The change reflected in this "displacement" of Work's store by "The General Store" is a small parable, diagnostic of the emergence of postmodernity in Chadds Ford. Throughout the following pages I will refer to Chadds Ford as a Site, indicating with the upper case my focus upon this "place" as a postmodern phenomenon. For my purposes its existence as a geographical region or a kind of community are secondary to its existence as a particularly vivid staging of advanced consumer culture. That means I will be centrally concerned with Chadds Ford as an image, an idea, an ideological discourse, an assemblage of texts. This is the focus I mean to signify with the word Site.

In more conventional social terms, Chadds Ford's postmodernity is institutionally manifest in two ways. First, it is a tourist site. Growing legions travel there to expend their leisure time. The nature of its attractions, the sights to be seen there, figure prominently in what follows. Second, Chadds Ford is suburban. It has been suggested that the anthropological study of contemporary America requires going to the "symbolic suburbs," emblem for the locus of core American values and themes (Varenne 1986:39). For my purposes I would recast that view by inverting and generalizing it. What makes the contemporary suburb a privileged Site of postmodernity is the way it foregrounds in everyday life the pervasiveness of the commodity form, of the simulacrum, of spectacle and an economy of sign exchange, to borrow some of the designations that have been assigned to the conditions of late consumer capitalism (Baudrillard 1981; Debord 1970). The suburb is the emblem in social life not of some cultural core with an identifiable content, but of the de-centered condition of postmodernity in general.

As both a tourist site and a suburb, Chadds Ford forces itself on the attention of someone interested in the documentation of our contemporary social order. From the perspective of postmodernity, these two social forms, tourism and suburbanism, can in fact be seen merely as transforms of one another—the suburb a kind of sedentary tourism of one's own everyday self, and tourism a mobile suburb devoted to the endlessly deferred accomplishment of that self as fully present and authentic. In terms of ethnographic theory, one shared feature of tourism and suburbanism, a feature foregrounded in Chadds Ford, is especially important. Both carry to a kind of extreme the privileging of visual experience. They share the snapshot as their definitive genre. Our roadside photographer is a tourist of his own suburban environment. Chadds Ford is above all something one looks at—a kind of landscape, an historical vista, a collection of museums and historic houses to peruse, a collection of architectural styles and allusions, an endless flow of photographs, paintings, postcards, and so on.

These visually coded texts can be profitably thought of as "auto-ethnographies," and Chadds Ford's cultural production in general we can regard as a perpetual flow of auto-ethnographic practice. The ceaseless reproduction of images of itself is its definitive activity. In *The Tourist*, an important book for the issues of concern here, Dean MacCannell identifies tourism as a massive project of collective ethnography, characterized generally by the marking of sites. It is no accident that Chadds Ford is a site in this touristic sense. Elsewhere MacCannell (1979) suggests that such things as road systems might be seen as ethnographic inscriptions, ethnographies that institutions and structures of power write about themselves.[2] The automobile is then a kind of stylus, and in my driving and redriving the Chadds Ford roads a kind of inscription was underway. I take this "auto-writing" as a paradigm case of the much more general postmodern practice of self-inscription conducted by institutions.

And "auto-ethnography" also implies "automatic." Such texts generally appear as if from nowhere, apparently free of any premeditation or labor. The Chadds Ford of this study constitutes itself precisely in such "spontaneous" auto-ethnographic practice. It is this Chadds Ford, the Site conceived of as a textual effect, that radically disrupts the role of the professional scholar/ethnographer, a subject I will return to in my conclusion.

The arrangement of the following chapters reflects an approach that I think is one kind of response to the ethnographic dilemma posed by the cultural conditions of advanced consumer capitalism. Chapter 1 is a collection and arrangement of fragments, a gathering of such auto-ethnographies as I have just referred to. Given the pervasiveness of tourism at my Site and the blurring of the line between ethnography and tourism that postmodernity entails, it seemed appropriate to consider this assemblage a set of Chadds Ford "souvenirs." It represents problematize the intentionality of creating souvenirs

TWI BB
TWI SENT B

the collection/collage function that constitutes one pole of what, for the sake of provocation and lack of a better term, I am calling post-ethnographic practice.

This particular collection includes things that are quite literally auto-ethnographies and souvenirs—postcards, texts from brochures, the words of Chadds Ford natives, an overview of local history from the back of a menu. These were in effect gathered up and "pasted in." Among the other fragments are maps and published statistics, excerpts from travel literature, fiction and popular history, photographs, repro-ductions of paintings, and my verbal representations of objects, scenes and events. Although I attempted to keep this chapter as much a "simple" collection as possible, I found myself unable to eliminate exegesis entirely. In keeping with the general premise of this study though, when interpretive commentary creeps in it should be read as just another textual fragment of the same order as the other souvenirs, another item in the collection.

Chapter 2 offers an historical overview, spanning the last thirty years, of the emergence and transformation of some key Chadds Ford institutions. I focus particularly on the local community celebration, Chadds Ford Days, as a barometer of fundamental shifts in the nature of cultural pro-duction at the Site. The transformation of this event registers quite vividly the inauguration of postmodernity as the hegemonic order in this deep suburb.

Chapter 3 constitutes a theoretical interlude. There I survey some of the current and for my purposes most useful commentary on postmoder-nity as a historical formation. Although this theoretical discourse is in-dispensable to a rethinking of ethnographic representation, it is generally conducted at a level of abstraction that obscures specific processes, forces and currents in the operation of advanced consumer culture. In the interest of adapting this abstract theory to a specific Site, I identify in the second part of Chapter 3 two basic rhetorical patterns that I think are especially characteristic of Chadds Ford's postmodern discourse. I am calling them vignette and veneer. Also in this chapter I identify what seems to me the signature theme of Chadds Ford cultural production, a theme pervasive in the souvenirs assembled in Chapter 1. I am calling it the myth of Tradition.

Chapters 4 and 5 apply the ideas developed in Chapter 3 to critical readings of some specific institutional texts. This activity of critical read-ing, along with the collection/arrangement function reflected in Chapter 1, constitute the poles of a dialectic which I identify with post-ethnographic practice. In Chapter 4 I return to Chadds Ford Days to show how in its current form it enacts the sort of flattened, hermetic ("imploded," "televisual") space typical of postmodernity. Although ostensibly a celebration of Chadds Ford's rich history and traditions, it is in fact this Site's most complete staging of advanced consumer culture.

Chapter 5 consists of a comparative reading of the gallery displays at two Chadds Ford museums, The Brandywine River Museum and the Christian C. Sanderson Museum, the former a primary institutional agent of the postmodern hegemony, the latter a marginal, largely unincorporated element in the contemporary discourse of the Site. The Brandywine River Museum is the official arbiter of the "Brandywine Heritage" of art, central to which is the monumental figure of Andrew Wyeth. Wyeth lives half the year in Chadds Ford and his paintings more than any other single thing codify the image of this Site. Chris Sanderson was a local school teacher who amassed a stunning collection of tourist souvenirs, personal memorabilia and historical fragments. The museum named for him is his former house turned into a gallery crammed with these oddments and curiosities. The juxtaposition of these two institutional texts constitutes a kind of allegory of hegemony/counter-hegemony and is meant to foreground the critical potential of post-ethnographic practice.

In the conclusion I return to the general theoretical dilemma that postmodernity poses to ethnography and lay out abstractly how the methods employed in this case study constitute one possible response.

Perhaps it is prudent to end this introduction with a caveat. While some of what follows conforms, at least superficially, to the conventions of "traditional" ethnographic documentation, it departs from most ethnography in one fundamental and obvious respect: This is not an attempt to "get close to," to understand and to describe the culture, values or world view of a certain set of people. It is by no means an account of daily life and experience in the deep suburbs. In fact, insofar as it is an account of postmodern practice at a Site, it *cannot* be this sort of ethnography. To state epigrammatically a point I will expand on in Chapter 3 and the conclusion, the destabilization of subjectivity (the much-rehearsed "de-centered Subject") that virtually defines the postmodern moment short-circuits received ethnographic practice. Even at its most "dialogic," ethnography has always depended upon the presupposition of centered subjects. What follows can be taken as an attempt to answer the question: How might one proceed ethnographically if the notion of stable subjectivity is perceived as a problem rather than assumed as a premise?

NOTES

1. This is the basic premise in the wholesale rethinking of ethnographic writing currently under way. Most of the relevant issues are raised in the volume *Writing Culture: The Poetics and Politics of Ethnography* (Clifford and Marcus, eds. 1986). See especially the essays by Clifford (98–121) and Rabinow (234–261).

2. MacCannell observes (1979:163) that increasingly ethnographic texts "are not written by anthropologists but by machines and institutions." He also suggests that under current historical conditions "the role of the ethnographer is ...effaced." The present study is indebted at several points to MacCannell's work.

1 | *Chadds Ford Souvenirs*

...the rest would be fragments of cloth, bits of cotton, lumps of earth, records of speech, pieces of wood and iron, phials of odors, plates of food and ...

James Agee,
Let Us Now Praise Famous Men

I

After five consecutive cold, rainy weekends, our Philadelphia apartment felt like a crowded elevator. Tempers and frustrations rose higher than the piles of soggy gloves. Casually I mentioned getting away for the weekend, "somewhere close by where we can..." when all three children started talking at once.

"Go skiing!" son Pete shouted.

"No!" pleaded daughter Ann. "I have a report due in art. I have to spend Saturday at a gallery."

Susan announced, "Saturday is my birthday, and Dad promised to take me to a French restaurant."

Just before the discussion broke into bedlam, their father came in from the den. "Let's go. I know a place where we can do all those things, and it's not far away."

Being a skeptic, I said, "Henry, if you find a place that will keep everybody happy, even I'll take skiing lessons."

Before I could change my mind, Henry said, "You're on. We're going to Chadds Ford." By the smile on his face I knew I had spoken too soon. As I helped pack the car, I wondered what I'd look like in traction.

Chadds Ford is only 28 miles southwest of Philadelphia. A gallon and a half of gasoline took us away from the bleak winter skyline of the city to the open country of Chester County.

At one time Chadds Ford was just one of many tiny Revolutionary towns along the Brandywine River. The rolling hills of southern Pennsylvania are studded with 18th century inns, old covered bridges, the neat, solid architecture of early German and Quaker settlers. Being art buffs, we immediately recognized the white winter landscape immortalized by Andrew Wyeth in his paintings. Nestled in the hip pocket of Chester County, Chadds Ford has changed little in the past century. Although it is now a well known art center, it has retained its small town flavor.

(Boyd 1979–80:28)

II

In 1905 Chadds Ford village, besides its cluster of houses and a Chadds Ford Hotel, was composed of "two railroad stations, a creamery, a lumber and coal yard, carriage works, two stores, grange hall, another hall, two churches, a harness shop, barber shop and a drug store, also two doctors" (Thompson 1973:154). A 1980 inventory of public spaces in the village included a post office, law office, real estate office (all housed in a restored, gambrel-roofed barn), a collection of tourist shops (the Barn Shops—a mini-mall housed in the outbuildings of a nineteenth-century farm), an art gallery (formerly the farmhouse) specializing in local artists and expensive reproductions of Wyeth art, the Chadds Ford Inn (restaurant and bar, formerly the hotel), the Cha Bet Boutique (dresses), another law office, an antique gallery, a groundwater technology firm, an aerobic dance studio, Hank's Place (cafe), two gas stations (one of them formerly the creamery), a small building being refurbished with wide plank siding, mullioned windows, and shake roof (soon to open as The General Store), the Artisans' Cooperative (outlet for Appalachian crafts), the Brandywine Battlefield Museum, the Brandywine River Museum (formerly the lumber and coal yard), the Chris Sanderson Museum (a private dwelling recycled as a display space for Sanderson's personal accumulations), and the John Chadd House (eighteenth-century house restored and opened to the public by the Chadds Ford Historical Society).

A little farther afield east and west along Route 1, the main thoroughfare through the village, one found assorted other businesses and attractions: to the east, Brandywine Battlefield State Park (commemorating the Revolutionary War battle fought around Chadds Ford) and the ruins of an old mill (architecturally "stabilized" by Birmingham Township); to the west, Chadds Ford Knoll (the first of many housing developments in the area), Chadds Ford West (a suburban business complex designed as a set of enlarged re-creations of eighteenth-century farmhouses and outbuildings), and a second structure restored by the Historical Society and opened to the public (the Barns-Brinton House, an early eighteenth-century dwelling and tavern).

As of this writing the inventory needs to be modified as follows: The General Store has disappeared and been replaced by a much larger building—designed, sided, roofed, and decorated in the same rustic mode. It houses the post office (moved from its former place in the restored barn just to the east), a bank outlet with drive-up window, a convenience food store, an Allstate agency, a law firm, a realtor's office, and an abstract company. The gambrel-roofed barn now houses several real estate agencies. Under construction directly behind the Barn Shops complex, itself refurbished and elaborately landscaped after a recent fire, is a large motel/bed-and-breakfast hostelry, to be called The Brandywine River Hotel. To the east of the village a second suburban business complex, The Commons, has been added. Unlike the earlier, less sophisticated Chadds Ford West, this office complex is sited back from the highway and secluded by vegetation. It is designed in the cluster condominium mode.

By 1983 the main village intersection (U.S. Route 1 and Pennsylvania Route 100) had been transformed by the installation of a traffic light and the addition of left turn lanes. The stop sign on Route 100 was no longer able to squeeze north-south travelers safely onto the busy four lanes of the main highway.[1]

III

There is little hope of finding an indisputable Chadds Ford, Pennsylvania, either in hard facts of geography or in a sociology of community. Like any name, Chadds Ford designates different things in different circumstances. The best we can hope for is to assemble a collection of designations. But however we care to locate Chadds Ford physically, demographically, or sociologically, it also exists as an idea, an image, a matrix of ideological discourses. Large amounts of energy are invested in producing, maintaining and distributing the *idea* of Chadds Ford.

As a Site, Chadds Ford does not belong to any group of people or set of related groups. Sites, as I am using the term, are not inhabited in that sense. As a complex ideological production—an ordering of texts—Chadds Ford hovers vaguely above an ill-defined locale, available to many degrees of participation, identification and reproduction. Like the topography of the middle Brandywine Valley seen through the picturesque haze of high summer, the internal contours of the Chadds Ford image blur and float free of firm connections. As an idea, Chadds Ford is heterogeneous and adaptable, expanding or contracting to suit the situations of its invocation. One can be absorbed by it, manipulate it or carry pieces of it, souvenirs, away to physically remote locations. Ambiguity, in short, is the fundamental condition of its existence. It is by virtue of this ambiguity, and the flexibility it allows the image, that Chadds Ford as a cultural production can engage such a broad range of participation. As the travel magazine implies, Chadds Ford can answer to a multitude of desires, and it's only a gallon and a half of gas away.

But we must begin conventionally by drawing some boundaries on the map and "siting" Chadds Ford in the literal sense of that word. The one institution that might serve as the basis for identifying a "Chadds Ford community," a site in the normal ethnographic sense, is the Chadds Ford Elementary School (grades 1–5). The school building sits at the intersection of three townships and the school district boundary corresponds more or less to their outline. The townships, located in the extreme southeastern corner of Pennsylvania where it borders on the northern knob of Delaware, are Pennsbury and Birmingham in Chester County, and Birmingham in Delaware County (see Maps 1 and 2). The souvenirs displayed in these pages were, for the most part, collected within these three townships. When I speak of Chadds Ford as a general physical location, an unavoidable fiction, I refer to this area, which corresponds more or less to the middle Brandywine River Valley.

The townships contain, of course, a number of named locales of various sorts. For example, there are the old places designated long ago because they were small settlements at crossroads. Parkersville, Dilworthtown, Mendenhall, and Fairville are some of the names. Much newer, but undoubtedly more indicative of how the majority of residents locate themselves today, are names like Chadds Ford Knoll, Radley Run, Cannon Hill, and Spring Meadows—names of suburban housing developments.

Among these Chadds Ford places, the one demanding most of our attention is Chadds Ford village, the particular settlement I have inventoried above. Here is the most obvious ambiguity of our Site: Chadds Ford names both a vague region and the specific village sitting at the intersection of Routes 1 and 100 just east of the elementary school. As we shall see, this mystifying dialectic of vagueness and specificity characterizes the cultural discourse of the Site generally.

Among the small settlements in the three townships, Chadds Ford village has been the most significant ever since the colonial period. The Great Road to Nottingham, main overland link between Philadelphia and Baltimore in the eighteenth and early nineteenth centuries, gave the village its start by intersecting the Brandywine River at this spot (see Map 3). John Chad, the original ferryman, gave the settlement his name. In the mid-nineteenth-century two railroad lines were built, the Philadelphia and Baltimore Central and the Wilmington and Northern, with their inter-

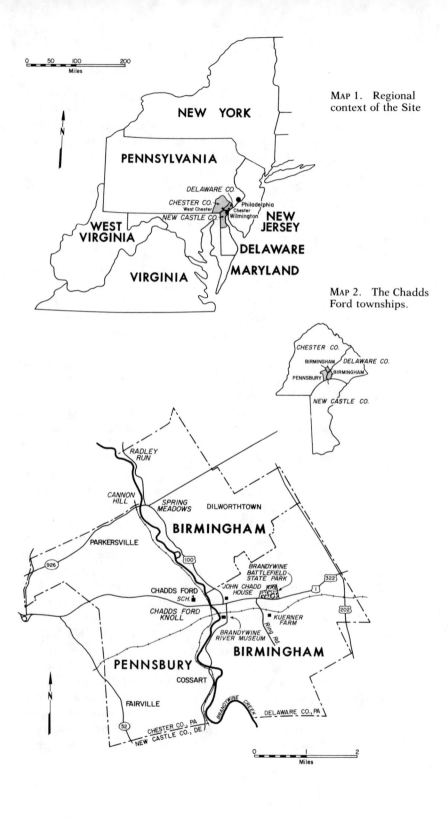

Map 1. Regional context of the Site

Map 2. The Chadds Ford townships.

section at Chadds Ford (see Map 4), or strictly speaking, at Chadds Ford Junction just across the river from the village (Hughes and McMullan 1982:35). This particular settlement, then, was the place through which the surrounding area had strongest contact with the larger world.

And likewise today, this village is without question the center of gravity in the cultural (re)production of Chadds Ford as a Site (see Map 5). An important type of participation in the discourse of Chadds Ford is the appropriation of its name, best reflected perhaps in the clamor for a Chadds Ford address as commodified in the form of the mailbox one can rent at the village post office. The desirability of the address manifests itself in the mild, half-amused resentment that "authentic" Chadds Ford residents display toward the more remote box holders.

IV

The Chadds Ford Inn, established in 1736, now belongs to the moderately priced "rustic inn" genre of restaurant so characteristic of the deep-suburban-tourist social order. Its menu suggests an image of hearty rural abundance and prosperity, running to beef, game, seafood, and heavy sauces. Turn to the back cover and you will find inscribed there a short course in Chadds Ford history.[2] This text runs together discrete and disparate moments to construct a continuous whole, a mythological past in which to root the dominant motifs of the Chadds Ford image. The windows of the Inn itself provide the unifying perspective:

> The windows of the Chadds Ford Inn looking out for over two and a half centuries onto Kings Highway, now U.S. Route 1, have seen a great deal of American history pass by—Indians and early settlers on foot, travelers on horseback, in farm wagons and carts, all the great officers of the American Revolution, Martha Washington on her way through from Mt. Vernon to spend the long winters at Valley Forge, General Lafayette in his coach on his return trip to the battle ground in 1825. Howard Pyle and his art students beginning with the summer of 1898, the sturdy New Englander, N.C. Wyeth, who walked out from Wilmington, Delaware the summer of 1902 to catch a brief glimpse of the Pyle class and came back the following summer to live until his death in 1945, his son Andrew Wyeth with his brother and sisters walking back and forth to their house on the hill in full view of the Inn, the young man from the West, Peter Hurd, who came in 1922 to study with N.C. Wyeth and married his eldest daughter Henriette, and now another generation, James Wyeth whizzing by in his sports car.

Here, conveniently condensed, is the "official" significant past of Chadds Ford, the standard package designed for quick assimilation and the transportability required by a tourist audience. The components appearing regularly in Chadds Ford's self-citation as an historically significant place are these:

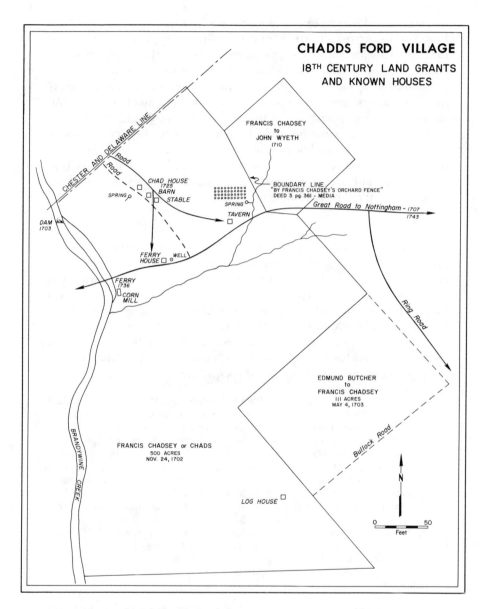

MAP 3. Late colonial Chadds Ford

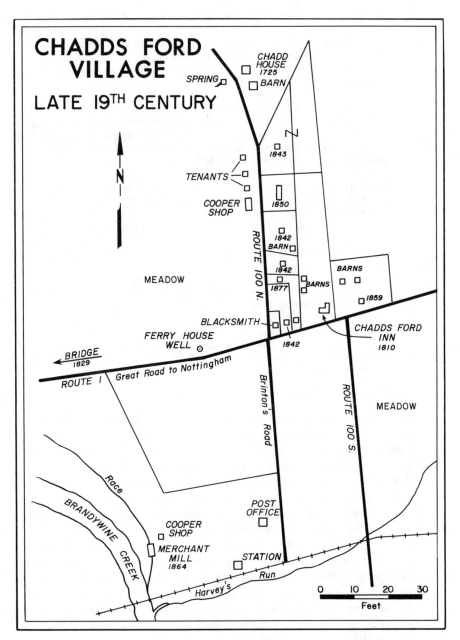

CHADDS FORD VILLAGE

LATE 19TH CENTURY

N

CHADD HOUSE 1725

SPRING

BARN

1843

TENANTS

COOPER SHOP

1850

1842 BARN

1842

1877

BARNS

BARNS

1859

MEADOW

ROUTE 100 N.

BLACKSMITH

FERRY HOUSE WELL

1842

CHADDS FORD INN 1810

BRIDGE 1829

ROUTE 1   Great Road to Nottingham

Brinton's Road

ROUTE 100 S.

MEADOW

Race

BRANDYWINE CREEK

POST OFFICE

COOPER SHOP

MERCHANT MILL 1864

STATION

Harvey's   Run

0   10   20   30
Feet

MAP 4

• a vague but important pre-Revolutionary period combining passing references to a Native American presence with the imagery of the pre- and early industrial social order. This historical realm currently occupies increasing attention in Chadds Ford cultural discourse. The resources of the Chadds Ford Historical Society are especially concentrated here

• the Revolutionary War, focusing on the Battle of the Brandywine (September 11, 1777), which was fought in the immediate vicinity. The object of intense professionalization, this historical moment has been monumentalized by the Commonwealth of Pennsylvania in its Brandywine Battlefield Park just east of the village.

• the turn of the century origin of the official artistic heritage, the Brandywine School. The common view acknowledges but tends to downplay the dominance of commerical art in the history of Brandywine painting. Either the "fine art" component of commercial illustration is emphasized or, more commonly, the Pyle school figures as the seedbed from which fine art has emerged in the second half of this century.

• the Wyeth family romance, which is today the dominant motif of Chadds Ford's cultural production. The mythology of generations is strong and merges with the imagery of residual agrarianism of the best-known Wyeth paintings to create a remarkably powerful mechanism of a sort for which we have no good name. It activates and maintains that global process whereby values and resources, ideology and material accumulations mobilize and transform from one to the other.

Our little passage from the back of the menu is interesting for more than its content. Note how it works rhetorically to create the impression of smooth continuity from one to the other of its historical moments. Generalized references to vague periods flow into details of "major event" textbook history; political and military references are juxtaposed to mention of cultural developments; elaborate family mythology and artistic genealogy drop us at the present and whizz off into the future in a sports car. Even the run-on syntax contributes to this effect. The whole thing assumes a rhetorical unity through the fixed perspective that looks out upon the road through the windows of the Chadds Ford Inn, a visually coded physical stability that analogically connotes temporal continuity. History is depicted as a spectacle, a pageant presenting a passive audience with an unbroken line of actors and scenes. The production and reproduction of texts about stability, completeness and continuity in the face of patent historical diversity, discontinuity and drastic selectivity is a major issue for our reading of this Site.

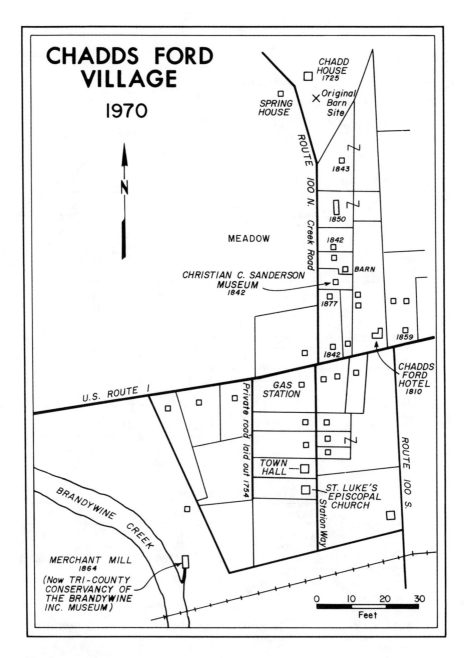

MAP 5

V

Some numbers:[3]

   Pennsbury Twp. (Chester Co.) = p
   Birmingham Twp. (Chester Co.) = BC
   Birmingham Twp. (Delaware Co.) = BD

TABLE 1 Total population

	1960	1970	1980	% increase 1960–1980
P	936	1,763	2,604	178
BC	453	834	1,584	250
BD	1,093	1,281	2,057	88
Total	2,482	3,878	6,245	152

TABLE 2 Black population

	1960	1970	1980
P	14	19	6
BC	30	4	1
BD	57	27	14
Total	101	50	21
% of total pop.	4	1.3	.3

TABLE 3 Median income (% of national median)

	1960	1970	1980
P	6,887 (118%)	15,806 (154.4%)	30,370 (138.6%)
BC	not reported	21,271 (207.8%)	43,482 (198.5%)
BD	7,803 (133.7%)	16,983 (165.9%)	27,319 (124.7%)

TABLE 4 1960, % of households with income of $25,000 or more (poverty level information not available)

P	11.3
BC	9.5
BD	12.7

TABLE 5 1970, % of households with income of $50,000 or more; or below the poverty line

	$50,000+	Below poverty line
P	2.8	4.0
BC	5.3	2.1
BD	10.3	2.8

TABLE 6 1980, % of households with income of $50,000 or more; or below poverty line

	50,000+	Below poverty line
P	19.4	0.8
BC	40.4	1.7
BD	21.5	1.4

TABLE 7 Valuation of homes (1960 information not available)

	1970	1980
P	$ 30,800	$ 89,600
BC	49,700	137,600
BD	32,800	110,300

TABLE 8 Median number of rooms per owner occupied home

	1960	1970	1980
P	6.4	7.6	8.0
BC	6.4	7.9	8.4
BD	6.2	6.7	7.0

TABLE 9 Persons per household

	1960	1970	1980
P	3.51	3.81	2.82
BC	3.48	3.66	3.41
BD	3.54	3.39	2.70

VI

The early eighteenth century and the Revolutionary War years constitute the classic period of Chadds Ford's mythological past. In this it is not unique,[4] nor is the shape of its recent history unusual among circum-metropolitan regions of the eastern United States. What does set it apart is the extremity to which it has carried modern socio-historical trends. Tourism and postwar suburbanization are the dominant facts of Chadds Ford's current social order. If it is true that everyday life in the West organizes itself increasingly around leisure pursuits and the cultivation of "lifestyle," then Chadds Ford is a quintessential example of the "post-industrial" order.[5] As a Site Chadds Ford specializes in the endless repro-duction, physically and ideologically, of an image that combines pre-industrial rural domestic economy, generalized agrarian rusticity and the abstract idea of tradition.

Although change has been rapid and visible on the land over the last twenty-five years in Chadds Ford, native perceptions of the transformation are necessarily limited. The native population after all is itself a function of the transformation. My conversations with Chadds Ford residents about recent developments in their area suggest to me a loose typology of his-torical perceptions.

Although few remain who view length of residence in terms of gen-erations rather than years, there are some old-timers with considerable historical perspective. Mary McMullan, long affiliated with the Chadds Ford School district and author (1980) of the school's history, is known as one of the people to talk to about life in the old Chadds Ford. For her, World War II marks the beginning of the transformation, which she sees as the decline of the old order of small-scale agriculture and the family farm. Chadds Ford village, with its creamery, rail junction, grange, ly-ceums, and pageants was an agricultural service center before the War, and that is what has changed for people like Miss McMullan.

A second perspective belongs to the segment of the Chadds Ford pop-ulation that moved there in the 1950s and 1960s. These people represent the first and classical phase of postwar suburbanization, which included both the creation of entirely new settlements out of old family farms (the early housing developments like Chadds Ford Knoll) and more elite sub-urbanization, that is, the purchase and restoration of old farm houses and mills.

Those who came in this phase are distinguished from the more recent arrivals, whose sudden and heavy in-migration in the 1970s provided the contrastive social component that transformed their suburban precursors into "established" residents. To the large numbers of newcomers, the earlier suburbanites, fewer in number and some in possession of "au-thentic" (i.e. non-development) properties, are the Chadds Ford natives. To these "native suburbanites" the significant moment of historical change in Chadds Ford is the decade of the 1970s. Suburbanization and the corresponding decline of small agriculture had been a steady process since the mid-1950s, but in the 1970s it achieved a new order of magnitude. Between 1970 and 1980, Pennsbury Township, the Chadds Ford area west of the Brandywine, saw no less than a 47.7% increase in population. And, even more telling for transformation of the landscape, occupied residences in the township increased a remarkable 96.2% (from 473 housing units to 926). As of 1980 there were two working dairy farms in Pennsbury Township; there were twelve suburban housing developments (Hughes and McMullan 1982:46, 97).[6]

At least some of the established residents distinguish themselves from the new arrivals on the basis of perceived motivations for moving to Chadds Ford. One kind of motivation is positive and includes all the classic Jeffersonian reasons for relocating in the suburbs: healthy environment, good place to raise children, an opportunity to work on the land, privacy, independence, and so on. In Chadds Ford we find added to these an interest in the historical and cultural significance of the place.

Opposed to such motivations, and usually ascribed to the new arrivals, is the negative impulse of escape, escape from the city or, more specifically, avoidance of minorities. The suburbanization of Chadds Ford has mainly involved out-migration from Wilmington, Delaware, and a common opinion in Chadds Ford is that the recent blossoming of subdivisions is a manifestation of "white flight" in the wake of court ordered bussing to desegregate Wilmington schools.

There is considerable irony in such an opinion, although no doubt there is more than a little truth to it. Some blacks lived in the Chadds Ford area as early as 1800 (Hughes and McMullan 1982:15), and as time went on they became an important part of the agricultural labor force, occupying tenant houses on the farms and even separate black settlements,[7] of which very little note is taken today. In 1905 a woman contemplating moving to Chadds Ford hesitated for fear she wouldn't be able to find "any white folks to associate with" (Thompson 1973:160). When the Chadds Ford School opened in 1925, it included, along with its regular six elementary grades and three middle school classes, a Union Room where "a suitable colored teacher was...employed to teach the colored pupils of the first six grades" (McMullan 1980:9), a situation that persisted until 1950. Of the eleven members on the school's 1931 baseball team, four were black (Ibid.:12).

Today, blacks are almost entirely absent from the Chadds Ford scene, absent from the physical place and from the official image of its past. The beginning of their disappearance and the first phase of postwar suburbanization were more or less simultaneous phenomena. Both were functions of the general social transformation that replaced the prewar system of agricultural production with an order that organizes itself around the production and replication of emblems and images. The suburban settlement pattern is an important means of such production.

VII

"Established resident" and "newcomer" are probably the native categories most characteristic of the postwar suburban order. In Chadds Ford they have a special force, because the ideology of tradition and connection with the past is such a key element in the image of the place. Residence, physical and temporal, weighs heavily in the determination of status. Status, of course, is manipulable according to the demands of specific situations. To assign our two categories of residence to the two phases of suburban settlement is conceptually helpful but also a great oversimplification. A definitive feature of Chadds Ford cultural production is the wealth of opportunity it offers for participation. The simple fact of how long one has lived there is colored by how thoroughly one "gets in the spirit" of the place. One can quickly appropriate, at least to a degree, the knowledge and interests of established residents. At the very least one can ally oneself with the positively valued side of another native social distinction in Chadds Ford: resident vs. tourist.

The eternal paradox of suburban settlement, especially in a place like Chadds Ford, where preservationist ideology is so prominent (see sec. XII), is that the new arrival immediately feels threatened by the general movement he has just realized for himself. The attractions of natural beauty, peace, space and privacy are ever in danger of effecting their own destruction. Yet it is through the desire and envy of those wanting to move to Chadds Ford that the resident validates her own residence. In a place like Chadds Ford, with its added cultural attractions of historical significance (Battle of the Brandywine) and artistic heritage (the Brandywine School, Wyeth), the suburban dialectic is inseparable from the contemporary structure of tourism. Tourist traffic may be a nuisance to residents, but its presence is a constant reminder that one inhabits an "authentic" place.

Over the last ten years, suburban tourism has become a major industry in the counties that surround Philadelphia. In 1980 the two counties that meet at Chadds Ford, Chester (predominantly suburban and rural) and Delaware (heavily suburban), had incomes from tourism of $139.2 million and $154.6 million, respectively (*Philadelphia Inquirer*, 7/11/82). In 1979 a "Discover the Brandywine Valley" promotional campaign was mounted by these two counties and the city of Wilmington, Delaware, to market the region where Chadds Ford is located (Ibid.). As we have seen, in the Winter 1979–80 issue of its magazine, *Discovery*, the Allstate Motor Club suggested Chadds Ford as a "gas-stingy weekend" vacation spot for Philadelphians constrained by energy prices. The Brandywine River Museum, the biggest tourist attraction at Chadds Ford, suggests its tourist "catchment" area in the mileage chart on one of its brochures (see Map 1):

Baltimore 74

Harrisburg 92

New York 128

Scranton 130

Philadelphia 28

Washington 112

Wilmington 12

In Chadds Ford, tourism and suburbanization form an uneasy symbiosis of attraction and validation out of which arises the cultural production I have loosely been calling the Chadds Ford "idea" or "image." We gain helpful perspective on this production by viewing Chadds Ford as a set of orientations to other places. It is far from being the self-sufficient rural community to which its image looks for inspiration. In fact, as a locale of suburban residence and tourist pilgrimage, one might even say it exists as a place to come to from other places. The odd thing is that the ideas of independence and self-sufficiency are important ideological products of this place that is so thoroughly dependent on other places. There are very few everyday commercial services available in the three Chadds Ford townships; no major commercial strips, no extravagant mall (the Barn Shops specialize in gifts, trinkets, souvenirs, and the like), no huge supermarket, no significant health facilities. For such personal services, and less tangibly, for social connections and personal attachment, there are two general orientations characteristic of Chadds Ford residence.

One of these is a very distinct alignment down the Brandywine River to Wilmington, Delaware. In some sense, Chadds Ford is a suburb of Wilmington. While that city has always figured in the Chadds Ford consciousness, the wave of suburbanization in the 1970s sharpened the focus considerably. Directly or indirectly, the DuPont Corporation, headquartered in Wilmington, is the economic dominant of present day Chadds Ford.

Less concentrated and undoubtedly weaker in quantitative terms, but also older and more common among long-time residents, is a general orientation up the valley toward West Chester, Pennsylvania. Like prewar Chadds Ford, West Chester was mainly an agricultural rather than industrial center. It was also a Quaker town (see Map 1).

In something of the same spirit, the more established residents in the western parts of the Chadds Ford area might look in the direction of Kennett Square, also originally Quaker and still agricultural, though now mainly as a center for the highly developed mushroom industry. This orientation is, I believe, rather a weak one. Kennett Square and its surrounding countryside has a strong regional identity (mushrooms, dairy, horticulture) of its own, one that contrasts sharply with Chadds Ford's. The two interpenetrate very little.

Route 1, running more or less perpendicular to the everyday spatial orientations of Chadds Ford residents, is without question the primary line of orientation for tourist movement. One can read the recent history of Chadds Ford in the disjunctions of scale along this axis. Driving west on Route 1 and coming to the edge of the Brandywine watershed (approximately at Route 202; see Map 2), one finds oneself surrounded by the familiar strip landscape of large parking lots, gas stations with outsized logos at the top of tall poles, and big brick surf 'n' turf restaurants. Go a few hundred yards farther on, over the edge of the watershed, and you get the feeling of having entered not just a different landscape, but a different scale of landscape. Chadds Ford village in particular gives this impression. It is organized at a walking pace and at human eye level. There are no sidewalks, as if the village were pretending it is still safe to walk on the shoulder of Baltimore Pike (Route 1). In fact, pedestrian traffic has had to take to the narrow and precarious strips of grass left between the road and the buildings when the highway was widened to four lanes. Tracks worn down to the bare earth, like cowpaths, mark the movement of tourists trying to walk around the village. The commercial signs, too, indicate an ambiguity of scale. All are oriented to the highway, but most of them are too small to be read easily at 55 mph (see Figure 1). The two notable exceptions are the sign at the corner Sunoco station and the one at the entrace to the Brandywine Museum, but even these give the impression of being big signs trying to remain unobtrusive. The gas station sign is perhaps only a third as large as the Sunoco sign at the intersection of Routes 1 and 202, and it is also much lower. The museum sign is also low, and its design conforms to the theme of hand-made rusticity.

The village of Chadds Ford is at a smaller scale than the highway that cuts through it. Although modern tourism operates at the scale of highways, the special quality of tourism in the Brandywine region is that the perceived authenticity of the Site depends on the impression it gives of being small-scale. The tourism is in part a response to the image of Chadds Ford as a place where life moves at a slower pace and in a smaller orbit.

FIGURE 1. View toward the Chadds Ford village intersection. Photograph by the author.

This quality of scale that draws the tourists also motivates some Chadds Ford residents to create situations for themselves where they can experience more intimately a pre-industrial scale of perception.

VIII

To define Chadds Ford as a set of spatial orientations is, on the one hand, a fairly straightforward matter of identifying the significant topographical, infrastructural, and social facts of its physical existence. On the other hand, spatial orientation also involves the identification of less tangible ideological facts. How is Chadds Ford oriented conceptually in a regional environment? What areas are recognized as Chadds Ford's "significant regional others"? A full account of such an ideological orientation would, of course, be a study in itself. However, two areas stand out particularly clearly in their regional dialogue with Chadds Ford.

A prominent Chadds Ford resident has published a children's book about characters and events in a place called "the Ford" (Wyeth 1979). The Chadds Ford insider will recognize the human models of the animal characters and the various locales where the events take place. In many respects, the bird's-eye-view map that precedes the text gives an accurate account of Chadds Ford's mythic geography. The Ford is a small, self-sufficient, and down-at-the-heels community beyond which its residents rarely venture. The narrative concerns the adventures of Ford residents when they do have cause to visit two nearby regions: the "hound and hunt country" to the northwest, home of the story's villain, who has "plenty of cash but no class," and the "vast estates of the Baron deFace" to the south, a manicured environment of formal gardens and palatial mansions supported by a fortune amassed in the production of black powder. These two areas constitute barely disguised references to, respectively, the "hunt country" of western Chester County, Pennsylvania, and the "chateaux district" of northern New Castle County, Delaware.

In the latter area, just across the Delaware border from Chadds Ford, the du Ponts have their private estates. Du Pont influence is strong in Chadds Ford, and du Pont gossip thrives there. It was du Pont money that got the Chadds Ford Elementary School built and du Pont money has underwritten the Brandywine River Museum and Conservancy.

Less directly, but more deeply and importantly, the hunt country of Chester County exerts an influence on Chadds Ford consciousness. It offers the model for a way of life that can be reproduced emblematically (miniaturized, commodified) in deep-suburban life-style. In the more expensive housing developments and on the larger individual properties of Chadds Ford one can actually have a barn and riding ring; and one finds any number of residents who say they moved to Chadds Ford so the children could have a horse.

To enhance these emblems with authentic experience, one can tour the hunt country itself, only a few minutes away, thus demonstrating the continuity between the cultivation of lifestyle in the suburbs and the structure of tourism. Go in mid-May and you can see the Radnor Hunt Races, sponsored by Resorts International and Beefeaters Gin. If you attend as a "special patron" ($50–$500), you can enter the contests that set the tone of the event: Best Picnic (tailgate or buffet), Best Vintage Car, and Best Hat:

> Food categories judged on originality, eye appeal and savory cuisine....Hats judged on individuality and style, vintage cars on appearance and harmony with the picnic theme.
>
> (Radnor Hunt Races brochure, 1981)

Even the general admission patron can bring a version (e.g., shrimp salad, spinach quiche, white wine) of the elegant picnic for a day on the racing green.

The chateaux district and hunt country are strong voices in the ideological environment of Chadds Ford. The former is a mysterious private realm of the super-rich, too remote for mimetic incorporation into daily suburban life, but for that very reason infinitely available as an object of speculation and gossip. Also, limited public access is available through a system of du Pont inspired and subsidized museums. The hunt country is also an elite realm, one modeled on English countryhouse life. The "culture of the horse" around which it is organized, however, is much more susceptible to mimetic participation than the almost regally aristocratic image of the Delaware estates.

IX

I have been using the word "image" in an extended sense roughly synonymous with "idea" or "conception," but Chadds Ford also involves an image in the strict sense of "visual representation." Chadds Ford is a certain look, a sight, a kind of landscape which, as a cultural production, involves not only a content, a repertoire of physical features, but a way of seeing as well, a repertoire of perspectives. One cannot "locate" Chadds Ford as an idea without locating it as a kind of visual experience. First, then, a few straightforward facts of topography.

Chadds Ford is riparian, topographically bounded on the east and west by the edges of the Brandywine River watershed. The river is the dominant geographical fact, splitting the area of the three townships roughly in half along a line from northwest to southeast. The Brandywine empties into the Delaware River at Wilmington, Delaware. The romantic picturesqueness of the Chadds Ford scene originates along the winding course of the middle Brandywine, and great amounts of energy, material and ideational, are invested in preserving the appropriate look. Here is an authoritative description of the middle Brandywine. The passage follows upon an account of the "singular harmony in the life of individuals, families, and whole communities" among the original Quaker settlers:

> A rich farming region, diversified with woods and many streams, it is a land of symmetrically curving hills, sometimes conical, curving into the side of valleys of the runs tributary to the Brandywine, and dropping rather sharply to the river, which here bends in graceful loops. It is a made country, and has been so since the mid-eighteenth century, in which only an occasional "barren" of serpentine is wasteland. The forest land is of rich and heavy timber in wood lots, and occasional mile-long stretches, the nesting places of hawks. There are many lonely trees of beauty and dignity, both in the water meadows of the creek and upon the hills otherwise bare. No visible soil waste or hasty exploitation in this excellent valley. The friendly families came to stay, and many are still there, or their descendants have come back to build country places on the hills.
>
> Hundreds of old houses are, externally, very much as their builders left

them, although their stone has weathered to autumn shades. These stone houses are capacious, with a chimney at each end, and an extension, of one story usually, of either stone of logs, which often was the original house. In the meadow below will be a springhouse, also of stone and usually under an oak or a sycamore, and beside, or behind, the home a vast barn whose blank walls of more hastily assembled stones are multi-colored. Old silver maples, a Norway fir, a white pine, and usually a cherry, are the protecting trees. Maples shade the lane.

But what is most distinctive of the Brandywine houses, by comparison with New England or Virginia, is the way they are settled comfortably against a rising slope. There is a Quaker reticence in their placing, seldom on the road, never showily set on a height, facing usually the southern sun, and not on the highway.

(Canby 1941:160–161)

Place this, a mid-twentieth-century description by a popular historian, next to a tableau from a mid-nineteenth century novel set in the same region:

The house, built like most other old farm houses in that part of the country, of hornblend stone, stood near the bottom of a rounded knoll, over-hanging the deep winding valley. It was two stories in height, the gable looking towards the road, and showing, just under the broad double chimney, a lime-stone slab, upon which were rudely carved the initials of the builder and his wife, and the date "1727." A low portico, overgrown with woodbine and trumpet flower, ran along the front. In the narrow flower-bed under it, the crocuses and daffodils were beginning to thrust up their blunt, green points.

A walk of flagstones separated them from the vegetable garden, which was bounded by the mill-race, carrying half the water of the creek to the saw and grist-mill on the other side of the road.

(Taylor 1866:25–26)

In their selections of objects, in some of their details, but most importantly, in the connotations of tone, these passages are interchangeable, though the one is the modern non-fiction sketch of a typical middle Brandywine landscape, while the other is a romantic nineteenth century re-creation of a late eighteenth century scene. Although both consciously associate themselves with a specifically Quaker milieu, they belong to a larger genre of romantic American vision—the idyllic image of cozy rural prosperity and tidy industry in a picturesque but safely domesticated landscape.

The Chadds Ford image as visual experience drinks deep at this romantic well, and these verbal descriptions are matched by countless paintings of the so-called "Brandywine School" of art. But the incorporation of this visual experience into the cultural production of the current Chadds Ford image involves certain important manipulations and adaptations. Foremost among these is the generalization of the romantic vision. The particularity of the Quaker associations has diminished, until today the image is diffuse and lacking in specificity. Small-scale agrarianism in a rolling wooded landscape infused with the feeling of cultural stability and depth in time: these are the qualities of Chadds Ford as a physical image. Their vagueness and generality is a basic condition of the cultural production that *is* Chadds Ford, serving to accomodate the broadest possible participation by blurring cultural, historical, and geographical distinctions.

We might take, for example, the lack of historical specificity. Chadds Ford cultural production homogenizes such disparate elements as the early eighteenth century domestic economy of water-powered mills and the mid-twentieth century world of residual rural values in the decaying economy of small-scale agriculture. In the generalized Chadds Ford image these scenes flow smoothly into one another. Somehow there obtains a condition that allows us to overlook such disjunctions as that between the tidy prosperity of the Quaker settlers and the rural disrepair evident in many of Andrew Wyeth's paintings.

X

One's sense of Chadds Ford as a unified landscape or consistent visual experience is influenced by a particular visual rhetoric, a uniform way of seeing that begins in the handling of point-of-view in Brandywine School paintings—especially Andrew Wyeth's—and the postcards available to tourists, and extends to the control of vantage points in everyday life. Without claiming that they constitute anything like a complete "rhetoric of seeing" in Chadds Ford, a few recurring features of the visual images produced there are:

1. a middle distance view of structures (typically barns or farm houses) or other focal objects (especially isolated stands of trees) across agricultural space (pasture, barnyard), often with some sort of interposed barrier (fence, water course) (Figures 2–4),

2. panoramic overview of the valley, often from a vantage point marked somehow as agricultural, with river and distant farmsteads as points of compositional focus,

3. steep-angle views up or down hill or other perspectives that emphasize a topography of hills and hollows (e.g., roofs or buildings seen above the crest of a hill) (Figures 5 and 6).

What we have in these patterns of seeing, of course, are the cliches of romantic agricultural landscape, a conventional framework within which an infinity of individual compositions can be worked out. It is above all

FIGURE 2. *Evening at Kuerners*, Andrew Wyeth. Private collection.

FIGURE 3.   Image from the Chadds Ford Days art exhibit. Photograph by
the author.

a landscape of nostalgia and desire characterized by glimpses of a way of life that is distant or partially hidden, but still visible and so possibly accessible. Chadds Ford topography is so popular among amateur landscape artists because of the ready access it provides to these conventional perspectives of desire. The visual experience of Chadds Ford is thoroughly assimilated to a generalized and widely familiar American look that transcends regional specificity.

These conventional perspectives are important to an account of the Chadds Ford image not only in what they show, but also in what they hide. An important criterion for the visual image of the place is that it be smooth, that there be no jarring elements that speak of a world outside the generalized agrarian idyll. The typical visual image is highly sanitized, free of all reference to the modern infrastructure of transportation, communication, energy and development. Wyeth paints the Kuerner farm from positions that leave out of view the paved roads, railroad tracks and high tension towers that are part of the reality. The postcard view of the John Chadd House (restored by the Chadds Ford Historical Society) (Figure 7) gives the impression that a smooth greensward runs from the main

FIGURE 4. Travel magazine image of "Wyeth's white world." *Discovery*, the Allstate Motor Club Magazine, Winter 1979/80.

house, past its outbuilding, and down through the trees to the floor of the valley. In fact, Route 100 cuts between the two structures. Similarly, one postcard view of the Brandywine River Museum (Figure 8), a low-angle shot meant to evoke the romantic image of the isolated mill, studiously avoids any reference to the heavy tourist traffic the museum attracts. The camera angle leaves out of sight the large parking lot. In short, anti-reflexivity is a definitive feature of these productions.

The impulse that informs the construction of these images carries over into the settlement pattern most characteristic of Chadds Ford today: the suburban housing development. Residential development is the dominant force in the radical transformation of Chadds Ford landscape and social order over the last twenty-five years. Its special quality, though certainly not unique to Chadds Ford, is a devotion to the preservation of the agrarian image represented in the paintings and postcards. The implicit promise of the developers is that one can actually inhabit these images.

Chadds Ford residential development belongs to a genre I have been calling "deep suburban" (Figure 9). As a middle landscape standing between rural and urban, it strives toward as complete an imitation of the agrarian ideal as possible. And it has that paradoxical quality of being both a place where people actually live and an idea of a way of life, represented mainly by the preservation, or wholesale creation, of the appropriate look. The controlling idea is that one will actually live at the vantage point from which the paintings are painted and the postcards

FIGURE 5. *Public Sale*, Andrew Wyeth. Private collection.

FIGURE 6. Travel magazine image of the Chadds Ford landscape. *Discovery*, the Allstate Motor Club Magazine, Winter 1979/80.

photographed. Ideally, the view from your windows will be of an undisturbed and agrarian scene, reproducing as faithfully as possible the perspectival elements of the generalized romantic landscape. The image of the rolling, intermittently wooded terrain determines the developers' choice of names for their subdivisions. Read together, the names of the twelve Pennsbury Township developments are a poem to a topographical ideal:

Ridgefield, Ridge Run, Hanover Hunt,

Fair Hill, Fern Hill, Hamorton Woods,

Raintree, Chaddwyck, Pennsbury

Heights, Hickory

Hollow, Pennsbury—East and West,

Chadds Ford

Knoll.

FIGURE 7.   John Chad House, postcard view

In reality, of course, practical constraints produce a range of approximations to this ideal. To illustrate, here are some examples of how image is reproduced, more or less completely, in the physical reality of habitation (see Map 2 for locations):

1. Chadds Ford Knoll, built in the 1950s and the oldest housing development in our three Chadds Ford townships, has the look of an early manifestation of the middle to upper-middle class version of this settlement type. Sitting on a slope above Route 100 just west of Chadds Ford village (see map 1), it is densely settled but given variety by the winding and looping of the roads along which it is laid out—as opposed to the uniformity of the cul-de-sac pattern. The lots are relatively small—averaging an acre or less—but the layout produces a variety of lot shapes and the topography allows some variation in house placement. The houses themselves conform to no standardized set of named styles, a feature like the cul-de-sac lay-out, of the more controlled and thoroughly "planned" developments; but they are mainly of the two-story frame "colonial" style, with a number of ranch houses mixed in. The street names establish the early American and Revolutionary War themes: Constitution Drive, Washington Lane, Mt. Vernon Place, Cannoneer Circle, Stirling Way, Lamppost

FIGURE 8. Brandywine River Museum, postcard view

Lane, Concord Way, Virginia Drive. Two decorative elements dominate: the American eagle (usually placed above the front door or on the garage) and sections of post and rail fence at driveway entrances. The latter decorates properties throughout the Chadds Ford area and beyond, giving it the quality of an emblem for the generalized agrarian image of the mid-Atlantic region.[8]

The density of settlement in Chadds Ford Knoll precludes the overall reproduction of the perspective that places one in agricultural open-space, (see above, perspective no. 1 of my brief list), though this point-of-view is individually produced in miniature in the form of the open lawn so centrally characteristic of suburban development. As an alternative, the development as a whole has used landscaping to create a general impression of agricultural periphery, a landscape of woodland punctuated by clearings. Furthermore, there is a continuity between this impression of immediate surroundings and the long-range view one gets from various points around the development. Vegetation is maintained to allow panoramic views of the valley (e.g., at the intersection of Washington Lane and Constitution Drive), with its picturesque alternation of woods and open space, As a whole, Chadds Ford Knoll cultivates the

FIGURE 9. Deep-suburban landscape ideal. Photograph by the author.

look characterized under no. 2 in my partial rhetoric of Chadds Ford perspectives.

2. Quite different in style and constituency, but devoted to the same visual ideology, is Radley Run Mews, a retirement-recreational develop-ment in the northern projection of Birmingham Township, Chester County. Here the visual experience has as its main resource the Radley Run Coun-try Club golf course, which rolls without hindrance almost to the doors of the Mews residents. Here the associations of small-scale agriculture are replaced by an equivalent, the imagery of the eighteenth-century English rural park. The golf course provides a panorama of idealized country landscape that is a self-contained and scrupulously maintained counter-part of the valley panorama framed at Chadds Ford Knoll. It is, so to speak, that valley panorama reproduced at a scale that makes it physically accessible (by electric golf cart). The theme of the development, expressed in its road names, is quite specifically that of the Revolutionary War, including special reference to the Battle of the Brandywine, the major skirmish of which occurred at Osborn Hill directly contiguous to the de-velopment. The structures in the development are organized linearly and are attached to one another in groups of two or three. They sit on very small lots, with separate garages arranged in rows. The garages are adapted reproductions of the Quaker horse shed, a distinctive architectural

form found throughout the Chadds Ford area, both in restored and recreated versions (Figures 10 and 11). As a component of the Chadds Ford image, this form symbolizes the Quaker history of the place, which otherwise is felt only weakly in the Chadds Ford idea.

3. For a third example of how the "Chadds Ford way of seeing" materializes in the physical organization of deep suburban settlement, I go a little beyond my arbitrary Chadds Ford boundary, to Cannon Hill in the southeast corner of Pocopson Township and just across the fork of the Brandywine from Radley Run. Its interest as an example lies in the unequivocal correlation of visual perspective and agrarian image with hard dollars and cents values in its marketing.

Cannon Hill is a collection of twenty-five irregular lots arranged along either side of a single cul-de-sac (Cannon Hill Drive), which follows more or less a ridge line approximately three hundred feet in elevation. In either direction from this line the slope falls unevenly, from a gentle roll at the southern end to a steep slide down to river level in the north. That the layout is meant to emphasize a downhill perspective (no. 3 in my categorization of perspectives) is reflected in the factors that determine lot prices (which average between $30,000 and $42,000). Of increasing value are the features corresponding to such descriptive categories as: "sloping to rear," "sloping with view," and "view of the river." Value is enhanced if the lot contains a "knoll" and also if it has woods, the categories of the latter being: woods, half woods, and densely wooded. A typical lot description is this: "3 acres, high woods, view of the river—$45,500." The lots range in size from 2.6 to 7.6 acres, the great majority of them being between three and four acres. They are advertised as "farmettes," which seems to mean they are large enough to accommodate a small barn or other outbuilding. Lots on which a horse might be kept are designated and priced accordingly.

Clearly, here is an example where the reality of a place is thoroughly shaped to conform to a general image. Physical organization strives to create a certain kind of experience, the look enshrined in countless Brandywine paintings and tourist images. A formal "Declaration of Restrictions for Cannon Hill" indicates the extent of control exercised in the interest of creating an appropriate and sanitary visual experience. Here are some excerpts:

> No construction shall begin upon any residence or accessory building on any lot, nor any major alteration made to the exterior of any existing building, until the plans and specifications showing floor plans, materials, colors, location and elevations of same have been submitted to and approved by the developer. All such plans shall have been prepared by and bear the seal of a registered

FIGURE 10. Quaker horse shed as suburban garage. Photograph by the author.

FIGURE 11. Suburban garage as Quaker horse shed. Photograph by the author.

architect or engineer. The intent of such approval is to insure that all structures at Cannon Hill shall exist in general harmony and character with each other, and the topography, vegetation and other natural features.

No fence, other than post and rail, or other continuous obstruction or barrier of like nature shall be erected or maintained unless approved.

No outside or freestanding TV, radio, short wave or similar arial or antenna shall be erected.

No fowl shall be raised or kept and no kennel for the breeding or boarding of dogs shall be erected or maintained on any lot.

No lot shall be used other than for residential purposes.

No dwelling house shall be erected on any lot which shall be designed for occupancy by more than a single family; however, this shall not prohibit quarters for domestic service.

The area of the old Indian Campground on lot #21, as indicated on the recorded plan, shall be restricted against building and earth moving for other than agricultural purposes.

4. Last, and perhaps most complete as an illustration of the material expression of Chadds Ford ideology through visual perspective, is Spring Meadows. This is a new development at the corner of Routes 100 and 926 in Birmingham Township, Chester County, just south of Radley Run. A collection of seventy-six lots carved from farm fields, Spring Meadows is arranged according to the principle of "cluster housing" currently fashionable in affluent, deep-suburban development planning (see Figure 9). The individually owned houses, situated uniformly on relatively regular lots, are concentrated or "clustered" in one part of the development property, while another part, or several other sections, are left as "open-space." The open areas belong to the development as a whole and are maintained collectively with fees regularly paid by the homeowners. Residents have some say in how these areas will be managed, subject of course to the constraints of the developer and the township. For example, they can have the fields mowed or leave the grass long, depending on which look the majority favors. Although a professional firm performs the general maintenance of the open areas, residents also have the chance to get involved with the land by doing minor landscaping, cleanup, etc.

Spring Meadows, as its name implies, devotes itself to the agrarian image. Its open-space consists of a "farm pond" near the entrance road and a large rolling field of grass that tends toward marshiness in the low areas. One corner of the open-space has been identified as the former site of an Indian settlement and the source of Indian artifacts. As in Cannon Hill, special provision has been made for its preservation.

The original farmhouse and its barn have been preserved as tangible evidence of the land's agricultural authenticity. Such preserved farm structures, maintained either as useable habitations or as picturesquely

Figure 12. Deep-suburban "Pennsylvania farmhouse." Photograph by the author.

decaying decorative elements (e.g., overgrown barn ruins) have become a common element in the development landscapes of this region.

The Spring Meadow houses, a mixture of spec and custom designed structures, mostly fall within a few stylistic categories, all of them with acceptably rustic associations. These include:

French provincial (square, unadorned exterior, hipped roof, corners suggesting massive stone block construction)

Tudor (facade combining stone or brick with "half timber" and plaster veneers, intersecting gables with multiple dormers)

Pennsylvania farmhouse (Figure 12) (facade and roofline suggest stages of building, main section with stone veneer and "addition" with simulated plaster facade, allusion to penteave)

New England cottage (frame, many shuttered windows in facade, symmetrical)

California modern (multiple sections, roofs at various angles, great expanses of glass, dark raw wood siding)

The developments are permanent vantages from which one has unlimited access to the visual experience central to Chadds Ford as an ideological production. They are the habitable counterpart of the conventional points-of-view in Brandywine paintings and tourist images. In some cases, for example the farmettes of Cannon Hill, we have the hint of a deeper involvement, a participation of doing as well as looking. Of course the suburban lawn always provides a sense of encounter with the land and faint agricultural associations cling to the miniature mowing and planting that goes on there. The affluent, deep-suburban housing development sometimes provides considerable opportunity for this sort of participation. One's lot might actually allow for a small barn and some farm animals or a horse.

XI

The inclination represented by developments like Cannon Hill and Spring Meadows is more fully realized by a segment of the Chadds Ford population that resides outside such settlements. In his description of the typical "old house" along the middle Brandywine, (see above) Henry S. Canby suggests that many of these properites are still owned by the "friendly families" that originally settled the area. This may have been true at the time of his writing (1941), but since World War II the same economic and demographic pressures that produced the phenomenon of the modern housing development has also resulted in the buying out of these old families by the members of an affluent class of white collar and professional elite, many of them associated with the research and development division of DuPont corporation, which is located a few miles downstream in Wilmington, Delaware. The authentic old farmhouses and mills, along with parcels of land comparable in size to the average property of the region's agricultural past,[9] came into the hands of people with the resources and leisure to refurbish the dwellings and pursue a kind of avocational agriculture. Real flocks of sheep might be raised, real crops of hay grown. In retirement, someone in this situation might cultivate a convincing image of an authentically agricultural life style. If unable to participate directly, one can at least lease land to the few "real" farmers still to be found along the middle Brandywine.

This deep physical involvement with the agrarian component of the Chadds Ford image is often accompanied by an equal commitment to the "Chadds Ford heritage"; that is, a commitment to the restoration, preservation, display and, most interestingly, participatory re-creation of Chadds Ford's "significant past." The Chadds Ford Historical Society is the institutional manifestation of this facet of Chadds Ford cultural production, and its officers and most active participants belong to a bloc[10] (or sub-bloc) with its occupations/economic base of considerable affluence rooted in DuPont and its ideological/avocational energies concentrated in active engagement with the agrarian/historical ideal.

In 1983 Virginia Johnson had just completed a remarkably successful term as president of the Chadds Ford Historical Society. Her six-and-a-half year tenure saw through to completion the Society's main projects: the restoration of two eighteenth century structures, the John Chad and

Barns-Brinton houses. Under her presidency the Society adopted the idea that the restored houses should be used actively by Society members, not just displayed; and the Society now operates according to the principles and ideology of recreational "living history." Its ongoing activities include the use of the restored houses as settings for the re-creation of colonial domestic arts (e.g., baking in a beehive oven), instruction in crafts appropriate to the colonial image (e.g., stencilling, calligraphy), and Society theme parties (e.g., Tavern Night and Herbal Luncheon).

Not surprising perhaps is the remarkable continuity between this public ideology of the Historical Society and the setting of Mrs. Johnson's private sphere. She and her husband live at Ravenroyde, one of those solid Quaker farmsteads idealized by Canby and Bayard Taylor. The house, its core dating to the late eighteenth century, remained in the Parker family, that of the original Quaker owners, until 1911. The Johnsons have lived there more than forty years and by current standards that makes them Chadds Ford old-timers. They took the name Ravenroyde from the original Parker homestead in Yorkshire (Hughes and McMullan 1982:14).

A considerable parcel of land goes with the house, enough to grow a hay crop and pasture cattle, and modern farm machinery sits nearby in evidence of a serious involvement with agriculture. Inside, the house is full of the solid objects of the appropriate past and the ephemeral clutter of an active present. Stacks of newspapers and magazines contend for space with antiques of various sorts, some apparently with parts missing and some, to the non-specialist, of obscure function. On my first visit to the house I found the parlor occupied by a tall, square object painted black and decorated in a faded floral pattern. With a small door on one side and the powdery smell of long-stored leather, it turned out to be an antique sedan chair like the one in which a gouty Franklin was carted around Paris. Mrs. Johnson, a bit to her dismay, received it as an unsolicited contribution to the Historical Society from a woman who originally bought it as an anniversary gift (thirty-fifth) for her husband.

Down some steps from the original parlor is "the big living room," which the Johnsons have added to their eighteenth century house. The sliding glass patio doors and large television in the corner notwithstanding, the room's construction uses elements scavenged from old buildings (beams from barns, etc.) to give a look and feel entirely consistent with the rest of the building. The architectural firm of John Milner, which specializes in the restoration and re-creation of such architecture and the harmonization of old and new elements, designed both this addition and planned the restorations of the Historical Society's two houses. Milner donated the design for the "cage bar" recently installed at the Barns-

Brinton House (which was also a tavern) in honor of Mrs. Johnson's retirement as Society president.

The walls of the Johnsons' addition are lined with Brandywine art, some by Mrs. Johnson herself. A large charcoal pre-study by N.C. Wyeth dominates the room, but when she speaks of Brandywine painting Mrs. Johnson lets it be known that the domination of the local art scene by the "Wyeth tradition" has caused a red flag of resentment to go aloft in certain quarters. Her own teacher for example, Tom Bostelle, prefers that his paintings not hang on the same wall as Andrew Wyeth's.

Though more equivocal in this regard than her art instructor, Mrs. Johnson expresses ambivalence about some of the trends and forces at work in the Chadds Ford scene; and this is quite consistent with the ideology implicit in both the public orientation of the Historical Society and her personal life-style. Saving a more complete history of the Historical Society for later, suffice it to mention here that the origin of this organization was closely connected to that of the Brandywine Conservancy and Museum, the institution that has assumed professional authority for the "Brandywine Heritage" of art and landscape. Put simply, the Conservancy operates from an ideology approaching pure preservationism, a commitment to defining and stabilizing the "authentic" scene—in both the land and the art—according to the standards of professional planners and curators.

This ideology mobilizes support through the dramatic image of a heroic struggle between forces of sane (read: professional and institutional) management and preservation and the chaotic destructiveness of modern development, a conflict rhetorically supported with Revolutionary War analogies:

> The environment which inspired these artists, and those who have followed, is again being threatened, this time not by the roaring of Revolutionary cannon. The serenity is now challenged by the roar of the indiscriminate bulldozer. This pressure contemporary civilization puts on a fragile landscape resulted in the formation of the Brandywine Conservancy in the late 1960s.
> (Brandywine River Conservancy/Museum slide show)

The original crisis from which the two institutions, the Historical Society and Conservancy, emerged in the late 1960s was the threat that light industry would gain a foothold near the village of Chadds Ford. The successful elimination of the unifying danger created a freer climate where ideologies could diverge. The Conservancy turned sharply in the direction of professional control, dedicated on the one hand to keeping the land as free as possible from the effects of modern civilization—which now includes suburban development—and concerned on the other hand with the professional legitimation of the Pyle-Wyeth artistic line, which in part means disassociating it from the current work of "imitators" and epigones.

The Historical Society operates on the avocational energies of amateurs. Its ideology of active individual participation in a significant past is paralleled by a belief in the active use of private land. This includes recreational uses such as avocational farming, leasing to professional agriculture and even sale for development purposes if one so desires. As of 1982 in fact, the Johnsons were planning to use some of their property for residential development according to the best principles of cluster housing.

I do not mean to suggest that these divergent ideologies belong to two clearly identifiable groups of people, nor that they stand in radical opposition to one another. One finds for example active members of the Historical Society who are also committed volunteers at the Brandywine River Museum. Personal connection to Chadds Ford ideology is situational, varying in depth and orientation according to local circumstances. Rather than imagining clearly opposed camps, it is better to think of two currents in the ongoing activity of a complex cultural discourse. Chadds Ford speaks in a voice with multiple inflections.

XII

James Duff came to the directorship of the Brandywine River Conservancy and Museum as the result of an executive search by a professional consulting firm. Tall and professorial, he seems a particularly orderly person, with a public style of tactful formality well suited to the job of culture management. His pipes sit neatly on a rack in an office where the desk is uncluttered and each object gives the impression of being permanently fixed parallel or perpendicular to something else. The wintertime view from the west window offers unwanted glimpses of Chadds Ford Knoll sitting just across the Brandywine, not far from where Knyphausen deployed Hessian artillary in 1777.

Mr. Duff speaks with sarcasm about the notion that Chadds Ford is a community, a place of human connectedness. It exists, he believes, mostly as a creature of romantic imagination. Whatever community there might be fades rapidly with the onslaught of the suburban developers. For him, the viable alternative is what he calls "personal synthesis," meaning the individual construction of an identity of place, as opposed to a wholesale appropriation of prefab forms (the developments) or the identity of organic community, which is no longer available in Chadds Ford. Mr. Duff expresses here rather clearly the ideology of that mobile managerial class that seems most at home in a postmodern environment of transportable, anonymous expertise.

If Chadds Ford village is the center of ideological production for the general Chadds Ford image, the institution Mr. Duff directs displays more vividly than anything else the sort of paradox of which that image is made. Paradox stands forth clearly in the space between the Conservancy/Museum's explicit ideology of preservation and the forms of cultural production by which it achieves its purpose.

According to Mr. Duff, the primary thesis of the Brandywine River Conservancy is that the natural environment of the Brandywine River Valley has generated a unique set of cultural accoutrements and a distinctive regional history. The Conservancy/Museum serves as a multi-disciplinary resource for the preservation of the definitive Brandywine environment — physical, cultural, and historical. Practically, this means offering its professional expertise in the stewardship of private properties through conservation and preservation easements:

> A conservation or preservation easement is a legal agreement between a property owner and a conservation organization. The property owner agrees to establish certain restrictions over some of his or her property and the conservation organization agrees to regularly inspect the eased areas for any violation and to uphold the conditions of the agreement.... The conservation or preservation easements accomplish the same goals, but with a difference in focus. A conservation easement is used to conserve land, while a preservation easement preserves the cultural integrity of historic structures.
> ("Green Is As Good As Gold," Brandywine
> Conservancy land stewardship brochure)[11]

Easement agreements "provide positive economic considerations" in the form of federal and local tax benefits.

The conservancy also promotes and coordinates other forms of conservation and preservation; for example, Chester County Act 515, according to which tax incentives are offered to the owners of land designated a "farm, forest, water-supply, or open-space" who covenant to preserve these uses for at least ten years. Also, in conjunction with the Chester County Historical Society, the Conservancy coordinates the Historic Sites Survey in the region.

Suburban development, concretized in the image of the "relentlessly advancing bulldozer," is the implicit villain against which the Conservancy arrays its political and economic machinery of professional stewardship. In its brochure on conservation and preservation, a series of drawings (Figure 13) depicts the process of environmental and cultural degradation as the replacement of woods and open-space by dense suburban settlement, the erosion of a picturesque watercourse, and the ugly modernization of an old farmhouse through inappropriate additions (driveway, garage) and subtractions (continuous cornice, penteave, panelled doors). The hard-edged geometry of parallels and perpendiculars (curbs, roadsigns, concrete abutments, eroded banks, rows of uniform houses) replaces the organic softness of the original scene.

The Conservancy's antagonism toward suburban development informs its policy and overt ideology, but viewed in the larger picture of social and cultural production, that antagonism is suffused with irony. I have suggested that the suburban developments are mechanisms for providing access to a generalized image of residual agrarian life and values. Paradoxically, many qualities associated with that life—close-knit community, deep and specific connection to a particular place, personal involvement with a unique past, a definite identity peculiar to the locale— are qualities inadmissable to the generalized image. Their aura but not their personal enactment is required, for the goal of suburban development is to enlist a broad range of participation (read: financial investment). A generalized, idyllic image of tidy, small-scale agrarianism, Chadds Ford's speciality, has proved very successful in attracting such participation, no doubt because it provides a ready-made setting into which people can import their personal associations. As a postmodern cultural production, the Chadds Ford image is an elaborate stage set in which one can imagine and enact the idea of a way of life.

The irony of the Brandywine River Conservancy is that in its devotion to preserving the *unique* heritage and landscape of the middle Brandywine, it too must produce and disseminate a generalized image capable of attracting support from remote sources. Paramount among these sources are the tourists, who come to see Brandywine art in the environment where it was painted, and a national — even international — network of the cultural elite.

This latter group is capable of mobilizing huge resources of wealth and prestige. The recent $7,000,000 nationwide endowment drive suggests the order of magnitude of these resources, and this partial list of endowment committee members suggests the audience to which the drive was pitched:

Lady Bird Johnson (honorary chair)

Ms. Wallis Annenberg

Mrs. Jo Jo Starbuck Bradshaw

Mr. Douglas Fairbanks, Jr.

FIGURE 13.
Landscape
degradation —
Conservancy
perspective.
From, "Green Is as
Good as Gold,"
Brandywine River
Conservacy
pamphlet.

Miss Nancy Hanks

Ms. Ali McGraw

Mrs. Gertrude Stein

Mr. Irving S. Shapiro (DuPont chairman)

Mr. Eugene Ormandy

Mr. Andy Warhol

The Brandywine River Museum above all serves to attract popular and elite patronage. It is a mechanism of subtle transformation through which the local specificity of this "unique part of the world," the main premise of Conservancy ideology, becomes the representative specimen of a generalized idea that can resonate with personal associations in places far remote from Chadds Ford.

This transformation from specific place to specimen to generalized image turns upon the paradoxical logic of preservationist ideology. The unique and special scene of Chadds Ford (or the Brandywine Valley) is in danger of being overwhelmed by the forces of progress and development. The available alternative is to throw up a financial and political fence of preservation behind which the local scene can perpetuate its uniqueness undisturbed. But for that fence to be an effective barrier requires the investment of material resources well beyond those available in the place itself. The solution (characteristically postmodern) is to make that barrier not an impenetrable palisade, but a velvet rope—to "museumize" rather than fortify.

The preservation of Chadds Ford depends on presenting it as a representative display, and it has the duplicity of any specimen. It is a unique case but "means" a general class. It is as synecdoche that Chadds Ford attracts the far-flung resources for its own preservation, doing so by assimilating its own uniqueness, the justification for its preservation, to a generalized image capable of tapping many and widespread springs of personal association.

XIII

The old mill building which is now the Brandywine River Museum symbolizes the Conservancy's simultaneous concerns with art, history, and the natural environment. Here is a remarkable architectural blending of old and new, of the indoors and the outdoors, all of it comfortable and dramatic, all of it clearly related to important human endeavor in art, commerce and land use.

The original mill was constructed in 1864. It was a grist mill which turned local grain into flour used here and throughout the United States. The building was utilitarian in design and function; handsome, but entirely practical. It produced flour until 1941. In 1971, it opened a new face to the public. Architect James R. Grieves of Baltimore transformed the building into a modern museum, adding contemporary spaces to the basic building while preserving its native, rugged character.

From the entrance, the mill looks only slightly changed. Its windows are now shuttered, but its brick walls are still studded with iron diamonds that once helped to hold the walls in place. Upon entering the courtyard, however, changes and additions are immediately apparent to the visitor. Here a group of sheds styled after a well-known architectural form of the region [Quaker horse shed] enclose patterns of paving stone. The courtyard is the site for many special activities, from crafts demonstrations to farmers' markets. Surrounding the Museum in large and well-known gardens are wild flowers and other native plants of the region.

Inside the building, curving glass walls offer a view of the River and its hills. Here the art of the Brandywine Valley is effectively related to the natural beauty of land and water which has inspired so much of that art. This Museum is extraordinary. Its galleries are housed in the renovated mill with its original rough white plaster walls and hand-hewn wooden beams. It is an ideal setting for viewing regional art.

> ("Preserving an American Heritage," Brandywine
> River Conservancy/Museum pamphlet, 1981)

As part of its self-preservation, the Museum offers a set of four postcard views of its building (Figures 14 and 15). Arranged into contrastive pairs, they efficiently reproduce Conservancy ideology. Throughout its self-presentation, the Conservancy rhetorically organizes its ideology in binary oppositions: "blending of old and new, of the indoors and outdoors," cultural preservation/natural conservation, and so on. Two cards are interior views, two exterior. One pair, an interior and an exterior view, both horizontally composed, is devoted to the gallery/old mill restoration. The other pair an interior and an exterior, both vertically composed, depicts the "circulation core" addition.

In their earth tones, weathered brick, rough-hewn wood and unfinished plaster, and in the square monumentality of compositional elements the restored mill pictures speak of landscape of the middle Brandywine. These apparent commitments to the specificity of the place justify an implicit claim to authority. The museum projects the aura of concentrated authenticity, the place where the authentic Chadds Ford experience is most readily available.

Yet the very act of circumscription implied here, based as it is on the portable authority of professional managers, involves de-specification and dissociation, the replacement of an active encounter with a place by the efficiently displayed and eminently viewable image of such an encounter. "Representative authenticity" is the oxymoron upon which the Conservancy/Museum depends.

FIGURE 14.   Brandywine River Museum — restored mill gallery. Museum postcards; photographs by Ernest Beadle.

FIGURE 15.
Brandywine River
Museum —
circulation core
addition. Museum
postcards;
photographs by
Ernest Beadle.

Figure 14 (cont.). Restored mill gallery — interior.

Figure 15 (cont.). Circulation core — interior.

XIV

If the binarized architecture of the Brandywine River Museum encodes a paradoxical but eminently successful ideology organized around a dialectic of specificity and generality or local rootedness and mobile expertise, the discourse conducted inside the building encodes a variant of the same dialectic. Such redundancy is, of course, characteristic of the postmodern Site. Here are some excerpts from a guide's discourse during a gallery tour in July, 1982:

> [Referring to the Andrew Wyeth painting *Roasted Chestnuts*] This is a boy named Alan Messersmith, who one day—he was a friend of the children, of the Wyeth children; and one day, uh, talked all the kids in the neighborhood into...y'know had this great scheme. They were going to get independently wealthy selling roasted chestnuts along the roads of the Brandywine valley. And most of the kids gave up after a few days. But Alan *stuck* it out; Alan *stuck* right alongside the highway until the snows came. And Wyeth painted him; did several beautiful studies of the ear and the head—and the steam.
>
> This is a little bit of an unusual painting to look at because at the same time that you seem to stare out there for a car, you're still staring down here at your feet. And then you want to look at the detail. And we almost have several ways to look, and [it] almost is...unrestful—again.

The same discursive structure operates in the this guide's commentary on Wyeth's Siri paintings:

> These nudes over in here are all of *Siri Erickson*. This is Siri. She was a young girl. She was first painted, in this painting over here [*The Sauna*], in the family sauna...her family...her father's sauna when she was fourteen years old. And Wyeth considers these a...a growth from Christina Olson, from the work...the paintings he did of Christina Olson. Christina died in January of 19...68? My dates...I get dates...I can barely remember my own birthday half the time, um, [checks her notes]...yeah, '68. And, uh, he started painting Siri the next summer, and he considers this an extension of his works with the Olsons. Some are done in watercolor, some are done in tempera. This is the first one he did, as I mentioned.
>
> He originally painted her with a towel across her chest. And he showed it to his wife Betsy, who said, "It doesn't look natural. Why don't you get her to take the towel off?"
>
> And Andrew said, "*My God*! Her father'll *kill* me. She's four*teen*!"
>
> So the next day he said, "Siri, would you be *willing*?"
>
> And she said, "Ya know, my father asked me last night, if we're in the, the uh, sauna, why do you have a towel wrapped around you?
>
> So Andrew said, "Go ask your mother or your dad, because this kind of thing can get real sticky."
>
> And she came back—said it was fine. They are a very unselfconscious family. Uh, when she was posing for that large one over in the corner there, where her arms are crossed, she was posing for that—she was fifteen at the time—uh, she *rushed* out the door, *picked* up a club, and *clubbed to death* a

woodchuck in her father's garden! Came back in, blood spattered on her legs, picked up her pose, and—that was it. Ya know, Wyeth thought that was pretty neat, ya know . . . that this girl . . . I mean, how many fifteen year old girls would, ya know, in the *first* place, stand there nude, and in the second place, club to death a woodchuck, and think nothing of it.

Uh, you can see her grow up [indicating the whole series of paintings]. This is one that I particularly enjoy [indicating *Indian Summer*] because of the flesh. Ya know, as an art teacher and an artist myself, people ask me, "How do you paint flesh?" And there are actually millions of combinations for flesh, and please enjoy these and look at them afterwards. There's [points to appropriate areas in the painting] yellow flesh and there's purples in there; and there's green-grays, and blue-grays and more, uh, brown-oranges in there. There's just so many combinations. There's heavy tan—there's light tan—and there's no tan [points to each]. You can enjoy all these different colors of flesh.

This is also an egg tempera, which is a hatched, uh, medium, where you have to put layers and layers of paint on it and it's all hatched, so the colors are almost woven together. Do you have any questions on anything on the second floor?

[No one does.]

The issues of color and composition, light and perspective, medium and oeuvre, are the stuff of the academy, universal categories through which a painting becomes fine art and the artist sheds his personal history. Clubbed woodchucks and the cute schemes of enterprising children run against the grain of professional art appreciation. Wyeth insists (and the curators of the museum acknowledge) that the paintings' anecdotal background is essential to an appreciation of his art. But in this Wyeth is expressing the acceptable aesthetic principle that his art draws the universal, the profound, and the mythical out of the concrete and ordinary. The gallery guides, however, often use anecdotes to create a sense of intimacy with the artist, to present him as a real person with real experiences and to identify themselves as insiders. In short, these anecdotes are implements of authentication, anchors to the specificity of place and person. The professional staff explicitly discourages the volunteer guides from spreading "Wyeth gossip," a mechanism crucial to Wyeth's inscription in the postmodern order. Instead, they urge them to emphasize the aesthetics and technical processes of his art. The discourse illustrated in these excerpts constantly reproduces the characteristic dialectic.

The Brandywine Conservancy/Museum insists upon its regional roots, its local tradition, yet simultaneously aspires to an ideal aesthetic world that acknowledges no regions, nor the contingencies of concrete time, nor persons with concrete histories. Wyeth is a Brandywine painter/Wyeth is a twentieth century master: this is the simplest formulation of one particular inscription of a paradox that in many forms pervades Chadds Ford's discourse.

Also, given the postmodern context, it should not be surprising that the stories told by this particular guide are oral reinscriptions of Wyeth's own anecdotes, themselves inscribed in *The Two Worlds of Andrew Wyeth*, a book of interviews conducted by no less an agent of cultural validation than Thomas Hoving (1978) for a major exhibit of Wyeth's work at the Metropolitan Museum.

XV

If Chadds Ford is a locale privileged with the aura of authenticity, Andrew Wyeth is its *genius loci*. Although his art is firmly within the modernist mode, as a cultural phenomenon Wyeth (or "Wyethness") is a decidedly postmodern institution. Symptomatic of this condition is the degree to which the public sphere of Wyeth spectacle merges with the private domain of domestic experience. At his home a short distance north of the village, just off Route 100, Wyeth lives and works in the expensively restored structures of an eighteenth-century grist mill, views of which appear in his paintings. The mill building itself "reproduces" (re-inscribes) the Brandywine River Museum in that it houses Wyeth's private gallery (third floor) and the office through which the business side of his artistic production is managed (fourth floor). The eighteenth-century milling machinery (grindstones, chutes, undershot millwheel, etc.) is being re-created on the first two floors.

The miller's house has also been carefully restored with native materials and archaic techniques to give it an authentically eighteenth-century look. For a garage, a re-creation of the Concordville Quaker Meeting horse shed has been appended to the house. A large front room patterned after the house George Washington used as his headquarters during the Brandywine battle has been added to the house. This makes the room a copy of a copy, since the original headquarters burned in 1931, later to be re-created by the Brandywine Battlefield Park Commission. The "depth of authenticity" in the Wyeth property re-creation extends even to the restoration of a dormant feud. By repairing the dam behind the mill as part of the recovery of the eighteenth century look, Wyeth has subjected a neighbor's property to periodic flooding. Sellers Hoffman, mill operator, and Joseph Hickman, local farmer, litigated over the same issue a hundred years ago (*Philadelphia Inquirer*, 6/15/81). We see here a whole material environment conforming to the "logic" of postmodern pastiche, a subject I will return to in Chapter 3.

In the range of Chadds Ford cultural production, Wyeth's home stands somewhere between the Brandywine River museum and the restored Quaker farmhouses and recreational farms of the DuPont elite. Although a private home restored with private funds, it has the self-consciousness, formality, and orderliness of a museum; and caretaker/handyman George Heebner hints of plans to open the property to the public after Wyeth's death. The museum-like quality of this site is of course a function of the wealth available for the production of its look, and this is inseparable from Wyeth's status as a major American artist: some would say *the* major American artist.[12]

The Chadds Ford location most associated with Wyeth's work is the Karl Kuerner farm, which sits a little east of the village, off Ring Road (see Map 2). Wyeth has painted some of his best known works there: *Brown Swiss, Evening at Kuerners, Spring Fed, Groundhog Day, Karl, Anna Kuerner*. Just at the edge of the property, where the now unused Penn Central Line crosses Ring Road, N.C. Wyeth and his grandson were struck by a train and killed in 1945. Here is Betsy Wyeth, Andrew's wife and business manager, speaking of the Kuerner property:

> The Kuerner farm is about a mile's walk from Andrew Wyeth's studio in Chadds Ford. Suburbia has changed this walk considerably in the last few years. Until the late 1950s the artist could cross cornfields and pastures and walk through a woods undisturbed. Nowadays he has to choose his path with caution to avoid meeting someone on the way—the land has been sold, large tracts subdivided, houses built, the brook in the woods dammed to create a pond and "no trespassing" signs warn him off. Even Karl Kuerner has sold a few acres of land here and there; but Kuerner's Hill remains unchanged, for Karl and his only son, Karl Jr, still farm the land.
>
> (Wyeth 1976:7)

Since this was written, Karl Sr. has died and suburban incursion, presented here as a hindrance to artistic creation, has whittled the farm to about one hundred acres. The famous hill is hemmed with rows of small lots and a rural condominium complex, Ringfield, sits a few hundred yards down Ring Road. Wyeth framed the property in his paintings and the modern socio-economic order has replicated that act on the very ground itself. The Kuerner farm is both an obsolescent remnant of the residual agrarian past and the site authorized by Wyeth's paintings as the official representative of that past. In this it reflects the overall situation of contemporary Chadds Ford.

The relation between the human and physical setting of Chadds Ford and its artistic reproduction is immensely complex, and this in a way thoroughly characteristic of the cultural discourse that makes Chadds Ford so typically postmodern. In part, the complexity derives from a bewildering replicative fluidity whereby the art and the actual setting tend to merge in quite literal ways, paintings taking on physical properties of the "reality" they depict and reality being transformed to correspond to its image in the art. Similarly, the boundary between the artist and his human subjects frequently blurs.

Wyeth above all exemplifies these tendencies. He speaks of such things as sanding a portion of a painting to give it the "perfect texture of the real wall" he was depicting (Hoving 1978:92). While Wyeth was painting *Young Bull* in Kuerner's barnyard, so the story goes, the animal subject acted up. In its thrashing about it splashed paint across the hindquarters of its own image. The marks were left on the painting, superimposing the contingent reality of the creative moment upon the meticulously constructed and controlled product of that creativity (Wyeth 1976:228–233).

Wyeth goes so far as to associate the physical substance of his medium, the natural colors used in tempera painting, with the Chadds Ford earth itself. "I like to pick it up," he says of this medium, "and hold it in my fingers. To me it's like the dry mud of the Brandywine valley in certain times of the year or like these tawney fields that one can see outside my windows" (Hoving 1978:34).

Similarly, Wyeth sometimes identifies so closely with his human subjects as to blur his own personality. While occupied with painting Karl Kuerner, for example, he adjusted his ethnic heritage appropriately, from French Swiss, (his "real" ethnicity) to Swiss German. Wyeth himself describes a striking example of this phenomenon:

> Once, while I was doing a painting of a Negro called Tom Clark—it was called *That Gentleman*—Halloween came along. I shaved every bit of hair off my head, I was absolutely bald. Then I put alizarin crimson all over my whole head and then took brown ink and rubbed it over very transparently and the red came through. I tipped my eyes with adhesive tape, enlarged my nostrils a little and I actually looked like Tom Clark. I was becoming part of my painting, really.
> (Meryman 1973:51)

My point here is that these tendencies in Wyeth and his art are not mere manifestations of a personal aesthetic philosophy, though Wyeth seems to consider them such. In fact they are concentrated, perhaps heightened examples of postmodern signifying practice as exemplified at Chadds Ford. They are matched by corresponding tendencies moving in the opposite direction but having the same effect of blurring the distinctions between artist and subject, "image" and "reality," or original and reproduction. This blurring proceeds from the apparently infinite replication of authenticity in Chadds Ford. As we have seen, the housing developments, chief villain in Conservancy ideology and dam to the artist's creative flow, are also a technique for replicating "in reality" the perspectives and scenery codified as authentically Chadds Ford by Wyeth's art. Even more specifically, particular paintings are reproduced by manipulating material reality. This is a phenomenon especially associated with tourism and usually takes the form of the search for the sites of individual paintings:

> We wanted to see the Kuerner farm. We own the book *Wyeth at Kuerners*, which reproduces 350 works by Andrew Wyeth in pencil, dry brush, water color and tempera—all depicting Hans [sic] Kuerner, and his wife Anna and their farm. We stopped at the local diner for directions "Maybe we'll see Andrew Wyeth himself," Ann said. "The people at the museum said he stops at this diner for coffee."
>
> "You'd know him if you saw him," we were told in the diner. "He wears ragged clothes—sort of eccentric. Always racing through town in his old T-bird, loaded with dogs."
>
> He wasn't there, but we got directions to Kuerner's farm. "Just go to the gas station," they said, "Turn up Ring Road. You can't miss it."
>
> Well, we missed it, becoming pleasantly lost on back country roads. Everything looked hauntingly familiar, and we knew we were in Wyeth country. There was a light dusting of snow on the ground as in many of his paintings. Wyeth seemed obsessed with white. "I love white things. Oh, I love white things," he says in the Kuerner book. We saw the play of light and shadow as the sun glanced over neat, orderly farm buildings and the rolling hills. We marveled at the textures, the stark bleakness, the unexpected beauty in common objects that Andrew Wyeth captured so well. Suddenly there it was. We laughed when we saw the Kuerner farmhouse because it looked so familiar. "It's just like being in one of those paintings," Pete said.
>
> We hadn't seen Andrew Wyeth in person, but somehow this was even better. The low winter sun was reflected off one of the windows, much like the scenes painted in "Brown Swiss" or "Evening at Kuerners." Ann took a picture of the Kuerner mailbox for her report, and we returned to the motel to pack and head home.
>
> (Boyd 1979–80:29–30; Cf. O'Doherty 1973,
> Logsden 1971, Wainwright 1967)

An act of distancing makes scenery out of topography, but what complicated ideological processes allow one to experience scenery through the categories of pictorial art? And even more perplexing, what transformation makes specific paintings the legitimizing antecedents of the physical locales they depict, so that the attraction of these geographical sites is their offer of participation in the painted image?

Christian C. Sanderson, to whom I will return presently, was a supertourist and, in his day, an eccentric because of how thoroughly he organized his life around tourism. Looking back from our present vantage, we might see him as a precursor of what has become typical of Chadds Ford cultural production. Sanderson lived in George Washington's Headquarters before it burned, and later in a little house, now the Sanderson Museum, just north of the village intersection. He was a friend of Wyeth and posed for some of his early paintings. In one of these, *The Schoolmaster*, he posed in front of a tree. In the picture Wyeth added a carving to the bark. Later, Sanderson took a penknife to the tree so that "reality" conformed better to the image. In the same spirit, on special occasions the curators of the Sanderson Museum hang a white shirt from a line on the building's side porch. A small tag hangs nearby identifying this tableau as *The Bachelor* by Andrew Wyeth, and inside one finds reproductions of the painting itself, as well as photographs of Wyeth in the act of painting it.

Perhaps even more telling than the mutual replication and interpenetration of "image" and "reality" is the replication of the artist himself. To some degree Wyeth is constantly reproduced in the countless painters, amateur and professional, who devote themselves to capturing the Wyeth "look" in their art. But the most revealing case is Karl J. Kuerner, grandson of the Karl Kuerner who figures so prominently in Wyeth's paintings. Karl Jr., the second generation Kuerner and also a subject of Wyeth's art, presided over the family farm-cum-tourist site. It is somehow fitting that his son, the third generation Karl, should be an artist in the Wyeth mode. Viewed as a general cultural process rather than a succession of individuals, we might see the development in these terms: the artist assimilates himself to and identifies with a particular setting—human and physical—and paints it; his images throw a frame around the setting (and its inhabitants), inscribing it and transforming it into a Site, something to be experienced only in reference to the images that authenticate it; the process is completed when the Site reproduces (re-cites) the artist himself.

Karl J. Kuerner—grandson—was coached in art by Carolyn Wyeth, Andrew's sister. His studio is the vacant tenant house, remnant of the prewar economic order, on the Kuerner property. His insistence on "making his own name" outside the Wyeth shadow is almost a required element in the ideology of artistic traditions and has the effect of emphasizing the generational connection. "Chadds Ford, long known as 'Artists' Country,' due to the reign of the legendary Wyeth family, has produced another astonishing talent in the person of twenty-five-year-old Karl J. Kuerner," says a card promoting his show at the Newman Art Gallery in Philadelphia.

In details of his career Kuerner seems to replicate the "idea of Wyeth." Talent apparent at an early age, a connection with commercial art, a sold-out first show, intimate knowledge of the subjects he paints: these are all biographical motifs that Kuerner and Wyeth share. If in some sense Wyeth is himself a cultural production, a key passage in the text of Chadds Ford, Kuerner represents the self-awareness of that discourse accomplished through postmodern processes of simulation.

XVI

Just east of the Chadds Ford intersection there sits a nineteenth-century farmstead—a brick farmhouse and several large outbuildings. In the 1950s the structures were done over as a tourist mall with a combined Revolutionary War/agrarian motif. These were the original shops:

Chadds Ford Gallery

Artisans' Coop for Unicef (since moved to its own building across the highway)

Battle Creek Pottery

Chadds Ford Travel

Collector's Cabinet (antiques)

Fudge Drum (candy)

General's Lady (women's clothing)

Mushroom Cave (rare reference to the mushroom industry of western Chester county)

Bookshop

Silver Shop

Turks Head Bazzaar

Village Craftsman

Wooden Shoe

Country Kitchen

By the early 80s the number of shops had dwindled. In 1983 there were these:

Chadds Ford Gallery

The Candle Shop

The Hayloft (gifts)

The Fudge Drum

The Milkhouse (snacks and ice cream)

Handarts Market

Feline and Friends

Colonel's Lady

Wooden Shoe[13]

These shops represent the low-priced segment of the tourist economy in Chadds Ford. Other segments in the division of economic labor are represented by the Artisans Cooperative and the Weymouth antique shop. The former is one of a number of northern outlets for the "authentic" products of Appalachian artisans. The latter specializes in relatively expensive antiques of regional association: large pieces of furniture, some of it Pennsylvania German, china, silverware, pottery, old paintings, and so on.[14]

The objects of the Barn Shops tend toward the miniature, the cozy and the cute. Miniature furniture for doll houses is a prominent item and one shop specializes in the paraphernalia of the "old fashioned Christmas." Comical miniature pigs in various media, (ceramic, cloth, wood) appear throughout the shops, a reference to the Jamie Wyeth pig paintings that are a special tourist favorite.

The Chadds Ford Gallery deserves special attention as a site overtly dedicated to image reproduction. If Chadds Ford cultural production is characterized by a seemingly endless series of replications of a generalized image, the gallery is a fitting symbol for the whole Chadds Ford scene. It is mainly an outlet for reproductions of Wyeth's art. Here the potential of the image to become an infinitely reproduceable commodity is most concretely realized.

The gallery building is the nineteenth-century farmhouse of the Barn Shops complex. With business offices upstairs, the first floor is the gallery proper. The walls of the entrance hallway, which runs straight through, front to back, provide space for special shows. On my first visit the works of some of the better-known local artists, who of course find no place in the Brandywine River Museum collection, were hanging here. Prices ranged generally from one hundred to several hundred dollars. This space has also housed an exhibit of posters from Wyeth's numerous museum shows ($50 to $100). Here, too, Karl J. Kuerner had his first one man show.

The two main rooms, what were the parlor and probably a dining room, contain the large and expensive reproductions of Wyeth's paintings. The typical "quality" reproduction can range well into the hundreds of dollars. In the case of a particularly popular or important painting, a few reproductions from the printing run might be reserved for signing by the artist. These are numbered and sold as items in a special edition, with prices from $1,000 to $4,000. Special portfolios are another reproduction phenomenon. A set of several images grouped by some unifying theme (e.g., the change of seasons) are sold as a package, enhancing their value.

The last room of the gallery, in the back of the house and probably once the kitchen, offers smaller and cheaper reproductions. In tone this room belongs with the rest of the Barn Shops out back, while the front of the gallery is more comparable to the moderately expensive antique shop just down the road. Unlike the front rooms, this back area has its walls densely covered with pictures. Down its middle is a bin of plastic-covered reproductions. The bin itself is a miniaturized reproduction of a free-standing manger. Along with the Wyeth works, some pure kitsch finds a place in this back room, for example Art Dembosky's comical drawings of pigs engaged in human activities. Prices here fall below $100.

The Chadds Ford Gallery represents the overtly commercial phase of a "general political economy" of Wyeth images (Baudrillard 1981:112–122). The reproduction of Wyeth's paintings and the shrewd management of these reproductions through special editions, limited printings, and size and quality of the image, articulate a commodity system accessible to patronage at many economic levels and ranges of interest, from the lowliest day-tripping tourist to the Wyeth connoisseur whose affluence falls short of the six figure price tag on an important Wyeth original.[15]

The highly controlled and calculated copying of Wyeth's paintings does not approach in volume that elusive form of reproduction: the replication of the general Wyeth look in the endless flow of paintings from the brushes of "Sunday painters" and of photographs from the cameras of Wyeth-stalking tourists. These activities, too, along with the massive infrastructure that supports them, are part of the economy of images in Chadds Ford.

One final example of Wyeth reproduction highlights the process of image commodification, in that it unequivocally disrupts the boundary that aesthetic ideology places between art and the collectible object. The Wyeths themselves have commissioned a craftsman, a goldsmith and jeweler, to produce a number of pieces based on motifs from Andrew's paintings. Some are to be jewelry produced in limited edition series; others will be one-of-a-kind *objets d'art*; all will be expensive. There were at one time plans for a joint show in which the three-dimensional objects would be displayed next to the paintings from which they were adapted.

The translation of painted image to crafted object is answered by a complementary movement in Wyeth's conception of his own artistic labor. He describes the tempera medium, for which he is best known, in terms of the tactile involvement with materials associated with the production of crafts. The dry colors are like the very soil he depicts in his paintings. The finished product has the durability so familiar as part of the handicraft mystique. The act of production is "like building, really building in great layers the way the earth itself was built" (Hoving 1978:34). The metaphor is at once geological and artisanal, natural *and* cultural, a typical blurring in Chadds Ford discourse. Most revealing is the metaphor for textile production. "You've got to weave it," Wyeth says of tempera, "as if you were weaving a rug or tapestry, slowly building it up" (ibid.:35).[16]

XVII

For the Bicentennial a local sewing group produced a "friendship quilt," an artifact particularly representative of the Chadds Ford scene (Figure 16). The "hand-made" quilt has pride of place among the crafts of suburban artisanal production. It combines the decorative and the utilitarian more emphatically than many crafts; its function is as appropriate to the present as to the past; it is eminently reproducible both cognitively and materially, having a fairly codified vocabulary of patterns and requiring fairly simple technical abilities; it is eminently consumable, witness its importance in the folk art and antique industry; and, perhaps most important, symbolically it is the very soul of pre-industrial domestic coziness.

The Chadds Ford friendship quilt has the added symbolic interest of being a collection of fragments brought together to evoke a general image of Chadds Ford history and culture. The quilt comprises individual squares, each one produced in isolation and depicting in applique an appropriate scene, locale or activity. Stitched together, the squares are meant to evoke a global image of the place. Here is a list of the quilt's contents:

- Lafayette Headquarters (building restored on the grounds of the Battlefield Park
- Dilworth oak (old tree with Revolutionary War associations)
- anonymous artist at work (emblem of artistic heritage)
- school children around a maypole (annual ritual performed by third-grade girls of the Chadds Ford Elementary School—emblem of community)
- Chris Sanderson (reproduction of a scene originally drawn by Jamie Wyeth for a Sanderson commemorative plate)
- octagonal schoolhouse (one of the generalized architectural forms symbolic of rusticity)
- The Brandywine River Museum (restored mill)
- winter skating on the Brandywine (another typical Chadds Ford activity emblematic of small community)
- Chadds Ford town hall (emblem of community)
- George Washington on his horse (central, double sized panel)

FIGURE 16. Chadds Ford friendship quilt. Photograph by the author.

- Karl Kuerner farm (locale of Wyeth's best known Chadds Ford paintings and supreme emblem of generalized rural imagery)
- granary (restored building on the Wyeth property used today as an office by Betsy Wyeth and the site of a recent major art theft)
- Christmas tree (the "old fashioned Christmas" is the Chadds Ford holiday *par excellence*)

- square dancing, with figures in colonial dress (community represented as costume tableau)
- Quaker family in buggy (emblematic of rusticity and heritage)
- cannon and crossed flags (emblem of the Battle of the Brandywine)
- fox hunt (peripheral to present-day Chadds Ford, but a significant emblem of the regional environment)
- Howard Pyle's studio (ruin of an old mill, now protectively "stabilized")
- Washington's headquarters (re-created on the grounds of the Battlefield Park after the original burned down)
- John Chad House (restored by Chadds Ford Historical Society— emblem of colonial domesticity)
- Chadds Ford Post Office (housed in a renovated barn)
- Brinton's Bridge (covered bridge, destroyed by fire)
- blacksmith shop (emblem of artisinal production)
- General Howe
- Scene of the Battle of the Brandywine

The quilt hangs on a frame as an introductory display at the local community celebration, Chadds Ford Days, the subject of Chapter 4. I propose that we view this object, like the Kuerner farm, as a representative artifact of Chadds Ford's postmodernity. In content it allusively sketches the overall Chadds Ford image; materially and ideologically it presents in small the paradoxes characteristic of that image.

Through the idealized mode of its production—the quilting bee—the generalized image of a quilt includes the ideas of organic community, unified action and conviviality. In this particular Chadds Ford quilt, image, object, and mode of production create a fabric of paradox and dislocation in which idealized archaism is a crucial part of the production. In producing the friendship quilt, the sewing group produced not only the object, but also the idea of "quiltness," with all its attendant associations. All these affective qualities of quiltness automatically infuse the objects and scenes represented in the quilt's text. The global idea of Chadds Ford appropriates the connotations of the artifact through which it is represented.

And there is yet another production involved in the quilt, simultaneous with and only analytically separable from the physical object and its affective force. I mean here the production of an encompassing attitude, a general perspective or rhetorical structure that enforces a limitation of vision. An opacity is installed that prevents inspection of the paradoxes flourishing around the quilt. The kind of paradox I mean is the one, again diagnostic of postmodernity, where both the thing and the idea of the thing are produced; a physical object is produced, but its materiality becomes equivocal in that it is inscribed with the simulacrum of the thing it purports to be. Such paradoxes are particularly evident in Chadds Ford, since the thing and the idea of the thing are so symmetrically opposed there. The ideas of close community, authenticity, early American rusticity, and traditionality that inform the image seem polarly opposed to the reality of the dominant suburban/tourist social order.

XVIII

Wyeth's comparison of his paintings to weaving, his commission of craft objects that reproduce motifs from his art, and the totalization of Chadds Ford in the form of a quilt: all these things suggest another pervasive theme of Chadds Ford ideology; namely, that artisanal production is the appropriate mode for the Chadds Ford image. An important part of what gets produced and endlessly reproduced in the advanced capitalist economic, social, and moral order of Chadds Ford are the simulacra of an *archaic* economic, social, and moral order. Subsistence, self-reliance and making by hand are its touchstones.

George Heebner is a Chadds Ford craftsman and devotee of Ayn Rand. His hands move in gestures at once mechanical and graceful, speaking of their thirty years' involvement with tools and reluctant materials. He tells of his work in restoring Hoffman's mill (now the property of Andrew Wyeth) with considerable reflexivity:[17]

> I've always been a very introspective individual. Not . . . I'm not the usual type of tradesperson, so to speak. Like I say, I was a chemist before this, and the training that I have is all self-taught. I've taken nothing on a professional level to do what I've been doing for the last thirty years. It's all been just a desire to achieve it. I do all the things myself. And I've never worked with a tradesman, whatever I've done. Like the masonry. I've never worked with a mason. And the carpentry—same way. 'Course, electrical and plumbing is sort of modern. But I've never worked with one of those, thank goodness. I really feel this was all to my advantage. I don't know, when I come up against a problem I don't say, "Well, traditionally we can't tackle that." You're licked when you say "It's not in the book, so therefore what's your next problem?"
>
> So in that sense, even with the plastering, but I've developed a technique of trying to make something look . . . [not] contrived, [but] like they did in the old days. In other words, try to make a stone wall that's not stone wall, say it's block underneath, and you want to make it look like it's plastered stone. If you contrive that to make little bumps here and little bumps there it's going to *look* contrived. But if you handicap yourself with the tool that you're using to plaster. . . . Instead of taking a plasterer's trowel you use, say, like a mason's trowel; and you can't do a good job with that but you try as hard as you can,

it looks much more natural, the finished product, than if you didn't handicap yourself. And you deliberately try. See deliberate is the key. I think its a natural evolved form on my part because I've never been taught how to do it.
(Interview conducted 6/27/81 at the Wyeth property)

Here is the postmodern craftsman, the meta-craftsman. His real skill lies less in making things than infusing them with the *idea* of craftedness. Training in the modern trades might well be a direct hindrance to his purpose. As in several other respects, the Wyeth context affords the most extreme and readable example of a general movement in Chadds Ford cultural production. In hiring Mr. Heebner, the Wyeth's created a quintessentially postmodern social role: specialist in the material production of the simulacra of archaic material production (cf. Jones 1975:129–139).

XIX

A bit more complicated and historically enlightening is the case of Joseph Messersmith. If Mr. Heebner is indigenous to the postmodern Chadds Ford scene, Mr. Messersmith seems a transitional figure who has had to adapt to the emerging socio-economic environment. His house sits at the end of a rutted lane off Station Way Road, not far from the village intersection. When he moved there in 1941 the house had no electricity, a pump outside, and a pot-bellied stove for heat. The walls were whitewashed. At first he had some animals and "farmed for fun."

Mr. Messersmith's hands seem too large-boned for his otherwise slight body and give the impression of moving at a slower, more controlled tempo than the rest of him. He is charged with nervous energy and his fingers are stained dark with the finish he applies to his tinwork.

Above the sofa hangs a large reproduction of Wyeth's most famous painting, *Christina's World*. Nearby is a pre-study of the boy's head in *Roasted Chestnuts*. The boy is Mr. Messersmith's youngest son, Alan. Here is Mr. Messersmith's capsule history of his working life:

What we did was make church windows, memorial church windows. It was called art leaded glass—art leaded stained glass. I been in that business for . . . well ever since I was seventeen. That article in the paper, that practically gives you the whole story. If you read that you know the whole story about the leaded glass business. Then of course we moved out here. Of course the Depression come along and when the Depression hits everything drops. Churches hadn't any money and architects aren't . . . got away from putting leaded glass in homes so we had to turn to something else. And so then I turned to painting [i.e. house interiors, etc.]. Then of course the War came along and when the War hits why then you go to the shipyards. I was in what they call the hardwood shop in the shipyard. I was in finishing, finishing quarters and furniture for the captain's quarters and the wheelhouse and things of that sort. That was in Chester Shipyard, Sun Ship Company. Then after the War, why then I came out and then got back in the glass business again—here and there as the business started to pick up. And then in between time, why, when business is slow, I got a job....Mr. Sweng [?] from the Park Commission [Brandywine Battlefield Park], he come over and asks me if I'd work on Lafayette and Washington's headquarters. So I started work over there, painting them inside, interior decorating inside and out. And I did that for quite a while and in between time I'd lay off that for awhile and go, if I'd get a leaded glass job, go to the leaded glass—and we'd make up windows. Had a studio in Philadelphia. We used to commute back and forth.

And then Andy came to me, Andy Wyeth came to me and he asked me . . . he had a palette someone gave him. It was a . . . what do you call it . . . a water paint palette. It was quite large and it was made out of real soft aluminum and it was bend all up on him ya know. So he asked me if I could make him a palette. And I looked at it and I says yeah. So he says he wanted it a little larger than the one he had. He wanted the cups deep because he wanted to use it for tempera work. And I said okay.—In fact I got one here. [pulls out Wyeth's palette and explains its construction and use].

In November Betsy [Wyeth] came to me and asked me to make Andy a chandelier that was over in Washington's Headquarters. And I had been painting over there ya know, so naturally I had the keys. The park is closed in the winter time. So we go in and I take the measurements of this chandelier and I made it for her. And there was some sconces on the wall and took some measurements. So this more or less got me started with the tin business. And from then on, why people had seen them ya know. And then along comes Chadds Ford Day. [account of the Chadds Ford Days celebration and the display of crafts there].

So after Chadds Ford Day, why it was some time afterwards, Mr. du Pont sent his architect up to see me, and they wanted windows made for the Essex House. Now the Essex House was up in Massachusetts. The du Pont Museum, Winterthur, got half of it and the Smithsonian Institute, they got the other half. And so I made the windows for that. That got me started on that. And then from there Old Salem, North Carolina, they have a village down there, a colonial village, and they seen me from the Smithsonian Institute. And so I got that job down there. And then Southhampton [Long Island], the first house built in New York State, the Hollyhock House, I got that. And then from there on, these architects get to know you, ya know. And more or less we went into restoration work of colonial windows. I did the Massey House over in Broomall. And the last one I did was Barns-Brinton, up here. That was the last one. So then from then we . . . I'm like the old soldier who faded away, you know. We just kinda went out of that business.

(Interview conducted 8/24/81 at Messersmith residence)

In personal terms this career seems a continuous whole, unfolding naturally in its series of contingencies—beginnings, developments, reversals and new beginnings—all unified by the implicit theme of Mr. Messersmith's manual skill. Viewed from a distance, however, the story typifies a general social movement, for Mr. Messersmith's career spans and indexes the transition from the industrial to the post-industrial, postmodern social order.

Even at the beginning, Mr. Messersmith was involved in a residual craft, the leaded glass window having been specialized to a decorative role. The informality of his training also suggests a residual system (he began his apprenticeship by sweeping out the shop for a dollar a day). The prewar decline and subsequent recovery of Mr. Messersmith's leaded glass trade involved a radical disjunction in the process of cultural production. His craft passed from the residual to the archaic, a cultural element "wholly recognized as an element of the past, to be observed, to be examined, or . . . to be consciously 'revived,' in a deliberately specializing way" (Williams 1977:122). The more or less simultaneous beginning of Mr. Messersmith's tinsmithing is an extension of his skill to another area of the self-consciously archaic.

But notice that it is just through this movement into the archaic that Mr. Messersmith incorporates himself into the emergent postwar social order of Chadds Ford, the order that has come to dominate the Chadds Ford scene and manifests itself in the culture of tourism, historic restoration and deep-suburban pseudo-agrarianism. In his tinsmithing and "restoration work of colonial windows," Mr. Messersmith recapitulates Mr. Heebner's social role. Like Mr. Heebner, he has become a producer of the idea of archaic craftedness. The self-devised finishing compound he uses to give his tinwork the dull patina of age is a tool, like Mr. Heebner's handicapping trowel, in the service of such image production.

Although retired from the leaded glass business, Mr. Messersmith has a thriving career in the re-creation of tin lighting fixtures modelled on colonial patterns. Apart from his private commissions, he markets his work through another typically postmodern institution, the crafts fair. He has participated in the large and popular Kutztown Folk Festival for some fifteen years, adopting the appropriate Pennsylvania German persona by growing a beard and dressing in the costume of the nineteenth-century farmer. He is also one of the founding fathers of Chadds Ford Days, now sponsored by the Chadds Ford Historical Society. For this crafts fair he dons the knee breeches, waistcoat and tricorn of the colonial craftsman.

XX

Amid such postmodern artifacts as the friendship quilt, Mr. Heebner's wall and Mr. Messersmith's tin, the sort of objects that have come to dominate the material world of this Site, one can find artifactual specimens that seem out of place, objects that don't blend very smoothly into the prevailing surfaces upon which Chadds Ford's postmodernity is inscribed. Here is one instance:

A photograph—a snapshot taken with one of the early ancestors of the Kodak Brownie camera. In the carefully composed tableau an elderly woman lies on her side at one end of a sofa, her hand cushioning her face. On the wall above her is a row of photographs, above that a shelf of bric-a-brac. On the upper left is a bust of a bearded man (Grant perhaps). The woman directs sad eyes toward the left foreground of the photograph, where a book sits propped open to a picture of Abraham Lincoln. A small American flag drapes over the top of the page. The scene is glossed by an entry in Hanna Carmack Sanderson's journal, Mrs. Sanderson being the reclining subject of the picture.

1865–1940

The morning of April 15th 1865 I was quite sick with some childish ailment on a long sofa in the living room, my father, on returning from the village post office excitedly told my mother something which caused her to cry out in distress many times. I called to her to know what it all meant, she came into the room tears flowing down her face as she said "Lincoln was shot last night and is dead now."

Today, April 15 betwen 9 and 9:30 a.m., Christie took my picture as I lay on that same sofa and at the same end as on that distressing day 75 years ago.

Hanna Carmack Sanderson, daughter of Capt.
Christian S. Carmack, Company 88th Pa. Vol.
Wounded Antietam September 17, 1862. For which
he was discharged.

(Thompson 1973:311–312)

The Christie referred to is Chris Sanderson, son of the subject. After his mother's death in 1943 he performed an annual ritual of commemorating her birthday by photographing his favorite photograph of her. When he died in 1966, a friend remarked of his large funeral procession in West Chester that the only thing missing from the scene was Sanderson himself standing on the curb taking a snapshot.

This mania for photographic commemoration is but one manifestation of a distinct mode of relating to the past, an historical sensibility that Sanderson displayed to an exaggerated degree and that, as I will argue in Chapter 5, is out of keeping with the smooth surfaces of Chadds Ford's postmodernity. Sanderson's memory is kept alive, rather tenuously, at the small museum that bears his name (Figure 17). A gateway at the back of the Barn Shops parking lot opens onto the yard of this museum. The "nature walk" laid out by the Brandywine River Museum/Conservancy leads from its restored mill, under the highway and across the flood plane, depositing one in a field just above the Sanderson Museum on Route 100. The John Chadd House is just a few hundred feet up the road (Figure 18).

But these physical connections notwithstanding, Sanderson and his institutional memory are hardly integrated into the general Chadds Ford discourse. The history of the emergence of postmodernity at this Site is among other things the history of the progressive displacement of Sanderson from his once central position in the cultural production of Chadds Ford. A recent travel magazine article on "Wyeth Country" rehearses faithfully the received mythology of the region, reproducing essentially the same imagery as the earlier Allstate Motor Club piece. Atypically though, it includes a reference to the Sanderson Museum. The tone of this passage gives some sense of the position Sanderson has come to occupy:

> Chadds Ford also has the Christian C. Sanderson Museum. In his time Sanderson collected just about everything. People brought him curiosities from all over the world. He was the kind of neighbor no one wanted; his 'valuables' exploded out of windows, out the doors, onto the porch, onto the street. After he died, some of his more avid fans cleaned the place up, sorted his treasures and put them in cases. You'll find sand from the digging of the Panama Canal, melted ice from the South Pole, a piece of Independence Hall and of Lincoln's log cabin.
>
> Sanderson was Andrew Wyeth's tutor after Wyeth quit school, and carefully preserved in an upstairs room are some very early sketches—drawings that one suspects Wyeth thought were long incinerated until they emerged one day from under piles of junk. The volunteer guides get a little fanatical as they show you around, insisting that you look at one more autograph, one more

FIGURE 17. Sanderson Museum. Photograph by the author.

rock, one more photograph. You wonder whether they'll permit you to escape, and, indeed, there is sorrow in their eyes as they let you go.

(Jakobson 1987:118)

In Chapter 5 I will propose Sanderson as an instance of noise in the system, a blip on the generally uniform screen of Chadds Ford's post-modernity. As the magazine description of his collection suggests, Sanderson and the Sanderson Museum have come to represent dirt, matter out of place, at this increasingly sanitized Site. The same travel article deplores the suburban development of the middle Brandywine valley, when ironically it is precisely the ideology of the highly managed suburban social order that identifies Sanderson as "the kind of neighbor no one wanted." That Sanderson was honored guest and recipient, along with Andrew Wyeth, of a community award at the first celebration of Chadds Ford Day in the late 1950s would seem to contradict such assessments by current shapers of tourist sensibility.

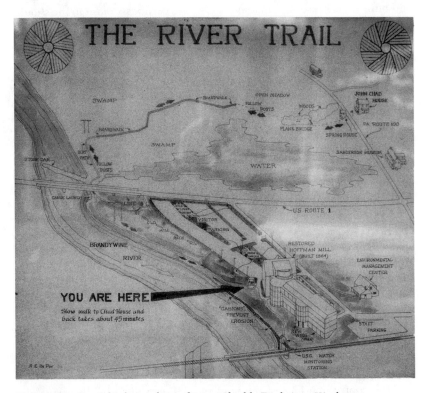

FIGURE 18. Spatial relationships of some Chadds Ford sites. Kiosk map, Brandywine River Conservancy and Museum.

As a rough spot in the otherwise smooth surface of our Site, Sanderson, his institutional reincarnation, and the objects associated with him, like the photograph described above, can be read as the aporia of Chadds Ford's discourse. Or better, he represents one of those "moments of truth" that, some would argue, can be extracted from even the most entrenched cultural dominants and turned to critical purposes. In such things as his rampant mania for photographic commemoration Sanderson both anticipates a full-blown postmodern sensibility and simultaneously pushes it to a point where its seams begin to show. There is a sense in which Sanderson is parodic of postmodernity, the social/cultural formation that tends to flatten parody into pastiche. However one frames him, Sanderson represents a small domain that appears resistant to easy incorporation by the discourse that has come to surround it.

XXI

The Barns-Brinton House, located a couple of miles west of the village and built in its present form about 1724, sits perilously close to the shoulder of Highway 1. Its front turns obliquely away from the traffic. The ghost of the eighteenth-century Great Road to Nottingham (see Map 3) speaks through the house's odd orientation.[18] Many of the themes and characters from the preceding sections loop through this place. Andrew Wyeth painted its portrait when it was still a tenant house. In his *Tenant Farmer* (Figure 19) a deer carcass hangs from a nearby tree and a ramshackle porch clings to the back wall, one of those unfortunate accretions deplored in Conservancy ideology.

The Chadds Ford Historical Society bought the property in 1969 and raised the money to recover its colonial form through the services of an architectural firm specializing in historic restorations. As Mr. Messersmith tells us, the window restoration was his handiwork. Proceeds from Chadds Ford Days, which annually reach about $20,000, maintain this house and the Historical Society's other property, the John Chadd House. Modern visitors to the Barns-Brinton House "may see and appreciate the beauty and workmanship of the artisans of the early eighteenth-century and enjoy the tavern room with its original panelling and walk-in fireplace" (Chadds Ford Historical Society brochure). The Chadds Ford Historical Society uses the building for its business meetings, for class instruction in various "colonial crafts" (e.g., stenciling, calligraphy, wreath making, herbal air fresheners), and for theme parties ("Tavern Night" and "Colonial Brunch"). Demonstrations of such things as open-hearth cooking and baking are part of the display for visitors.

The controlling idea of the Society is "living history," the principle that a remote period, in this case early eighteenth-century colonial Amer-

FIGURE 19. *Tenant Farmer*, Andrew Wyeth. Private collection.

ica, can be made available to direct experience. Practically, this means the Barns-Brinton House must not just sit there as a sterile monument. It must be put to active use.

As the above list of uses indicates, there are two sides to the living history concept. One involves using the house as the authentic setting for the re-creation of colonial domestic economy. Guides in authentic recreations of colonial costumes, the cooking and baking demonstrations, herbal gardening, spinning demonstrations: in such things the Historical Society emulates, on a scale appropriate to its financial resources, the living history museums, villages, farmsteads, mills and so forth that have become such a common feature of the American cultural landscape.[19]

The other side of the Historical Society's idea of living history is that the past of a place, its daily activities and values, can be integrated consciously with the lives of people now living there. For the most committed members of the Historical Society, participation in the Chadds Ford idea includes participation in the image of colonial domestic economy. Taking up a "colonial craft" as a hobby, decorating or restoring one's own home according to the colonial theme, and attending the Society's colonial theme parties are three clear examples of "living history" in this second sense.

Tavern Night will serve as a specific case. The Barns-Brinton House was used for some time as an inn and tavern, as well as a family residence. The idea of Tavern Night is to re-create the tavern atmosphere in the form of a cocktail party for Society members. Colonial drinks—mulled wine, punches, ale—are offered, along with food deemed appropriate to the image: cheese, fruit, popcorn, ham, and biscuits. The entertainment includes ballad singing, a magician, and, in one of the rooms upstairs, colonial board games. The house is decorated with some of the products of the craft classes, (e.g., corn husk wreaths). Some of the organizers dress in period costume.

The overall effect at these parties is less an integration of past and present than a licensed transgression of the boundary that marks off the museum display. Theater meets museum in these events. Tavern Night is a decidedly postmodern event enacted in the dramatic space of living history. A certain level of "authenticity" must be maintained to keep the colonial theme active. So, for example, the party goers' uncolonial coats must be hung "backstage" (i.e., in the basement where the modern amenities are located), rather than from the row of re-created eighteenth-century coat pegs that circle the main tavern room. Yet there is no deep commitment to maintaining the integrity of the image. If a magic act seems appropriate eighteenth-century entertainment at Tavern Night, it bothers no one that the magician wears a three-piece polyester suit and sports a rosebud in his lapel. The whole thing operates according to a rationale of "appropriate" or "strategic" authenticity.

When we view the Barns-Brinton House in relation to its surroundings, the question of scale forces itself upon us. The endless replication and redundancy that is so constitutive of Chadds Ford cultural production inevitably involves the processes of miniaturization and enlargement. Flexibility of scale is part of the general flexibility that characterizes what I have been calling the Chadds Ford idea or image.

The Barns-Brinton house sits a few hundred feet beyond "Chadds Ford West," a group of buildings in which office space is available for rent (Figure 20). Three of these structures sit in an even row facing Highway 1. All are designed to suggest the eighteenth-century house form so common in Chadds Ford vicinity. Collectively the three buildings reproduce or allude to many of the external elements of the Barns-Brinton House: penteave, balancing chimneys, small paired windows in the gable, rustic materials (plaster, stone, brick). In scale, however, they are of a different order of magnitude, one appropriate to the world of modern business and the busy highway which they face from behind the buffer of a parking lot.

FIGURE 20. Barns-Brinton House (looking toward Chadds Ford West).
Photograph by the author.

The odd thing about viewing the Barns-Brinton House in this setting
is the ambiguity of scale. It seems almost as valid to see the restoration
as a miniaturization as to see these other buildings as enlargements. The
ambiguity itself, of course, and not the objective fact of "authentic scale"
is the salient fact for our understanding of Chadds Ford cultural
production.

In an upstairs room of the house a large section of interior wall has
been cut away and the aperture framed as a kind of educational exhibit.
The internal elements of wall construction are revealed and marked with
explanatory text. Downstairs in the main tavern room the restorers found
some of the relatively elaborate original wall panelling still intact. Thus
they could reproduce with complete accuracy the pieces that were needed
for replacements. The simulations, however, were done so that their color
differed very slightly from the originals. The overall effect is not at all
jarring. The gestalt of the whole room as an accurate recreation of original
appearance is not disrupted. But one can also look more closely and see
the honest admission that the room is a restoration.

These two surfaces at the Barns-Brinton House, one in which a gap
has been opened and one in which a lack has been supplied, demonstrate
in a concretely material way a theoretical distinction that will be the

subject of Chapter 3. The contrast between them, and also between the two sides of the bifurcated architecture at the Brandywine River Museum, will serve as emblems of the two major rhetorical figures that seem to me to organize much of the ongoing discourse at this Site. I will call them postmodern veneer and vignette. But before turning to these theoretical considerations, first some history.

NOTES

1. The main fieldwork for this study was conducted intermittently from 1980 through 1982. Unless otherwise specified, all present reference is to that period. I made one extended return visit in the summer of 1985 and a brief tour in May, 1987. Although Chadds Ford had certainly changed in the intervening years, the changes appear to me as extensions or completions of things already present in the early 1980s.

2. I am referring here to the 1981 menu, which included dishes such as Calves Liver Bercy (natured calves liver sauteed in a brown sauce with shallots and Dijon mustard, $10.95), Rock Cornish Game Hen ($13.50), and Lobster Imperial ($14.95). At that time it appeared that young professionals and singles socialized in the bar on Friday and Saturday nights. While the dining room tuned its atmosphere to color prints of fox hunting, the bar was dominated by a print of Jamie Wyeth's rebel-without-a-cause portrait (*Draft Age*) of Jimmy Lynch (local character and Wyeth friend) in wraparound shades and leather jacket.

3. For the most part I would leave these national census figures to speak for themselves, just warning that they be read cautiously. They are just as much souvenirs (fragments, textual constructs) as anything else offered here. Note, for example, that in 1970 the national census jumps the upper limit of reported household income from $25,000 to $50,000 (Tables 4 and 5). But the $50,000 limit remains for the 1980 census. In comparing Tables 5 and 6 one must adjust for the inflation of the 1970s so as not to overestimate the significant jump in families above the $50,000 level between 1970 and 1980.

These figures suggest that of the three Chadds Ford townships, Birmingham in Chester County underwent the most significant demographic changes between 1960 and 1980, while Birmingham Township, Delaware County, although reflecting the common trend, has been somewhat slower to change. Pennsbury Township, Chester County, falls somewhere in the middle. For comparative data, see Muller 1982.

4. This is certainly the "classic past" of New England and the Mid-Atlantic states generally, though in the latter the Civil War is perhaps its equal. See Lynch 1972:30.

5. "Postmodern" and "post-industrial" are not interchangeable terms, though they are obviously related. The latter is more specifically a socio-economic category, the former a socio-cultural one and the one more appropriate to this study. On the concept of post-industrial, see Reisman 1958, Bell 1976, Kumar 1978.

6. Though I have no statistics, it is quite apparent that of the other two Chadds Ford townships, Birmingham, Chester County is more suburbanized than Pennsbury, while Birmingham, Delaware County is somewhat less subdivided. In the latter a number of fairly large properties appear in the plat books and these have affinities with the large estates of the Du Pont "chateaux district" just across the border in New Castle County, Delaware. Also, the Girl Scouts of America and the Archdiocese of Philadelphia own land in Birmingham Township, Delaware County.

7. See for example the passing reference, in a 1905 letter, to "the town of Africa, a colored village" in the Chadds Ford vicinity (Thompson 1973:153).

8. Since the colonial period provides the dominant historical image for the area under consideration, snake fence would be the more appropriate emblem, post and rail having replaced this form of fencing only in the nineteenth century (Glassie 1968:226).

9. Properties in the neighborhood of 100 to 250 acres seem to have been typical of eighteenth-century Chester and Delaware Counties. The original grants were "generally from 100 to 500 acres" (Lemon 1972:65, chapters 4 and 6 passim). In 1780 the largest landowner in Pennsbury Township held 507 acres, the second and third largest holdings being 350 and 327 acres (Heathcote 1932:206).

10. Antonio Gramsci's concept of *bloc* is perhaps not entirely appropriate to the situation described here. But something other than the standard sociological categories is required to account for the Chadds Ford social organization. It will have to embrace the "complex cultural and ideological processes taking place in everyday life within civil society" and "the building of popular alliances that transcend an exclusive class basis and coalesce around psychological-historical forces at work during a given historical moment" (Boggs 1976:81).

11. This brochure is no longer issued by the Conservancy.

12. For a highly positive academic appraisal of Wyeth's art, Corn 1973:93–165. For the negative modernist response to Wyeth's growing popularity in the 1960s, see Kuh 1968, Jacobs 1967, Alloway 1967.

13. Since 1983 one of the barns has been gutted by a fire and the whole complex has been refurbished and visually "upgraded" with decorative elements (wrought iron railing, etc.) and landscaping. A new motor hotel has gone up behind these shops.

14. This shop was closed as of 1985, but by 1987 it had reopened, presumably under new management.

15. The recent flap over the revelation of the "Helga paintings" was seen by some as the calculated result of a cunning market strategy. These paintings were done, one critic suggests, precisely with their suitability for mechanical reproduction in mind (Schjeldahl 1986). My own view is that individual calculation is of minor significance in comparison to the massive institutional and ideological mechanisms that form the necessary conditions for the Helga *cause celebre* and the Wyeth phenomenon in general.

16. The movement from art to craft and craft to art is another interesting issue in the cultural production of our age. Wyeth speaks of his art in craft terms, and somehow this enhances its aura. Conversely, many people who engage in what are commonly considered craft activities aspire to the designation of artist. Fine woodworkers, for example, often find that the time spent on a piece of furniture dictates a price tag beyond what most people will spend on a craft (i.e., primarily utilitarian) object. One procedure for getting established as a "craft artist" is to find and cultivate a patron, that is, a collector of one's works who can be persuaded to donate a piece to a museum. The producer then confirms his or her artist status by commissioning a poster depicting the object and indicating that it is part of a museum collection.

17. Since this and subsequent transcripts are of interest to us here mainly for their content and not as performances, I have not gone to great lengths to depict performance features. I indicate special emphasis with underlining and distinguish hesitations from purposeful, rhetorical pauses, the former indicated with three dots, the latter with a dash. These conventions hold throughout.

18. This route passed the building on the side away from the present highway.

19. Some time ago Kevin Lynch reported (1972:52) that there were "more than 125 museum villages and extensive city walking tours . . . in forty-two of the fifty states." Surely the number has greatly increased since then. See Anderson 1984.

2 | *Some History*

Take the notion of tradition:...it makes it possible to rethink the dispersion of history in the form of the same.

Michel Foucault,
The Archaeology of Knowledge

A Chadds Ford Time Line:

1703—Francis Chadsey (English Quaker) purchases 500 acres along the middle Brandywine

1736—John Chad (son of Francis Chadsey) has established a ferry across the Brandywine by this year

1777—Battle of the Brandywine (September 11)

1866—Bayard Taylor publishes *The Story of Kennett* (a popular romance set in the Brandywine Valley)

1882—Christian C. Sanderson born

1898—Howard Pyle establishes a summer art school at Chadds Ford

1903—N. C. Wyeth moves to Chadds Ford

1905—Sanderson moves to Chadds Ford

1906—Sanderson and his mother take up residence in the farmhouse used by Washington as headquarters during the Brandywine Battle

1917—Andrew Wyeth born

1921—during this year 9,257 people visit Sanderson in his home

1922—Sanderson forced to leave the Washington Headquarters, moves to West Chester; Sanderson opens one room of his West Chester house as The Brandywine Museum

1931—Washington's Headquarters burns to the ground; Sanderson returns to Chadds Ford and moves into the "Little Gray House," later to become the Sanderson Museum

1937—Sanderson's house electrified; Wyeth's first one man show (sold out the first day)

1943—Sanderson's mother dies on Christmas morning (becomes the subject of Wyeth's *Christmas Morning*); Wyeth, *The Hunter* (published as October 16 cover of the *Saturday Evening Post*)

1945—N.C. Wyeth struck by a train and killed near the Kuerner farm

1947—state forms a Brandywine Battlefield Park Commission (Sanderson not included)

1948—Wyeth, *Karl* (Karl Kuerner) and *Christina's World* (probably his most famous painting)

1952—Brandywine Battlefield Park and reconstructed Washington's Headquarters dedicated (Sanderson snubbed and vows to participate in no future park ceremonies or activities)

1953—Wyeth, *Snow Flurries*

1956—Wyeth, *Roasted Chestnuts*

1957—Work's Store (Chadds Ford general store) closes (soon to be replaced by a gas station); Chadds Ford Knoll, first housing development in the area, is laid out; Wyeth, *Brown Swiss* (perhaps his most important painting of the Kuerner farm)

1957–58—a Federation of Brandywine Communities formed to resist a powerline planned for the valley

1958—first Chadds Ford Day (Sanderson and Wyeth [in absentia] honored as community's leading citizens)

1959—second Chadds Ford Day introduces display of local crafts; September 11, Chris Sanderson Museum officially opened to the public in the front two rooms of the Little Gray House; Wyeth, *The Mill* (depicting his own property in Chadds Ford)

1960—Wyeth, *Young Bull*

1961—Wyeth, *Tenant Farmer* (Barns-Brinton House)

1962—Wyeth family art featured at Chadds Ford Day (small profit generated from admission fee charged to cover insurance costs)

1963–67—Chadds Ford Day apparently not celebrated in these years

1965—Battle of the Brandywine commemorated by the state at Battlefield Park (Sanderson gives brief address)

1966—Sanderson dies

1967—Tri-County Conservancy formed (its immediate purpose to resist an industrial park planned for a meadow near the village); Conservancy buys Hoffman's mill (at that time a coal and lumber yard) that will become the Brandywine River Museum

1968—Chadds Ford Historical Society chartered; Society buys the Chad House and property; Chadds Ford celebration revived, now as Chadds Ford Days (located on the grounds and in the mill purchased by the Conservancy); Chadds Ford Art Heritage show that is part of the celebration codifies the definitive Brandywine tradition of art

1969—Chadds Ford Historical Society purchases the Barns- Brinton House; Wyeth, *The Virgin* (one of the Siri paintings now owned by the Brandywine River Museum)

1971—Brandywine River Museum opens to the public (Chadds Ford Days still held in the museum courtyard)

1972—10,000 of Sanderson's snapshots sorted and displayed at the Sanderson Museum are free for the taking by photographic subjects or their families

1974—Chadds Ford Days has moved to the meadow near the post office (formerly the planned site of the industrial park, but now Conservancy property)

1975—major Andrew Wyeth show at the Metropolitan Museum of Art

1977—major Bicentennial re-enactment of the Battle of the Brandywine (co-sponsored by the Battlefield Park and the Chadds Ford Historical Society; 15,000 tourists attend); Chadds Ford Days moves this year to its current fairgrounds site off Route 100 (the event becomes primarily a colonial crafts fair)

1979—a major endowment campaign begun by the Brandywine River Museum (Ladybird Johnson named its honorary chairperson)

1980–82—primary period of fieldwork for this case study

1981—Summer Kitchen (see Chapter 4) is added to the Chadds Ford Days crafts fair; left turn lanes and stop light installed at village intersection; The General Store opens near the intersection

1985—dedication of the new addition (including an Andrew Wyeth gallery) at the Brandywine River Museum

1987–88—An American Vision: Three Generations of Wyeth Art (international art exhibition sponsored by AT&T)

1987–88—composition of the present text

The segment of the above chronology I will dwell on here is roughly the twenty-five year period beginning in 1957. That year is conveniently marked by the closing of the old general store in Chadds Ford, the appearance of the first planned suburban development in the area, the formation of an indigenous community organization to resist unwanted development in the Brandywine Valley, and Andrew Wyeth's completion of the painting *Brown Swiss*, arguably his most important depiction of the Chadds Ford landscape. The next year saw the first staging of the Chadds Ford Day celebration.

Symbolically at least, these events inaugurate two decades of social and cultural transformation. By the end of this period Chadds Ford is a new kind of place, the kind of Site that virtually exists through the generation of such fragments and souvenirs as I have collected in Chapter 1. An account of this transformation is necessarily a history of emergent institutions and an interpretation of the discourses that surround these institutions. Most relevant in the Chadds Ford case are the institutions devoted to natural and cultural preservation. Collectively they produce and endlessly reproduce the legitimizing discourse that sustains the Site.

Not surprisingly, the most overtly symbolic event that this Site has to offer, the Chadds Ford Day(s) celebration, turns out to be the best guide to the emergence, transformation and consolidation of the new cultural order. In Chapter 4 I will look closely at the current form of this event and show how it is perhaps the "purest" expression of advanced consumer culture that the Site generates. For present purposes a history of Chadds Ford Days can serve as a rather precise index to the processes from which this cultural order emerged.

Since 1968 Chadds Ford Days has been under the auspices of the Chadds Ford Historical Society, which was chartered in that year. Prior to that time the celebration was organized by a Chadds Ford Day committee. As part of its 1976 Bicentennial activities the Historical Society produced a taped lecture/slide show that reviews the organization's first eight years and, before that, the origin and development of Chadds Ford Day. The illustrated lecture mainly serves to introduce new members to the Society's "tradition." In other words, the Society has undertaken to traditionalize itself as an institution, and more importantly, to traditionalize Chadds Ford Days as a community event. Given that the Society has existed only since 1968 and that the celebration is but a decade older, one might even say the Society is, without knowing it, traditionalizing (and legitimizing) the cultural order from which it has itself emerged.[1]

Reading between the lines, one can infer from this document a great deal. The Historical Society presents the history of the event as a continuous "tradition" of celebration. As a result, important historical disjunctions become obscured. Their traces remain visible however, and by discovering the fissures papered over in the Society's account of itself we can begin to understand the transformations of Chadds Ford's current cultural order as it has emerged, become institutionally hegemonic, and ultimately penetrated the farthest corners of everyday discourse at this Site.

Here then is the "official" version of the origin of Chadds Ford Days as recounted in the Society's Bicentennial tape entitled "The Village That Stood Fast." The delivery, slow and measured, is punctuated by brief musical interludes that divide the whole account into logical segments. The narrator's impeccable diction, her British accent, and her rather self-conscious striving for rhetorical effect lends the presentation an air of formality and authoritative decorum. This account is in much the same key as the thumbnail history on the back of the Chadds Ford Inn menu:

> We are people who happen to live in a valley of particular beauty; and we mean, quite simply, to keep it that way. The year is nineteen hundred and seventy-six, the 200th anniversary of this nation's founding. Possibly the single most useful thing to come out of this special festive time is the fact that it has caused people all over the country to pause and take stock of themselves. Whence have we come? Where are we going?
>
> And so it's fitting that we, the Historical Society of Chadds Ford, should choose this time to look at ourselves. Where did it all begin, and why? What have we learned that might be of value to other communities? And where do we mean to go from here?
>
> Let's turn back the clock for a moment to nineteen hundred and fifty-eight. Strangers passing through Chadds Ford on that sunny September day might have been astonished to observe, there on the grassy hill above Route 1, the gallantries of wig and tricorn. There were backwoodsmen, and Indians, and demure pinafores. And could that really be Howard Pyle at his easel in front of Lafayette Hall?
>
> What they were seeing of course was the first of those wonderful extravaganzas: Chadds Ford Day, nineteen hundred and fifty-eight. What caused us all to gather on that lovely sunny day, there in front of Mr. Work's now vanished store [site currently occupied by the Sunoco station], dressed in our finery? We were, it seems, simply a group of neighbors who had begun to feel that there was something very special about this valley, something profoundly worth protection from the inevitable encroachments of industry. The seed of historic awareness had already been sown. Howard Pyle and his students had captured it on canvas; Chris Sanderson had evoked its magic to countless school children; and now there was a happy coming togther of local people— like Arabella Cleveland, Jane Gregory, Millie Jones, Marian Crumb, Alice Goetz, Pete Morgan and many others. It was they who had the gumption to do something about it.
>
> What evolved then, out of light-hearted planning sessions such at this, was a big, neighborhood costume festival. It was, as Millie Jones was to write later, "a means for the diverse peoples of the Brandywine community to learn what their neighbor's talents were, to come to know each other better, and share a mutual interest in the preservation of the beauty of this countryside. Little did they know, sitting there in the sunlight in front of Mr. Work's store,

where it would all lead. That first Chadds Ford Day was a resounding success. Over a thousand friends and visitors attended it.

There were Indians and powdered wigs, there were top hats and there were parasols. One of the most delightful features of the day was a diminutive tour of costume scenes posed before some of the historical local houses. Here, for example, a little group in front of the John Chad House, which includes, incidentally, a relative of the original Elizabeth Chad, Anna Davis. Here a leisurely game of croquet on the lawn at Work's. This neighborly conversation took place outside General Howe's headquarters. And here, a group of ladies gather outside the Brandywine Baptist Church. There were spinning wheels, and Sunday best finery, and a matching pair of Chadwick papooses who captured the hearts of us all.

For the first time there was in the old Howard Pyle house an exhibit of Wyeth family paintings organized by Millie Jones. And there was music by the Heavenly Bound Choir, and patriotic songs by Jack Morgan. Finally, there was time to sit in the gentle September sunlight and conjure up images of days gone by. It was, in short, a splendid occasion, one that marked the beginning of a long and happy tradition.

Of it the Wilmington News Journal of that time wrote, "Historic Chadds Ford Day, for all of its light hearted pageantry, clearly indicated they've got something to protect." And, in this same paper, Jane Gregory is quoted as saying of the area, "Grow it must, but we hope to find a way to let it grow by making history and scenery its best economic assets." We may take pride in the fact that this was said in nineteen hundred and fifty-eight.

Certainly something has happened to our sense of the past if eighteen years can be said to constitute a "long" tradition. In the Historical Society account we see only the surface of the first Chadds Ford Day celebration. Much deeper in its detail is Joseph Messersmith's personal recollection of the event, which he recounts as an episode in the chronicle of his working life as a craftsman [see Chapter 1, sec. XIX]. Mr. Messersmith is one of the handful of people who were involved in the first Chadds Ford Day and still participate some twenty-five years later. He is able to tell us not only about the event itself, but also about a prior institution not mentioned in the Historical Society's narrative and about the specific situation that precipitated these new institutions. Judging from newspaper records, Mr. Messersmith has mixed together aspects from the '58 and '59 celebrations, but that matters little for our present purposes. His account is larded with digressions that, while they might be tangential to the topic of Chadds Ford Day, invest his story with an authoritative depth of knowledge generally lacking from the "official" Historical Society version, where authority derives more from its oratory than from its content:

> ...And then along comes Chadds Ford Day. So, ah, we had ... the powerline wanted to come through, and so the people in Chadds Ford got together—they *didn't* want that powerline to come through Chadds Ford, because they coulda' re-routed it, see, up to Dilworthtown and out that way. So that's ... they started

to fight it and so the power company, they ... we organi ... we had a ... we got together and we formed an organization—called it the Federation of Brandywine Communities. And we got a charter and we started this organization and its main purpose was to fight the powerline. Well this more or less brought the people together, ya know? And so we would have meetings and neighbors would meet one another. So they said, somebody got the bright idea—I don't know who it was—we would have a Chadds Ford Day to celebrate the Battle of the Brandywine. So this is how Chadds Ford Day was born.

And there was a big barn right opposite the Chadds Ford Hotel [Chadds Ford Inn]—where that vacant lot is now?—there was a long barn there. And it was narrow but long and there was people—I can't think of their name ... well, anyway, they were builders and they had rented this barn. If I'm not mistaken it belonged to Mrs. Eachus. And, because she, see at one time, when we first moved here, there was a man by the name of Quimby — he was in the plumbing business. And he owned *all* around here, he owned a lot of houses on Station House [Station Way] Road and he owned along the Baltimore Pike there, owned the barn and that big house that was next to the barn and that little house, that little place that's got all fixed up now [the "General Store"], that was a little garage like. And so 'course when he died, Mrs. Eachus was a relative of his, of some kind or another, I don't know. But nevertheless she inherited all this property, and he owned down Route 100 here too. And so these people, the builder rented that barn from Mrs. Eachus.

So we wanted to have a Chadds Ford Day and somebody says there's a big barn—why not use that. So we go to the builders and asked 'em if we could use the barn. Cause he had all his equipment and stuff stored in there, materials and so on. So he said yeah, we could use it. All we had to do was move the stuff back ya know. *So* we get together and we go down and we look the barn over and we moved all the things back and made like a big aisle down the center of it ya know. So, we said well we gotta have something to cover all this junk up that's in the back there ya know. Building materials and all that ya know. So they got a rope, started from the front and went all the way down to the back and took it all the way around. There were these posts ya know that were up, to hold ... the barn was sorta shaped like this, ya know. And there were posts ya know in there. And they went all around the big posts. And the ladies got together and they got all their *quilts; beautiful* patchwork quilts and we layed them over the rope. And this made the background, the backdrop ya know? And then people that was in Chadds Ford, it was amazing how many people were skilled that was here. There was Mrs. Tullock. She made beautiful ceramic, ya know, things like that figure work there, ya know. That type—and it was like I remember she had a doll—it was about that high— and the lacework all around that doll—*open* lacework, ya know—ceramic—it was beautiful. She started right from scratch. She had the kiln and she fired it. Painted 'em and fired 'em. Then there was, oh, ah, Maletti I think, no, it wasn't Maletti; I can't think. Anyway, he worked Philadelphia Electric—he retired—and he made ... *looms.* And his wife weaved the clothes, made all their cloth on these looms and then she'd make their *clothes.* And then she'd also made rugs ya know, on the looms. And he had different sizes, he made different sizes of looms. He had ... he was quite clever at it; beautiful things ... piece of work. And, oh, there was *so* many people had *so* many things that we filled that barn up! From one end to the other, all the way around, ya know. Everybody had a little stall. And I was in the back and there was another fella made cabinets, he was back next to me. And I had a display of the stained glass windows and . . . then I had this tinware. And, in the meantime, prior to that, I had made windows for 1704 House [another restoration in the area] and installed 'em. And so I had a panel, an extra panel that I had made, and I had that on display and I was showing that this was a panel from 1704 House. Well . . . this was—we didn't *sell* anything, it wasn't . . . the object was just to display, that's all . . . and just have a good time and to have *fun*, ya know.

And everybody got in costumes. Mrs. Ladd, a lady over here by name of, do ya know Mrs. Ladd? She had the most *beautiful* selection—collection of *old* dresses. And she got 'em all out and she loaned 'em to the girls, ya know, the different ones. And my—she loaned my daughter one, and oh, the Chadwick girls, and the different people, ya know. And they *all* got dressed up.

Don Tullock he was master of ceremony, and Chris Sanderson. And then we had a . . . then there was three boys got together and they had the, they had the fife and drum corps. Then we had a parade, we started up, I think, by John Chad's house and come on down and around and around by the hotel and they had built a platform and Don Tullock got up . . . made a speech. And then Chris Sanderson got up there and he made a speech all about the Battle of the Brandywine. And we had a good time.

And then up at the Baptist Church they had the, in the basement we had a art exhibit—Andy's [Wyeth] paintings and different ones around had paintings and then they put them in ya know, for display. So in the meantime—oh, this thing was really advertised; they advertised it real good because a lot of the, they had three or four public relations people from DuPonts that lived in the community up here over at Atwater Road. I forget; I'm terrible with names. I forget names, but I know them if I see 'em. But anyhow they got the communications out in the papers and so forth and gave this, big write ups. And we had a big crowd. And in the mean time Mr. du Pont, he comes along and sees some of my little glasswork. And so that's how Chadds Ford Day was born. We were celebratin' the Battle of the Brandywine.

And my boys, they were in it. And like I said they were all in costumes. And my oldest boy . . . my youngest boy, Alan, he was dressed like a Indian, he was bare from here up, ya know. With paint and horns out on his head piece. And the Chadwicks, they were Mrs. Chadwick, she was dressed up like a Indian squaw and she had two twins at the time, little ones, and she had them dressed up like little Indians. And then she had a son and the son he was dressed up like a Indian along with my boy. And they had their flint guns ya know. And course he was the gunsmith, Chadwick was the gunsmith down here at the time.

It appears that the Historical Society description of the first Chadds Ford Day is highly selective, highlighting the things that came to dominate the Society's activities in the 1970s and 1980s. Mr. Messersmith's perspective as a craftsman and longtime Chadds Ford resident, though it too is selective, reveals to us a more complex event than we might have imagined from the slide show version.

First of all, the tape's vague references to the threat of "the inevitable encroachments of industry" and to the need for protection against them take on substance in Mr. Messersmith's account of the resistance to a proposed powerline. The first Chadds Ford Day, it turns out, sprang directly from an ad hoc political institution—the Federation of Brandywine Communities — devoted to mobilizing the forces of powerline resistance. Neither of the two accounts suggests that Chadds Ford Day was a planned strategy of this resistance; and it was probably not conceived explicitly in those terms. Nevertheless, the ideas of community self-awareness and self-esteem that pervade the first phase of the celebration strongly suggest its instrumental relationship to political purposes external to the event itself. In this respect, the Historical Society account, though it leaves out crucial facts, is perhaps truer to the general atmosphere that prompted the celebration than is Mr. Messersmith's implication that Chadds Ford Day was born of the desire to commemorate the Battle of the Brandywine. To him the event seems to have come about as an accidental by-product of the meetings over the powerline issue—somebody's "bright idea" for a celebration—rather than as a creature of that political issue itself.

After describing the first Chadds Ford Day, the Historical Society slide show surveys the highlights of the event over the next few years of its celebration. During these early years the Day was observed in several different ways and in different places around Chadds Ford, although its main elements (historical costumes, parade, speeches, etc.) stayed constant. In 1959 the festivities were conducted in the "square" (read: parking lot) next to the Chadds Ford Inn. In 1961 the celebration took the form of a costume picnic on the grounds of the Battlefield Park. "It would be impossible with the time at hand," the narrator tells us on the tape, "to chronicle anything but the highlights of those successive Chadds Ford Days. But a pattern had been set, and it continues to this day."

This Historical Society account of Chadds Ford Day is a particularly clear case of traditionalizing discourse. Controlled by the idea of continuity, it portrays the history of Chadds Ford Day as a continuous evolution proceeding directly from the early to the late 1960s, and it gives no hint of any break in the celebration. Mr. Messersmith's personal recollection doesn't iron the past so smoothly. He reveals that Chadds Ford Day disappeared for a time[2] and then was revived in 1968 as a fund raising tool of the newly formed Historical Society, which was created to purchase and restore two historic Chadds Ford sites. Here is Mr. Messersmith's account, picking up where his description of the first Chadds Ford Day leaves off:

> So that's how Chadds Ford Day was born, I imagine. Then this kept up for a few years and then all of a sudden it stopped. And then the Chadds Ford Historical Society started together...oh...Well what started the Chadds Ford Historical Society, as far as I can recall ...uh...Hoffman, up here on Route 100? the Hoffmans? they owned the John Chads House. And I think it

was up for sale. They was going to sell it. And so people got together—"Oh, the John Chads House, its a historical house," ya know? And I think this is what started the Historical Society. They organized and . . . to save the John Chads House.

And, after that was purchased . . . Originally, when . . . now I got this from Sweng [?], who was one of the supervisors or commissioners of the park [Brandywine Battlefield Park]. He told me that the park had purchased forty-nine acres. This was where the Clevelands lived. Lafayette's headquarters and Washington's. And the reason they had made it . . . they had it written up that they were going to have fifty acres, with the idea in the back of their minds that they were going to get John Chads House, with one acre, which would have made it fifty acres. But they had only purchased the forty-nine acres; but I think it was drawn up so they were going to have fifty. This was Weldon Heyburn's project, the park was. But then when John Chads House came up for sale, as I understand it, why then the Historical Society got together and *they* bought the house.

And then course they said, "Now we're going to have to raise some money." So they had another Chadds Ford Day. But this Chadds Ford Day, then, was down . . . then, in the meantime, in the meantime the syndicate bought the old mill—Weymouth and the du Ponts and so forth [referring to the Tri-County Conservancy, now the Brandywine River Conservancy]. And they had fixed it all up, ya know. And they had the courtyard out there, ya know, the cobbled courtyard. And so we had a Chadds Ford Day in there. And from then . . . And the next time[3] I think we had it in the field next to the park, next to the barn . . . post office out there. That originally was a barn, where the post office is. And we had a Chadds Ford Day there. And they've sorta grown out of that, due to traffic and one thing and another.

So, then, after that, then . . . oh, what's his name? Who built those houses up next to the Barns-Brinton House? . . . Well, anyway, he bought that . . . he put that up for sale . . . Oscar Burns! . . . Oscar. He had bought that ground and this [i.e., the Barns-Brinton house] and so forth. And he sold 'em . . . they raised money to buy the Barns-Brinton House. And then, more or less Chadds Ford Day was revived.

This revival of Chadds Ford Day cannot be understood without relating it to the major changes that occurred in the institutional structure of Chadds Ford cultural production in the late 1960s. This new Chadds Ford Day, or rather Chadds Ford Days, since the new economic function of the event required that it be extended, was an entirely different sort of celebration—virtually a different species of event from its early 1960s counterpart, the Historical Society's traditionalization notwithstanding. The immediate cause of the institutional innovations from which the Chadds Ford Day revival proceeds is absent from Mr. Messersmith's account, but the Historical Society tape affords it major emphasis:

> In the spring of 1967 an event occurred which was to prove a turning point for the whole community. Plans were announced to build a factory in this field, just behind the present Chadds Ford Post Office. There was an immediate public outcry. A handful of interested persons calling themselves the Friends of the Brandywine joined together to save this open space. In March

of that year the Tri-County Conservancy was born and the forty acre meadow purchased. In the fall of that same year, the fine old grist mill, known locally as Hoffman's Mill, came under the auctioneer's hammer. It too was bought by the Conservancy. And so began the whole astonishing story of the Brandywine River Museum. If any single thing served to consolidate our determination not to relinquish this part of our valley to the insatiable appetites of commerce, that threat of an industrial complex in our meadow was it. Perhaps Chadds Ford will one day go down in history as the village that said no, the village that stood fast.

The situation of a decade earlier seems to repeat itself: a little community threatened by the encroachments of industry draws together and heroically resists. This time the enemy is given a name. It is a factory proposed for the meadow next to the post office. Though the taped lecture tends to suggest that the situation in 1968 repeats that of a decade earlier, there is a telling inversion in the discourse that recounts these two moments of resistance. We might read this inversion as the trace or reflex of a historical disjunction that the discourse otherwise obscures. In the story of the first Chadds Ford Day the creation of the event is itself the crucial fact. The institutional and political conditions under which the event was originally produced are left vague. In the second story of resistance, the institutional and political situations are explicit and central, while the fact that the celebration is a new creation and a different kind of event goes unreported.

This reversal in the discourse bespeaks a fundamental transformation of Chadds Ford Day(s), a change conveniently marked by the mid–1960s hiatus revealed in Mr. Messersmith's account (and a change symbolized perhaps by Chris Sanderson's death in 1966). To put it simply, the event ceases to be an independent, locally oriented celebration and becomes the organ of a new institutional order. This new order is professionally managed, highly rational, and characterized by the concentration of power in the hands of a mobile class of experts associated with specifically *cultural* institutions. In Chapter 5 I will look more closely at these new conditions and relations of (re)production.

Reading the traces in the Historical Society discourse and drawing upon Mr. Messersmith's recollection, we may distinguish, then, two distinct phases of the Chadds Ford Day(s) celebration: late 1950s through early 1960s; late 1960s and after. For the second of these, the period of the event's resurrection (beginning in 1968), the Historical Society account depicts a climate of great institutional solidarity in Chadds Ford. Three institutions are associated in this retrospective image of the time when the village "stood fast"—the two museums I will compare in Chapter 5 and the Chadds Ford Historical Society itself, as represented by its restored house:

Plans were already underway for the emerging Brandywine River Museum. The dream of Chris Sanderson, whose death in 1966 had been a loss to us all, had been realized by the opening of a museum in his home. And now the preservation of the John Chad House was a challenge to each of us. Somehow it seemed as though these diverse things, inspired by a common goal, were coming together as an entity.

Just as the continuity of the Chadds Ford Day celebration is an illusion created by the discourse of the lecture/slide show, so this sense of strong institutional solidarity distorts the reality of the situation in 1968. Judging from subsequent developments, which must have already been visible when the slide show was produced in 1976, the initial institutional solidarity was a temporary and rather superficial formation. The breakdown of this solidarity is now quite complete, and the contemporary state of Chadds Ford Days, which reflects this institutional fragmentation, marks yet a third phase of the celebration, one in which it has largely ceased to be a community festival and become a commercial crafts fair constructed around the ideology of living history.

The overall development of the Chadds Ford Day celebration has a certain logic, but certainly not that of the simple, continuous and organic growth that the Historical Society slide show suggests. Rather it is a logic of disjunction and shifting relations between residual and emergent cultural forms.[4] To summarize, the development of the Chadds Ford Day celebration divides into three main phases. The first phase (late 1950s and early 1960s), while it marks a basic departure from prior forms, involves the mixture of emergent tendencies with residual patterns. The second phase (late 1960s to mid 1970s), which begins with the revival of the celebration in 1968 after a mid 1960s hiatus, involves an event in which the emergent elements of the first phase have become entrenched and the residual elements have been greatly reduced, if not eliminated altogether. The third phase (mid 1970s and after) is characterized by the full realization, the internal elaboration and, eventually, the self-sustaining routinization of the trends that were consolidated in the second phase.

It is tempting to cast the Chadds Ford situation of the late 1950s in the standard mold: small community and rural life are callously degraded by the heedless expansion of modern industry. This probably characterizes much of the native perception of the situation at the time and no doubt there is more than a little truth to it. In these terms, the first Chadds Ford Day might appear to have been motivated by an ideology of *traditionalism*, that is, an insistence upon the authority of past lifeways by an obsolescent social group or institution in response to the forces it perceives as a threat to its continued existence (Eisenstadt 1972:22). Traditionalism in this sense was certainly a factor in the early Chadds Ford Day celebration, but for present purposes the real interest of this first phase of the event lies in its combination of elements belonging to an increasingly obsolescent social and cultural order with the first glimmerings of new formations that will not fully come into their own for another decade.

It is impossible to draw up parallel lists of what is residual and what is emergent in the early stage of the Chadds Ford Day celebration, since these tendencies were blended in the continuity of the event and there is no single dimension along which they can be distinguished. But based on a knowledge of what Chadds Ford Day has become, we can sift out some of what was anticipatory from the elements that derived from an older system of social relations and that would not survive the consolidation of Chadds Ford's new order.

For many years Chris Sanderson observed the date of the Brandywine battle in some fashion or other, usually including the delivery of his spirited lecture on the subject.[5] He was, as in all his commemorations, scrupulous in marking the exact date of the event, no matter on what day of the week it might fall. And this "ritualistic" observation hangs on at the Sanderson Museum, where the exact date is still marked, though now as much in memory of Sanderson as to commemorate the battle. Once an official Chadds Ford Day was inaugurated however, the act of commemoration was allowed to float to the weekend. This seemingly trivial development is actually part of a whole shift in outlook and historical sensibility. The origin of a Chadds Ford Day in 1958 is the first step in a development where commemoration ceases to be an end in itself, as it was for Sanderson, and becomes an alibi for something else. In other words, the creation of a formal community event ostensibly intended to commemorate the battle actually marks the passage of true commemoration into the realm of the residual.

Looking back from the ideological vantage of 1976, the Historical Society account of the first Chadds Ford Day makes no overt mention of the Revolutionary War battle. Instead of commemoration, the significant themes are community awareness, resistance to industrial development, and costuming. Given only this account, one would miss the commemorative aspect of the early celebrations altogether, for commemoration had come to play only a very minor role in the second phase of Chadds Ford Days; and by 1976 it had virtually ceased to figure in the Historical Society's discourse. Nevertheless, the residuality of commemoration did not preclude its presence in several forms during the first phase of the celebration. Chris Sanderson's lecture, indeed the very fact of his presence during the early years of Chadds Ford Day, injected a commemorative element into the proceedings, since, as we will see, his whole life seems to have been organized around commemorative activities. Mr. Tullock's patriotic speech and Jack Morgan's patriotic songs belong to the same residual realm. Explicit patriotism, too, hardly figures in the current Chadds Ford Days celebrations. Perhaps the most clearly residual aspect of commemoration and patriotism in the first phase of the event was their official inclusion as formal presentations delivered from a platform set up for the purpose. The spirit of the grange, the lyceum, the prewar small town Fourth of July can be felt in these elements of early Chadds Ford Day celebrations. They are completely absent from the resurrected event of 1968.

More ambiguous in terms of the mixture of residual and emergent is the costuming emphasized in both the Messersmith and Historical Society accounts of the first Chadds Ford Day. The original event was primarily an open-invitation community costume party, with Chadds Ford history as its theme. The Revolutionary War was by no means the only image enacted. As the Historical Society text indicates, tricorns, top hats, papooses, parasols, croquet, spinning wheels, Howard Pyle, and powdered wigs were freely mixed. The celebration was very much in the spirit of those little neighborhood gatherings or block parties that include dressing up and parading, especially by the community's children. In this first Chadds Ford Day there was no attempt to coordinate or restrict the costuming; anything "historical," including Mrs. Chadwick's Victorian vintage dresses, was acceptable. Also, the "authenticity" of the costumes was not a significant issue. A news photo from a report on the 1958 celebration shows a young boy decked out in a commercially marketed "Indian" vest emblazoned with "Tonto" (*West Chester Daily Local News*, 9/20/58). The whole point was to generate a sense of community by allowing for the widest possible participation of local people.

This historical costuming had a strong affinity with a decidedly archaic form—the local pageant. During the mid and late 1930s the production of pageants was a prominent feature of cultural life in Chester and Delaware Counties.[6] Usually sponsored by civic organizations, American Legion posts, schools and other locally based institutions, these pageants were produced by professional firms—notably for the Chadds Ford vicinity, the John B. Rogers Producing Company of Fostoria, Ohio (Thompson 1973:294–295). The pageants were open-air dramatic spactacles based on popular stories (e.g., "Ramona" and "Rip van Winkle"), original plays ("A Fantasy of Fairyland"), or, most important for present purposes, local history (Ibid.:295–298). Two such historical pageants, "Historic Delaware" and "Historic Chester County," would have consisted of dramatized scenes and costume tableaux strung together chronologically and connected with a poetic commentary (Dierolf 1953:34). Although the scripts and productions were developed professionally, in performance pageants were a thoroughly popular form of amateur theatrical in which cast and crew were drawn from the local population (Ibid.:12). The line between a pageant of this sort and a large costume party could be quite thin.

Chris Sanderson provides a human link between formal pageantry and the early phase of the Chadds Ford Day celebration. He was much involved in the productions of the 1930s, providing the historical outlines from which the dramatizations were adapted and assuming various roles in the pageants themselves. He was Squire Cheney, a local hero of the Battle of the Brandywine, in the "Historic Chester County" pageant and he had the title role in "Rip van Winkle." When he donned the costume and persona of town crier, as he did for numerous celebratory and festive occasions, including some of the early Chadds Ford Day celebrations, it was very much in the spirit of the historical pageant.

Certain details of the costuming at the first Chadds Ford Day especially echo this pageantic spirit. Along with the general fact that various periods of Chadds Ford history were reflected in the costumes, the reference to someone impersonating "Howard Pyle at his easel" and to "the diminutive tour of costume scenes posed before some of the local historical houses" suggest an element of staged pageantry. The costume parade, as a formal display of historical allusions, also has a touch of the pageant about it. In fact, in the costume tableaux and the costume parade we have echoes of two basic pageant forms: dramatic enactment on a fixed stage and the procession of costumed characters (Dierolf 1953:33–36).

The echo of pageant, already a residual element in the first phase of Chadds Ford Day,[7] was heard faintly in the revived event of 1968, which still included the costume parade of the earlier celebrations. However, in the first phase the parade was a highlight of the day, while in 1968 other activities greatly overshadowed it. Today it is absent from the celebration.

The importance of costuming remains unabated however, and it would be easy to see this as a major continuity in the history of Chadds Ford Days. On closer examination, though, it turns out to be one of those superficial, outward continuities behind which a fundamental transformation has occurred. The costuming that figures prominently in the current Chadds Ford Days is informed by an ethos drastically different from that underlying the historical pageantry of the celebration's earlier phase and its antecedent local theatricals. The costuming of today's celebration devotes itself to the presentation of a single, unified historical image, the living history conception of eighteenth century country life in the mid-Atlantic colonies. In contrast to the eclectic historicism of the early Chadds Ford Days, this image is thoroughly conditioned by an ideology of closely monitored authenticity.

In Chapter 4 I will discuss at length the Historical Society's devotion to the increasingly popular model of "living history." Live actors, appropriate and authentic costumes, authentic historical settings that have been authentically restored and furnished, and appropriate activities using authentic implements and techniques: these are the key elements of living history, and the Historical Society pursues them to the degree that its relatively limited resources permit.[8] Most of its energies are directed toward producing and presenting an image of the colonial domestic activities—foodways, gardening, spinning and weaving, various crafts, leisure activities—that fit the settings provided by its two restored houses.

Pageantic costuming and living history costuming are radically different forms that enact entirely different ways of relating to the past. The historical pageant uses costume narratively and dramatically to re-create in spectacle specific events, actions and characters. Living history employs costume pictorially (archaeologically) to help create a generalized and "authentic" image of a past way of life. Perhaps we see an ambiguous mixing of these two modes of costuming in the "diminutive tour of costume scenes" singled out for special mention in the Historical Society slide show. I have already pointed out the place of costume tableaux in pageantry. However, it seems likely that the Historical Society of 1976 perceived the little tour as an anticipation of the living history procedures that were just coming into special prominence at the time of the Bicentennial and that have since become the guiding principle of Society activities.

We have seen in the costume parade a residual element that briefly survived the transformation to the second stage of the Chadds Ford Day celebration. The opposite case would be the brief glimmer at the end of stage one of an emergent element that would become fully realized only in stage two. The Historical Society tape provides an example of this in its commentary on the 1962 celebration, the last one before the five year hiatus in the staging of the event. In that year one of the highlights was a special exhibit of Wyeth family art. This in itself might be seen as an emergent element anticipating the 1968 art show which was to codify the Brandywine Heritage of painting. But just as important, and in fact directly connected, was the imposition for the first time of an admission fee. It became necessary to charge this small fee to defray the insurance coverage of the Wyeth paintings. To everyone's surprise, a small profit was made and a modest fund began to accrue. A hint of the economic potential of the event was discernable even then.

Speaking about the craft exhibit, Mr. Messersmith emphasizes the non-economic nature of the early Chadds Ford Day celebrations: "We didn't *sell* anything, . . . the object was just to display, that's all . . . and just to have a good time and to have *fun*, ya know." Yet this lack of overt economic motive was combined with professional marketing of the event as a whole, through the good services of some DuPont public relations people. As a result, along with its dominant properties as a community costume party, the celebration had a touch of the tourist attraction about it. It drew a crowd, the Historical Society tape tells us, of about a thousand visitors. Perhaps the appearance of minor economic and marketing elements in an otherwise non-economic event reflect an emerging form of self-validation in which the presence of tourist others is an important criterion for establishing authenticity. If the purpose of the early Chadds Ford Day celebrations was to confirm the existence of a Chadds Ford community (in response to an outside threat), then perhaps it employed both esoteric (self-display) and exoteric (display for tourist others) means to this end.

Messersmith's account makes it clear that a political motive, resistance to the power company, was behind the movement for Chadds Ford self-awareness from which the first Chadds Ford Day grew.[9] Of course economic forces on a grand scale (the scale of highways and powerlines) were involved in these developments. But in itself, the first phase of the event was substantially non-economic, a few emergent economic elements notwithstanding. In sharp contrast, the resurrected celebration was shot through with economic motives.

For all its rhetorical artifice, the Historical Society lecture betrays a real sense of amazement at the response to the 1968 Chadds Ford Days. Mr. Messersmith was impressed by the "big crowd" of one thousand at the first Chadds Ford Day, but the 1968 celebration, now extended to a full week, drew 25,000 visitors, involved ninety-one volunteer workers, and was covered in the New York press. It attracted "visitors from every state in the union." The book sale alone—an innovation of the event's new economic purpose—brought in $22,000. This was not just a community celebration picking up where it had left off a few years earlier; it was a new kind of event altogether, conducted at an entirely different order of magnitude.

Far from being a repetition or continuation of the 1958 situation that prompted the first Chadds Ford Day, the events of 1967–68 invert the power relations of that earlier time. The series of large steel pylons now to be seen marching down the middle of the Brandywine Valley is blatant evidence that resistance to the powerline came to naught in the late 1950s, or at least to no more than a power company agreement to paint its towers green so they would be a little less obtrusive. Of course there are complicated political and economic reasons why the power company was not to be denied, but certainly one factor was that at the time the forces of resistance to "the encroachments of industry" were local and quite limited. The scope of the early Chadds Ford Day celebrations was correspondingly limited. Apart from a certain poetic interest, perhaps it indicates something about the scale of the event that the number of tourists attending the first Chadds Ford Day was about the same as the toll of American dead at the Brandywine Battle.

Whereas in 1958 the industrial threat was the "power company," almost a mythical embodiment of Industry, in 1968 the enemy was, according to popular recollection, a hat factory. The industrial park proposed for the meadow near the post office would have contained only light industry. The absence of such a park from the Chadds Ford scene attests to the power of the new institutions that sprang up in response to this industrial threat, and it is no accident that the most notable of these institutions—the Tri-County Conservancy (precursor of the Brandywine Conservancy and Museum) and the Chadds Ford Historical Society—were concerned with the scenic, cultural and historical resources of the middle Brandywine. The ideology of preservation bound the Conservancy and Historical Society together during the late 1960s and produced a temporary alliance, one aspect of which was a shared sponsorship of the renewed and transformed Chadds Ford Days.

The tremendous success of the 1968 event was, the Historical Society lecture tells us, a result of one thing in particular: the art show. As we have seen, the production of pictorial art had long been a recognized part of the Chadds Ford cultural landscape, and art shows were included in the Chadds Ford Day celebration from its inception. Even in the first phase a distinction was made between Wyeth family art and the rest of Brandywine artistic production, but the image of a clear, well-formed and above all *definitive* "tradition" had not yet coalesced. Chadds Ford Days 1968 was the official occasion for public enactment of this definitive traditionalization of Brandywine art. It provided the excuse for the presentation to a mass audience, through touristic display and the national press, of an authoritative "Chadds Ford heritage."

The catalogue of the 1968 art show, "The Chadds Ford Art Heritage: 1898–1968," places this definitive heritage in the codified schema of Chadds Ford's mythological past (see Chapter 1, sec. IV): first the "children of the forest, the Leni-Lenape, fishers of shad, travelers of trails"; then the "steady yeomen using stone and wood in simple Quaker fashion" (conceived in this version of Chadds Ford history as the first Chadds Ford artists); in turn, they are followed by Pyle, whose "studio was an ancient mill where the rush of water toward the Brandywine creaked a massive wheel, once used for grinding grain"; then on to N.C. Wyeth, his children and their spouses and *their* children and *their* spouses. The art heritage is traced along lines of blood, marriage, and pedagogy. Eight artists were included in the show: Pyle, N.C. Wyeth, Carolyn Wyeth, John W. McCoy II, Andrew Wyeth, Rea Redifer, George A. Weymouth, and James (Jamie) Wyeth. N.C. was Pyle's student, Carolyn and Andrew were N.C.'s children and his art pupils, John McCoy was N.C.'s student and married one of his daughters, Ann. George Weymouth, Chairman of the Board of the Brandywine Conservancy, married *their* daughter Anna. Carolyn carries on the pedagogic tradition, teaching art in the studio set up by her father. James, Andrew's son, studied with her, as did Rea Redifer (Meyer 1975). With the subsequent elaboration of the more general Brandywine heritage, Redifer was dropped from the tradition and relegated to the ranks of lesser Brandywine artists, where the countless amateur and Sunday painters are lumped together with those professional artists currently working along the middle Brandywine who are without strong Wyeth connections.

The middle phase of the celebration, late 1960s to mid-1970s, was decidedly and necessarily economic, in that it corresponds to the time when the institutional infrastructure of the "new" Chadds Ford Days was being established. The Chadds Ford Historical Society reaped the immediate economic benefits of the traditionalizing art show that proved such a draw to the tourist audience. Enough money was brought in to buy the John Chad House and this, combined with various other fund raisers conducted with Conservancy assistance over the next few years, put the society firmly on its feet, its two historic sites purchased and their restorations underway. None of this would have been possible without the aura of the Brandywine heritage as an attraction or the institutional structure that sprang up to produce and maintain this aura. In retrospect, however, it is hard to avoid the cynical view that the Conservancy/Museum "used" the Historical Society, its restoration projects, and the revived Chadds Ford Days celebration as the locally based, legitimizing occasion— the alibi—for initiating its much more comprehensive projects of cultural and natural resource management, projects addressed to a national mass audience. In the long run the major economic beneficiaries of the cultural developments in the late 1960s have been institutions operating at a scale that quite transcends the cultural micro-climate of Chadds Ford.

Whether we take the cynical perspective or not, there is no denying that the history of Chadds Ford Days from the mid–1970s to the present reflects a breakdown of the institutional solidarity that served the interests of both the Conservancy/Museum and the Historical Society in the late 1960s and early 1970s. The last tangible link between these two institutions was severed recently when the Historical Society moved its records from the space allowed it in the library of the Brandywine River Museum to the now fully restored Barns-Brinton House.

The third phase of the Chadds Ford Days celebration corresponds to this breakdown of institutional solidarity and reflects the attendant specialization of labor in Chadds Ford cultural practice. The areas of cultural preservation staked out in the late 1960s by the Conservancy and the Historical Society have undergone analogous but quite separate processes of secondary, internal elaboration and routinization. For the Conservancy this has meant a process of elite, professional museumization and the development of an eminently consumable myth of traditionality, issues I will return to in Chapter 5.

Much of the artistic production that was pared away in this process of tradition-making because it could not be easily integrated with the official, streamlined version of the Brandywine art heritage was taken up by the Historical Society and incorporated as one component in the third phase of Chadds Ford Days, namely, the art show that is now one of the "anchors" of Chadds Ford Days.[10] Likewise, the crafts display that had always been a part of the event became in its third stage the key attraction. Chadds Ford Days today is primarily a crafts fair with a vaguely colonial theme.

Needless to say, these two dominant elements of the current celebration have little in common with their first phase precursors. The overall transformation of Chadds Ford Days can be characterized as a partially residual community festival becoming an advanced consumer spectacle, a living history craft fair, by way of a transitional stage in which it contributed to the economic and ideological validation of the new social/cultural order.

The Historical Society accomplished the initial purchase, the physical stabilization and some of the basic restoration of its two eighteenth century houses with the financial rewards of its temporary alliance with the Conservancy and the Brandywine art heritage. With these things achieved and no major new projects on the horizon, the Society began to direct its energies toward the active use of its sites and various elaborations of the living history image. Along with the simple maintenance of its two houses, it opened them to the public and eventually hired trained guides to wear authentic eighteenth century costumes and demonstrate various colonial domestic activities; it set up classes to teach colonial crafts and domestic techniques; and it established a series of colonial theme parties at which Society members could pretend to enact colonial forms of conviviality in authentic settings.

Chadds Ford Days had become by the early 1980s the stabilized economic instrument that supports these secondary elaborations of the definitive living history image. As a whole, the event has been thoroughly routinized. In the first stage Chadds Ford Day was physically dispersed.

It had the whole village as its arena: the flag raising and cannon salute at the town hall, the parade along Station Way Road, the staged scenes at historic sites, the platform for speakers in the Chadds Ford Inn parking lot, the craft display in the barn, the art shows in the Baptist Church and Lafayette Hall, the picnic at Battlefield Park. And its shape was not fixed from year to year. Because of the special conditions of cultural production and its new economic motive, the celebration of the late 1960s and early 1970s was localized on the property of the Tri-County Conservancy, first in the mill courtyard and then in the nearby meadow owned by the Conservancy. But even in this phase the physical shape and the scope of Chadds Ford Days were subject to some variation from year to year.

No such flexibility is evident in the third phase of the event. Every year it is celebrated (or perhaps "staged" is the better word) at one end of a particular floodplane meadow north of the village intersection. And along with this geographic containment, the event has turned in upon itself to create the sort of enclosed, entirely self-referential space that, as we will see in the next chapter, many theorists associate with the historical conditions of late consumer culture. In my three years of observation, all the changes to occur in Chadds Ford Days were internal rearrangements of existing elements, elaborations of already established images, or, in the case of the Summer Kitchen, more complete realizations of the logic already in place. These physical stabilities correspond to the economic fact that by the early 1980s the event had become balanced at a point where it could be expected to generate about $20,000 annually for the support of Historical Society activities and maintenance of its living history image.

This figure suggests that on an imaginary scale registering the impact and influence of cultural institutions under current historical conditions, Chadds Ford Days and the historical society which sponsors it would place rather low. Certainly the Brandywine River Museum/Conservancy operate at a different order of magnitude. The Historical Society's total available funds at the end of 1981 were $78,953; at the end of 1980 the Brandywine Conservancy had an operating fund (not including its plant and endowment funds) of $1,267,569. The contrast between the two institutions that these figures suggest is accurate in one sense. The Brandywine River Museum and the discourse on deposit there are connected to national and even international networks of cultural hegemony well beyond the ken of the Historical Society. Yet it will be my argument in Chapter 4 that Chadds Ford Days and the type of cultural discourse it represents reflect a "more advanced" form of cultural practice or a more fully realized staging of consumer culture than any of the other Chadds Ford institutions I will discuss. But before I can turn to a close reading of this discourse, I must step back from my Site and consider some of the abstract properties of the cultural order that contemporary Chadds Ford embodies so completely. First, then, some theory.

NOTES

1. Based on his questionnaire profile of American community festivals, Larry Danielson (1972) finds that for the most part such events as Chadds Ford Days have emerged only since 1940. But John Gutowski (1977) observes that "the modern American festival has a broader provenance, deeper antecedents in both American history and ancient European tradition . . . than Danielson recognizes." For an overview of the history of American festivals and fairs and a survey of the rather meager scholarly literature on them, Gutowski 1977:204–219.

2. Announcements of a Chadds Ford Day are absent from local papers between 1963 and 1967.

3. Newspaper accounts suggest that the event was celebrated on the grounds of the mill as late as 1971, the year the restored structure opened as the Brandywine River Museum. By 1974,however, the celebration had moved to the meadow near the post office.

4. "The residual, by definition, has been effectively formed in the past, but it is still active in the cultural process, not only as an element of the past, but as an effective element of the present" (Williams 1977:122). "By 'emergent' I mean, first, that new meanings and values, new practices, new relationships and kinds of relationship are continually being created" (Ibid.:123).

5. Thomas R. Thompson, Sanderson's biographer, possesses a tape of this lecture and has put together a series of slides to go with it. In this form Sanderson's account of the Battle of the Brandywine is still occasionally heard by school groups and local historical societies. It would make an interesting comparison to place this production alongside the continuous slide show/lecture that plays in the visitors center at the Battlefield Park. In fact, the whole issue of the slide-illustrated taped lecture as an expressive form that resides on the boundary between vernacular and professional bears looking into.

6. On the pageant movement in America, Dierolf 1953; for the view of a seminal figure in the movement, Mackaye 1912; and for a classic sociological study of pageantry, Warner 1959:103–225.

7. That the pageant as a complete form was still alive at this time is demonstrated by the fact that the 1959 Chadds Ford Day was deferred a week so as not to conflict with the Downingtown Centennial Celebration. The nearby community of Downington celebrated its centennial with, among other things, a full-blown historical pageant—"Downingtown Centurama."

8. An important model for the Chadds Ford Historical Society's living history image is the "Colonial Plantation" located in Ridley Creek State Park, several miles northeast of Chadds Ford. It is an open-air museum and "working" farm meant to re-create as fully as possible rural colonial lifeways in eastern Pennsylvania. The Historical Society has the resources and facilities to re-create only a small segment of the image presented at the plantation, namely, the sphere of the hearth and household life. For the historical background of the movement of which the Chadds Ford Historical Society is a latter-day manifestation, see Hosmer 1965 and Anderson 1984. Also see Wallace 1981 for an excellent critical history of the history museum movement. For some perceptive discussions of the ideology of history museums, see Lowenthal 1979 and Lynch 1972:29–64.

9. The specific political manifestation of the controversy was reported in local papers as a zoning battle between residents and township supervisors over the issue of commercial development (*West Chester Daily Local News*, Op-Ed, 9/20/58).

10. I use this term in the technical sense used by planners of shopping malls to designate the flagship department stores that are the focal points in mall layouts (Jacobs 1984:29). For Chadds Ford Days the anchors are the art show at one end and the Historical Society demonstration area and Summer Kitchen at the other.

3 Chadds Ford as a Site of Postmodernity: Veneers, Vignettes, and the Myth of Tradition

There is no longer any transcendence or depth, but only the immanent surface of operations unfolding, the smooth and functional surface of communication. In the image of television, the most beautiful prototypical object of this new era, the surrounding universe and our very bodies are becoming monitoring screens.

Jean Baudrillard,
The Ecstasy of Communication

I. THE CULTURAL LOGIC OF POSTMODERNITY AND ITS RELATION TO THE SITE

Something significant happened in Chadds Ford between the late 1950s and the early 1980s. Or more accurately, a whole series of complex, interconnected transformations occurred and collectively accomplished a thorough retooling of cultural production at this Site. The emergence and subsequent mutation of the Chadds Ford Days celebration provide a kind of map to these changes. It is only with considerable ambivalence that I am characterizing this shift in Chadds Ford's cultural discourse as the emergence of postmodernity as the new cultural dominant of the Site. In the context of this case study it would be preferrable I think to say that these transformations entail the early inscription and increasingly sophisticated reproduction of Chadds Ford *as* a Site—an assemblage of auto-ethnographic texts. But without doubt the current discussions and debates about postmodernity provide the best place to start constructing an analytical apparatus—a language, a set of concepts, points of comparison—capable of producing an adequate reading of Chadds Ford.

Not the least of my reservations about "postmodernity" as the umbrella term for the cultural dominant of this Site is the word's contested status (Pfeil 1986:125). There is anything but agreement on how it ought to be applied—"on whether postmodernism is a period, a tendency within a period, an aesthetico-philosophical category transcending, indeed deploring, periodization, much less [on] exactly who or what would constitute the definition of the term even if one of these options were elected" (Bernstein 1987:45).

Inevitably, there have begun to appear from the welter of discourse on postmodernity attempts to typologize and track the sources of its theoretical variants (Arac 1986, Huyssen 1986:179–221, Bruno 1987:61). For purposes here the crucial distinction is between those approaches which view postmodernity as merely the most recent episode in the "formalist narrative of art movements and moments" (Pfeil 1986:125), a phase in the autonomous history of aesthetic styles, and those approaches which use the word to designate a whole discourse/practice, with distinct, if not easily definable, relations and conditions of cultural production. According to the latter view, postmodern styles of expression are the symptoms of something much more fundamental. It is of course this second conception of postmodernity, however fraught with difficulties it might be, that holds some interest for ethnographers of contemporary consumer culture.

Among those who understand postmodernity as a broad social/ cultural formation that grows ever more pervasive in contemporary life, Frederic Jameson has been the most systematic and influential theorist in identifying its characteristic features (Jameson 1984a; Stephanson 1987). His generalizations about this cultural order, the onset of which he links to the emerging discourses of the 1960s (Jameson 1984b), have both inspired astute readings of particular cultural texts and occasioned productive critical debates about cultural practice under the conditions of advanced capitalism. Perhaps Jameson's most controversial claim is that there is a more or less direct connection between postmodernity as a cultural order and capitalism in its "third" or multinational phase. This correspondence is analogous to and displaces in history the correspondence between modernist culture and second phase or "corporate" capitalism.

Such totalizing abstraction is typical of the theoretical discourse that surrounds the concept of postmodernism. The "empirical" studies that proceed from this theorizing tend to focus on isolated phenomena from the realms of elite and mass culture—literature, visual arts, architecture and urban landscape, film, television, mass advertising—to show how they enact the cultural agendas of postmodernity. As compelling as these analyses often are (Morse 1985, Sorkin 1986, Miller 1986, Bruno 1987, Mainardi

1987, Best 1987/88, Herron 1987/88),[1] including Jameson's own (1984a passim.), they tend to remain detached from all but the most generalized of contexts. Rarely do they attempt to identify and analyze the concrete apparatus of mediating institutions that stand between particular cultural texts and the material forces and relations of which these texts are the ideological expression.[2] One sees in this lack of attention to the concrete means of cultural production an as yet unoccupied terrain in the exploration of postmodernity. It is my contention here that an ethnographic practice of some sort is indispensible to the colonization of this territory.

If there is any truth at all to the view, and I believe there is, that postmodernity names a distinct cultural formation, then like all such formations it is not monolithic or uniform. It arises at different times in different places, it inhabits various institutional contexts, it deploys a range of rhetorical technologies and it achieves hegemonic dominance with varying degrees of success and penetration, depending on local conditions. Perhaps most important of all, cultural practices that remain unincorporated by postmodernity, alternative or even oppositional discourses, might take a great variety of forms and intensities depending on particular circumstances. We can also assume that the postmodern order changes internally in ways that may be peculiar to specific contexts. The development of Chadds Ford Days is an accurate map to the emergence and consolidation of postmodernity at this Site, but it will not be a useful guide elsewhere.

These sorts of specificities are precisely what seem most lacking in current discussions of postmodernity. I have suggested in the introduction that the conditions of postmodernity seriously complicate and call into question the received practices of ethnography. It seems to me equally true that some form of ethnography must be brought to bear in the interest of productively complicating the empirical analysis of postmodernity.

Thirty years ago, about at the time when the lineaments of an advanced consumer culture were coming clear, Roland Barthes (1972 [1957]) was assembling his collection of modern mythologies and extracting from them in broad outline some of the key ideological components of the contemporary scene. In a concluding essay he readily acknowledges that though these ideological themes and structures are pervasive, they are by no means uniform. Rather, they distribute themselves in what he calls "micro-climates." He resigns himself to the fact that in his generalized reading he is not "able to carry out any real study of the social geography of myths. But it is perfectly possible to draw what linguists would call the isoglosses of a myth, the lines which limit the social region where it is spoken" (149).

I take Chadds Ford to be just such a micro-climate—a specific region, though perhaps not in the strictly geographic sense, where a particular dialect of postmodernity is spoken. An adequate account of the discourse at this Site calls for an approach which keeps in view the broad structures and processes that allow us to speak of postmodernity as a recognizable entity, but one that is also sensitive to the "dialect variations" within this hegemony. Such an approach must tend in the direction of ethnography. For all the conceptual difficulties that his work entails, Frederic Jameson is still our best guide to the general properties of postmodernity, and it is to these broad "constitutive features" that we must briefly turn.

Jameson's explication of the gross structures of postmodernity takes the form of a set of homologies among three domains: space and materiality, time and historicity, and the nature of human subjectivity. The master metaphor linking these domains is something one might loosely characterize as "depthlessness." Under the cultural regime of postmodernity all material substance (spatial depth) tends to be flattened into infinitely reproduceable images projected onto glossy surfaces; all sense of historical connectedness, of a meaningful past and a projected future (depth in time), are displaced by an intense focus on present experience; and experience itself ceases to be a matter of individual perception and personal emotion (ego depth) and becomes a decentered condition of free-floating "intensities" that cannot be said to inhabit bounded consciousnesses.

From these conditions of cultural production proceed all the stylistic features understood as symptomatic of postmodernity—the "temporal disconnection and fragmentation" (Stephenson 1987:31) of narrative and historical discourse, the centrality of collage and pastiche in the arts, the eclectic allusions to past styles and periods in architecture and "nostalgia" films, the "schizophrenic" vividness of mass culture imagery, "the exhilaration of the gleaming surface" (Stephenson 1987:30), and so on. It will be of some benefit, I think, to illustrate these general diagnostic features with some specific instances as a first move in the direction of an ethnographic practice adequate to Chadds Ford as a particular Site of postmodernity.

Postmodernity is above all a regime of surfaces, a fact which, as we shall see, has considerable analytical power for a reading of Chadds Ford. Reality under this regime assimilates entirely to inscription. The "fundamental mutation" that prompts the growing discussion of postmodernity as a distinct cultural dominant with its own identifiable logic is the transformation through which "the object world itself...become(s) a set of texts or simulacra" (Jameson 1984a:60), which is to say, inscribed surfaces. Where Van Gogh's *Peasant Shoes*, representative of high modernism in the arts, evokes "the whole object world of agricultural misery, of stark rural poverty and the whole rudimentary human world of backbreaking peasant toil" (Ibid.:58), its postmodern counterpart, Warhol's *Diamond Dust Shoes*, is characterized by "a new kind of flatness or depthlessness, a new kind of superficiality in the most literal sense—perhaps the supreme formal feature of all postmodernisms...." (Ibid.:60).

The official announcement of postmodernity in the visual arts can perhaps be dated to Leo Steinberg's 1968 essay "Other Criteria," in which he uses the word to describe an "altogether new kind of picture surface" particularly evident in the work of Robert Rauschenberg (Crimp 1983:44). This "flatbed" surface (a term from the jargon of mechanical reproduction, i.e. printing) is one that "can receive a vast and heterogeneous array of cultural images and artifacts that had not been compatible with the pictorial field of either premodernist or modernist painting"(Ibid.). This new kind of surface disrupts the notion of "natural" vision, of spectatorship as the act of individual consciousness, and in this it sets an agenda for later postmodern artists. As we shall see, the idea of dispersed or decentered spectatorship has important implications for my reading of Chadds Ford Days as a decidedly postmodern event.

The "logic" of such surfaces is the logic of collage. One might say that Rauschenberg's surfaces composed of fragmentary images silkscreened from photographs of classical art works, advertising, news imagery, and the like, complete the logic of mechanical reproduction implicit even in the earliest modernist experiments in collage. The introduction of collage into the realm of the high arts, perhaps "the single most revolutionary formal innovation in artistic representation to occur in our century" (Ulmer 1984:84), makes possible a phenomenon we might call "pure surface," that is to say, the surface that depends upon or refers to no reality beyond, beneath, above itself, "the depthless, styleless, dehistoricized, decathected" surface (Eagleton 1986:132) absolutely pure in its self-referentiality. It is the sort of surface that reduces all reality to a set of equivalent images, with any given image subject to infinite reproduction or substitution.

A key characteristic of such surfaces is their automatic propagation, the seemingly mechanical operation through which they replicate their characteristics by drawing in, processing and reproducing as projected images potentially the whole world. The visual arts again provide convenient instances of this capacity for the postmodern, self-referential surface to assimilate and reproduce the world as an endless, self-generating series. Jameson's example of Duane Hanson's hyperrealist polyester figures illustrates this operation. The viewer's "moment of doubt and hesitation as to the breath and warmth" of these figures has the effect of returning "upon the real human beings moving about . . . in the museum, and . . . transform[ing] them also for the briefest instant into so many dead and flesh-coloured simulacra in their own right. The world thereby momentarily loses its depth and threatens to become a glossy skin, a stereoscopic illusion, a rush of filmic images without density" (1984a:76–77). The characteristic feeling/tone in this world of glossy surfaces and inscribed images is a "waning of affect" through which our received notions of human emotion are rendered inoperative as individual subjectivity is dispersed. Jameson characterizes this tone as euphoric, as an hysterical sublime, by which he seems to mean a kind of eroticized giddiness, a sense of free, illimitable, uncontrolled movement across surfaces, a four-wheel skid on the highway (Ibid.:64).

Jameson argues that "the modifications in aesthetic production" symptomatic of postmodernity have been most "dramatically visible" in architecture and it is there that postmodernity has been most centrally raised as a conscious theoretical issue. This privileged realm of architecture also provides the readiest point of articulation between Jameson's generalized anatomy of postmodernity as a cultural and social order and the present focusing of the ethnographic impulse on a specific postmodern Site.

At two points in his essay Jameson discusses architectural forms per se, and each bears usefully on the present study. In all his eclectic collection of postmodern symptoms, perhaps the purest material manifestation of the new order is

> the great free-standing wall of the Crocker Bank Center (Skidmore, Owings and Merrill)—a surface which seems to be unsupported by any volume, or whose putative volume (rectangular, trapezoidal?) is ocularly quite undecidable. This great sheet of windows, with its gravity-defying two-dimensionality, momentarily transforms the social ground on which we climb into the contents of a stereopticon, pasteboard shapes profiling themselves here and there around us (Ibid.:62).

In fact, "the distorting and fragmenting reflexions of one enormous glass surface to the other can be taken as paradigmatic of the central role of process and reproduction in postmodernist culture" (Ibid.:79).

I suspect some theorists of postmodern architecture would argue that the sort of structure Jameson identifies as paradigmatically postmodern is, as an isolated design style, more properly considered Late Modernist (see for example Jencks 1986:2–7). But Jameson is not really talking about self-conscious schools of architectural practice. He is speaking more abstractly of a massive shift in the whole material environment, the object world as ideology. In that sense the huge, apparently freestanding, two-dimensional glass surface, or better, the mirror-glass surface, is indeed one of the most "complete" signifiers of postmodernity. It signifies the postmodern agencies that absorb and project all contexts as surface effects or simulacra; it signifies the very technology of reproduction, which centrally defines the postmodern moment; as a physical facade it signifies the operation of capital in its latest and most refined phase. The mirror-glass surface is

> the sign of untouchable knowingness, paralleling the multinational head-quarters and bank buildings of Southern California and its imitators. There, the mirror-glass skin of the building throws back all inquiries to the inquirer, suggesting that today's corporation is to be appreciated precisely for its claim to high-tech universality, that the material product is not important — all that matters is the shiny sac of pure capital, the ultimate postmodern abstraction (Gitlin 1986:139).

One might add as well that mirror-glass is one-way glass, the glass of covert surveillance that presents itself as a surface in which one observes oneself. Self-surveillance merges with surveillance by an unseen, anonymous, untouchable other. This dual quality of such surfaces can be taken as a signifier, then, of the distinctly postmodern agencies of information gathering that become increasingly indistinguishable from agencies of social control, in that they operate with the full participation of those toward whom the surveillance and control are directed.

Most importantly of all, the extended mirror-glass surface is perhaps the purest signifier of signifying play itself, of endless and automatic image reproduction and substitution. It is the very embodiment of self-referentiality in that its primary effect is to convey the brute fact of surface.

As we have seen in Chapter 1, the mirror-glass surface appears at the Site of this study as the skin of the addition to the flour mill made over into the Brandywine River Museum. That institution and the land conservancy to which it is bound are without question the most visible agents of the postmodern order as staged in Chadds Ford. This particular Chadds Ford surface provides my initial link between Jameson's generalized diagnosis of postmodernity and the concrete cultural discourse of the Site. But before making this connection more explicit, we first need to take note of Jameson's other architectural paradigm, John Portman's Bonaventure Hotel in Los Angeles.

Of most relevance to this study are Jameson's observations about the space, or "hyperspace," of the soaring hotel lobby. "I am tempted to say," he says, that such space makes it impossible for us to use the language of volume or volumes any longer, since these last are impossible to seize. Hanging streamers indeed suffuse this empty space in such a way as to distract systematically and deliberately from whatever form it might be supposed to have; while a constant busyness gives the feeling that emptiness is here absolutely packed, that it is an element within which you yourself are immersed, without any of that distance that formerly enabled the perception of perspective or volume. You are in this hyperspace up to your eyes and your body (Jameson 1984a:82–83).

The obvious paradox of such postmodern hyperspaces is that they are volumes constructed so as to behave like surfaces. They are volumes which disperse individual subjectivity by suppressing or confusing their own three-dimensionality and invalidating easy determinations of higher or lower, front or back, thus making it difficult for subjects to locate themselves. This concept of hyperspace provides a good example of how attempts to totalize postmodernity need to be tempered and qualified by concrete observations of particular postmodern environments. There is a very specific way in which the notion of hyperspace applies to Chadds Ford.

First, it applies less to the treatment of physical space and materiality at this Site than to the domain of temporal space and historicity. Perhaps the definitive feature of Chadds Ford's postmodernity is the pervasiveness of an "historical hyperspace" in which depth in time is displaced by fragmentary surfaces. The essential qualification, though, is that depth in time is not simply obliterated by these postmodern surfaces. Rather a whole panoply of simulacra *signifying* historical depth and authenticity become the very texts inscribed upon such surfaces. It is not that depth and volume are simply suppressed, as they seem to be in the physical hyperspace of the Portman lobby, nor is it exactly that surfaces are deployed to fool the eye with the impression of depth. It is more accurate to say that Chadds Ford's postmodernity trades heavily in the reproducible simulation of depth, in depth as consumable imagery, in historical authenticity as a commodifed surface effect.

The Site of Chadds Ford exists as a play of postmodern surfaces, but the fragmented signifiers at play are signifiers of a temporal depth that has no actual existence behind, above, below or before those surfaces. This is the Site's distinctive version of the postmodern paradox. One can be still more specific and say that Chadds Ford specializes in reproducing the simulacra of a particular species of depth in time, namely, Traditionality, a topic I will return to presently.

Jameson's compelling discussion of postmodernity as a regime of surfaces provides an effective symptomatology for the basic diagnosis of this new (or by now not so new) cultural dominant. As we have just seen, though, the constitutive features he identifes might well be realized in quite distinctive local variants. And if one wants to move beyond the level of diagnosis, the theoretical discourse of which Jameson is the best representative ceases to be of much help at all. It can guide us in the identification of the effects of the postmodern order, but it is little concerned with the tangible apparatus that generates those effects. For example, it cannot help us much when we ask the question of how it happens that the depth and historical authenticity so central to the imagery of Chadds Ford are manifestly surface effects generated in a reproductive technology that contradicts the very notion of authenticity. And through the workings of what mechanisms does it happen that no one seems particularly disturbed by, or even aware of the paradox? Or to put it another way, how can Chadds Ford be so advanced and successful as a Site of postmodernity when the image and ideology it actively projects, an image of rootedness in time and authenticity of place, are everything postmodernity is not? How does it happen, and this is to suggest why Chadds Ford provides such an interesting laboratory, that postmodernity can turn to its own purposes (make over in its own image[ry]) even those moments that one might naturally look to as the best foundations for critique and resistance?

The answers to such questions require an approach that I am inclined to call ethnographic. They are questions about the specificities and local manifestations of postmodern discourse and about the institutions that sustain such discourse. If it is true that postmodernity is spoken in a range of dialect variations, it seems reasonable to assume that the discourse in any one of these dialects is likely to have its own distinctive conventions, or what one might call its rhetorical apparatus. If Chadds Ford is any indication it also seems true that postmodern micro-climates can organize their discourse around particular themes. In other words, under specific conditions of production there might be certain kinds of rhetorical and thematic constraints placed upon the supposed "free play" of postmodern discourse. Our next step then in moving toward an effective ethnographic practice will be to identify and explicate the rhetorical forms and the ideological themes most characteristic of this particular Site.

II. A RHETORIC OF SURFACES

One way to start is with a tour of, literally, some Chadds Ford surfaces. The Brandywine River Museum presents at our Site the surfaces most readable as rhetorical structures. For the schematic purposes of this chapter I will ignore some of the ideological complexity of this building, recovering it later when I deal with the museum as an institutional purveyor of a particular ideology. For the time being I will concern myself with its literal surfaces, its interior and exterior walls, as characteristically post-modern texts.

As we have already seen in the "official" postcard representations (Chapter 1, sec. XIII), the museum building is conceptually binarized. Its design divides it down the middle. I propose that this bifurcation can serve as a kind of indigenous model for a useful distinction between two basic postmodern rhetorical patterns that figure prominently in the discourse of the Site. Since the rhetoric of postmodernity is perhaps most easily grasped as a rhetoric of surfaces, I will characterize these two figures as surface effects—veneer and vignette.

The mirror-glass wall of the Brandywine River Museum can serve as a paradigm of the characteristically postmodern rhetorical figure I am calling *postmodern veneer*. In its simple sense, of course, veneer refers to covering a cheap substance making up the bulk of some object with a thin layer of finer material. In its metaphorical extension, veneer means a superficial and artificial outward display that hides an underlying reality. Speciousness, inauthenticity, and deception are often implied.

It is not hard to find material forms in Chadds Ford that it seems reasonable to consider veneers in this simple sense. The development houses laminated with a thin layer of artificial stone masonry and prefab plaster, and houses with superficial half-timbering externally appliqued for purely decorative purposes are obvious instances of veneering in the literal sense. Materials valued because they are picturesque, or that are perceived as in keeping with the generalized image of the place, are superficially applied to otherwise undistinguished structures made of standard building materials and conforming in many cases to standard design formats.

But the postmodern veneer as a characteristic structure of contemporary discourse is different from veneer in this simple sense. It refers to those sorts of surfaces, literal or metaphorical, that do not just hide some underlying substance, but that completely dissolve or de-materialize that substance. This is not to say, of course, that the substance is physically demolished. Rather it becomes framed as an image in an endless chain of automatic reproduction, so that it ceases to make sense to distinguish between substance and simulacrum, original and copy, depth and surface. One could say that the postmodern veneer involves not so much the lamination onto one substance of a finer, more valuable material, but rather the lamination onto one substance of the image or simulacrum or idea of itself. And at that moment of postmodern veneering all is rendered insubstantial. It would be incorrect, then, to consider the postmodern veneer as involving simple deception or inauthenticity. The so-called depth models that distinguish between authentic and inauthentic cease to make sense in the postmodern context (Jameson 1984a:61–62).

The reflecting glass curtain wall, or more accurately, the mirror-glass surface expanse, which Jameson identifies as perhaps the purest material emblem of the postmodern order, I would appropriate for this discussion as the clearest material expression of postmodern veneer. At the Site of Chadds Ford such surfaces are paradigmatically represented in the architecture of the Brandywine River Museum: in the curving glass skin of its "circulation core," a shape inspired, we are told in the institutional literature, by the barn silo. Visitors to the museum look out through this glass as they make their circuits through the building, from the gallery entrances and exits to the stairs and elevator, from gallery to restrooms, from gift shop and restaurant to gallery, and so on. The exterior of the glass surface presents itself to the visitor who strolls along the paved paths of the landscaped bank of the Brandywine, with its artfully arranged vegetation, its benches fashioned from discarded mill wheels, its hyperrealist bronze sculpture of a reclining cow, and its wire-mesh retaining wall, built to prevent the Brandywine from exercising its natural inclination to shift course with the spring floods (Figure 1).

The oddest and, I would suggest, definitively postmodern property of this mirror-glass surface, this postmodern veneer, is that it accomplishes the logical impossibility of being one-sided. Whether the surface is viewed from outside or from inside, its one-way mirroring allows it to reproduce a single image, literally the same text and not just two impressions of the same image. That text is, of course, the Brandywine River and its bordering vegetation, the automatically reproduced simulacrum of the natural environment that legitimizes the museum/conservancy.

When I say the image reproduced on/by this surface is single and that the surface is one-sided, I do not mean of course that the optical experience of individual viewers is the same inside and out. Looking out the window wall one sees the course of the Brandywine as in a postcard view, Nature framed and subtly "distorted" to make it "hyperreal" by a slight green tinting to the glass. Viewed from outside, the mirroring glass reproduces the external environment as rows of large quasi-impressionist fragments of reflected Brandywine vegetation. Conceptually though, the surface accomplishes in a single gesture the transformation of a material context into a surface effect that, though optically dual, can hardly be said to have a verso and recto. Our full appreciation of such postmodern surfaces requires that we bracket out, though this is only possible as a theoretical exercise, the stereoscopic mode of perception that presumes individual, self-contained consciousnesses as distinct nodes of reception and inter-

FIGURE 1. Hyperrealist cow beside the Brandywine. Photograph by the author.

pretation. In other words, we need to acknowledge the decentering of the subject in its assumed capacity as the individual physical locus of visual experience. Much of postmodern art makes such decentering its point.

Another version of much the same point is to say that postmodernity, through the infinite self-referentiality of its reproduced inscriptions, tends in many of its realizations toward the complete dissolution of material surfaces. Although the metaphor of projection onto surface is perhaps the best we can do in trying to capture postmodernity in the language available to us, in fact the purest expression of postmodernity would be the image that completely does without any material mediation, the simulacrum that exists without being inscribed on any surface, literally or metaphorically.

Leaving aside such technological curiosities as holograms (Eco 1986:3–6), the surface of polished glass is perhaps the most accessible correlative of the property I'm trying to capture here. To identify such surfaces as characteristically postmodern is to restate the postmodern hegemony of simulacra, of automatic mechanical reproduction, of glossy image and spectacle, all of which tend asymptotically toward a fully dematerialized world. The mirror-glass wall accomplishes a double dissolution: it reproduces the physical environment as an inscribed image, emptying that context of its materiality, and it simultaneously renders invisible its own material existence *as* a surface.

This specular "logic" realized in the architecture of the Brandywine River Museum was made even more explicit and self-referential in the recent (1985) addition to the building. On the river side this new addition extends the mirror glass of the circulation core back along a flat plane that culminates in a second glass cylinder, precisely replicating the "original" convex tower [Fig. 2]. Structurally the building now echoes itself and, optically, reflections abound. The two glass cylinders reproduce (and de-materialize) in reflection the Brandywine scenery, and the surface of the building now quite literally reflects itself, which is to say, this surface dissolves in an infinite series of reflections of reflections of reflections.

Although the architectural deployment of mirror-glass is paradigmatic of postmodern veneer, Chadds Ford offers up innumerable other surfaces with the characteristic properties of this rhetorical/discursive figure. At the end of Chapter 1 (sec. XXI) I described two specific surfaces, wall segments in the Barns-Brinton House, and suggested that, trivial as they might be, these passages from the general text of the Site exemplify discursive strategies pervasive in Chadds Ford. I have now identified one

FIGURE 2. Circulation core and 1985 addition. Photograph by the author.

of these strategies as postmodern veneer, and one of the tavern wall segments demonstrates its basic mechanism as vividly as the mirror-glass of the museum. It also demonstrates some of the range of variation of this rhetorical figure.

The framed cut-away upstairs at the Barns-Brinton House quite literally presents the construction of the wall as a display "hung" upon the wall. The frame, the protective glass, and the explanatory labels textualize the depth of the wall and its internal machinery. As the thing itself, the "depth" of the wall, becomes a representative specimen, it loses substance as a material reality, though it alludes to or recalls that order of reality. How different our reaction would be to the same wall segment if the plaster had merely fallen raggedly away to reveal unevenly the underlying lath and masonry. By framing and foregrounding the wall's materiality, by presenting it as spectacle, this surface segment produces the same veneering effect as the mirror-glass of the museum.

Just from among the souvenirs gathered in Chapter 1, Joseph Messersmith's tin, George Heebner's plastered wall, and the Chadds Ford friendship quilt share the basic property of postmodern veneer, namely, the inscription onto surfaces of the *image* of material processes, social relations, and historical circumstances. While these surfaces do not literally perform the optical feat of dissolving material substance, they produce the same effect by displacing and annulling material processes and relations of production through the substitution of their simulacra. Messersmith's tin surface dulled with a special compound to create the impression of age and wear textualizes the use value of these objects. They immediately become objects that display the *idea* of use through time and their actual utility either disappears completely or becomes marginal and a source of surprise ("Not only is this an exact replica of a colonial lighting fixture, but it has been wired to actually run on electricity!").

Much the same is true of Heebner's wall, a surface inscription of the image of rough workmanship and the artisan mode, and the friendship quilt, which textualizes both Chadds Ford's depth in time (through the iconography of its squares) and processes of communal production (through the quilt-form itself). These three cases represent that immense variety of veneered surfaces that depend on techniques of distressing, antiqueing, or otherwise archaizing objects, which is to say, techniques for mystifying their material production and existence by inscribing them with texts about materiality.

In proposing veneer as a designation for such phenomena I am merely giving a species name to processes widely recognized as diagnostic of postmodernity. The naming is also meant to suggest that these processes ought to be viewed as rhetorical/discursive practices. They do ideological work. Whether veneer is the best rubric or not, for purposes of this case study we need some designation under which to collect the properties and examples of this connected discursive practice so that it can be distinguished from another rhetorical form that I think is even more important for an account of Chadds Ford's distinctive postmodernity—a form I will call vignette. The distinction I am drawing with this terminology is crucial to my account of Chadds Ford as a distinct postmodern micro-climate. But before turning to vignette it is worth identifying two varieties or subspecies of the postmodern veneer, only one of which is typical of this Site.

I have made much of Chadds Ford's self-referentiality and auto-ethnographic self-inscription. But this is not to say that these controlling processes of reproduction and self-citation are "aware" of themselves *as* processes. One might go so far as to suggest that the ideological efficacy of Chadds Ford depends upon a misrecognition of itself. The obvious changes that have occurred there over the last twenty-five years can be couched in the familiar "machine-in-the-garden" terms of the encroachment of the modern world on rural village life[3], or be perceived as the depradations of industry and suburbanization, and so on. But it simply would not do for Chadds Ford cultural production to theorize its own postmodernity, that is, become fully conscious of its pervasive textuality. Were it to do so, Chadds Ford would have to be categorized as a different kind of postmodern Site than the one I am attempting to depict in this study. The closest approximation we have to this other kind of Site, one that is not only infinitely self-referential but also aware of its textuality and capable of textualizing (and commodifying) even this very awareness, is the theme park. Of course we might turn this around and say that Chadds Ford is a species of postmodern Site for which we have no good name but that might be described as like a theme park minus the self-consciousness. One symptom of this lack of detachment is the seeming absence of a self-directed sense of humor in Chadds Ford's cultural production. For the most part Chadds Ford takes itself quite seriously.

My point is that the veneers at this Site, although arising in postmodern processes of self-reflection, are generally unreflexive—even actively anti-reflexive. They are rarely if ever framed so as to reveal an awareness of themselves as rhetorical/discursive constructs. To generalize this observation we would have to say that Chadds Ford belongs to a special mode of postmodernity, let's call it the postmodern vernacular, characterized precisely by this self-referentiality minus reflexivity.

I will be contending later on that this vernacular mode is in many ways a more "advanced" formation than the self-conscious postmodernity that dominates most discussions. Jameson's analysis for example takes its illustrations largely from the theoretically self-aware productions of high culture—formal arts, letters, and philosophy. He generally glosses over the fact that postmodernity entails the breakdown of the distinction between elite and mass/popular culture. As a result, he presents a representative sampling of postmodern veneers that are highly reflexive, fully aware of their textuality and constructedness and intent on making that awareness apparent. Paradoxically, the least self-conscious veneers he cites, those closest to a vernacular mode (hence their usefulness in the above discussion), are the architectural examples—paradoxical because it was probably in high-style architecture that postmodernity first came to theoretical consciousness. It seems a bit odd that Jameson did not draw examples from more overtly self-conscious postmodern architecture. I will just cite one small instance from that domain to illustrate what I mean by a self-conscious postmodern veneer, as opposed to the vernacular, unreflexive variety characteristic of our Site and typified by the mirror-glass surface.

James Stirling's addition to the Staatsgalerie in Stuttgart (completed 1984) is a particularly notable instance of a consciously postmodern aesthetic at work (Jencks 1986:18). At one point on the ground level of this building several large blocks have apparently tumbled out of the wall to lie randomly in the grass. A gaping, irregular hole mars three courses of the block stone surface. But of course it is apparent to most everyone, at least after the initial surprise, that these blocks have been scattered thus on purpose. Inspection of the hole reveals that the structure is not made of solid stone after all. The stone slabs are only cladding veneered onto a steel supporting frame and not set in mortar. The interior seen through the hole is a parking garage, for which the hole itself and the thin gaps between the fixed blocks provide necessary ventilation. The romantic image of stone ruins in a garden is wryly juxtaposed to the modern reality of mass transportation and high-tech construction.

We have in this instance postmodern veneer at its most reflexive. Not only is history, in this case the history of classical and romantic architectural styles, laminated onto a surface as historicist imagery, but the *fact* of that inscription is itself made part of the text. In the self-conscious veneer such revelations become the point of the discourse. "One can sit on these false ruins and ponder the truth of our lost innocence: that we live in an age which can build with beautiful, expressive masonry as long as we make it skin-deep and hang it on a steel skeleton" (Jencks 1986:18). I believe that the reflection prompted by such self-conscious surfaces is not generally the sort that leads to critique. In fact, the hyper-reflexivity of the postmodern order is one of the key mechanisms it deploys to accomplish its own ideological reproduction. Self-revelation and unmasking become part of the textual game and help immunize the system against radical change. The tone of postmodernity's self-conscious surfaces is ironic, but of the distinctly detached sort that Jameson calls "blank irony" (1984a:65), that is, an irony that operates somehow without any stable position of judgement, a free floating irony in which any apparently definitive position is subject to further ironization. There is no master code.

Such self-consciousness is barely visible in Chadds Ford. The raw material, massively redundant, is there for accomplishing it, and in part this study is an attempt to add that layer of reflexivity. But the Site operates mainly in the vernacular, unironized mode of postmodernity. For the critical reader of this Site there is a strategic advantage to the fact that Chadds Ford has not (or not yet) absorbed and commodified its own critique. It is thoroughly postmodern in its self-citation, but it has not complicated that process by consciously presenting its textuality as part of its own discursive practice. Its discourse is not cynical. This Site has, however, invested heavily in a rhetorical strategy that seems equally effective for purposes of ideological reproduction—the strategy I am calling vignette.

I once chanced to fall into conversation with a regional representative of the Gannett newspaper *USA Today*. In the midst of a long monologue about the publishing business and this particular paper, he informed me that in some neighborhoods in Detroit—although he was not explicit, cues led me to think he meant inner city, probably black neighborhoods—it was fashionable to steal the *USA Today* paperboxes. With the doors removed these boxes were being installed in living rooms as television stands. Certain portable models fit neatly into the space intended for the newspapers.

At first this information seemed merely amusing, but upon reflection it struck me that it had some conceptual significance. Whether the information is apocryphal or not there is a structural principle at work here that seems distinctly postmodern, with analogues across the whole cultural field of contemporary life. It is no secret, and the publishers make no bones about the fact, that *USA Today* is an attempt to make print journalism as much like television as possible. The graphics, the short articles, the emphasis on entertainment are all meant to reproduce the typical effects of broadcast journalism and of TV in general. The television inserted into the paperbox implicitly acknowledges the connection. But it has another effect as well. It raises a question of priority, an ambivalence about levels of reality and representation. Is the older mode—print journalism—the substance (background, authentic origin, etc.) and television the image (inscription, text) played off against it? Or is it the other way around? Is the gesture a tacit acknowledgement of television as the inescapable background of everyday existence against which the newspaper seems a residual text about archaic modes of communication? Is it a substitution of paperbox for TV stand or TV stand for paperbox? The overall effect, I would suggest, is a ceaseless oscillation between these positions, with no way of deciding between them. The rhetorical outcome is that all attention becomes concentrated on the oscillating play itself.

Although this parable of the paperbox may seem all too trivial a case to generalize from, one assumption of this study is that postmodernity is most visibly at home in just such fragments. The rhetorical structure at work in this example, it turns out, pervades the postmodern discourse of Chadds Ford, and I am giving it the name *postmodern vignette*. As with the veneer, we find its paradigmatic realization back at the Brandywine River Museum. The reader will recall that I am taking the formal and thematic division in the architecture of the Museum as an unacknowledged model, generated by the Site itself, of a rhetorical distinction widely applicable to the discursive practice of Chadds Ford as a whole. If the mirror-glass circulation core and its extension embody the rhetoric of veneer, the restored mill/gallery exemplifies the logic of vignette.

The most obvious distinction between the two architectural modes of the museum, as coded by the postcards, is between "open" space and closed space. The circulation core is suffused with "natural light," opens onto panoramic views of the countryside, and emphasizes the fluid continuity of an interior space open from one level of the building to the next. The gallery, on the other hand, is entirely closed (the apertures behind the shutters visible on the outside of the mill are blocked by the interior wall of the gallery). The gallery levels are completely separate boxes and each level is elaborately articulated with partitions. The light is dramatically artificial—bright, flat, and uniform. The distinction I want to make between veneer and vignette as rhetorical forms of postmodern surfaces can, at least for a start, be couched in terms of this open/closed binary. Veneer in the simple sense designates a surface that literally hides some reality prior to it. Postmodern veneer, however, does not simply hide some prior reality or underlying substance. Rather, it dissolves materiality itself through the agency of simulation and inscription. Simple veneer can be accomplished with pre-industrial and industrial production technologies. Postmodern veneer requires a post-industrial technology of automatic, mechanico-electronic reproduction.

In either case, however, veneer involves some sense of a space, a material substance, an historical reality, beyond the veneered surface itself. This is patently true with simple veneers, but even the postmodern veneer cannot be conceptualized without reference to something that has been flattened, dissolved or inscribed as image (simulacrum). Philosophical questions as to the existential reality of this prior "something" are irrelevant for present purposes. The crucial point here is that veneer suggests a two-dimensional surface that can never fully escape at least a trace allusion to something external to it. Or to put it another way, veneer is a kind of framing strategy that involves the marking of boundaries. At least a minimal sense of an "outside" is necessary to the operation of veneer.

Vignette is my name for the sort of surface that constitutes a completely hermetic space, with absolutely no cognizance of a reality beyond itself, either as a hidden, underlying substance or as a prior authentic materiality that has been flattened into surface image. The notion of frame does not apply here, in that vignette designates a fully self-contained world of signifying practice which recognizes no outside. The vignetted surface extends infinitely.

Obviously I am not using the word in its popular acceptation as "a short descriptive literary sketch" or "a brief incident or scene" (*Webster's Collegiate Dictionary*). Rather I would emphasize its technical meaning in the visual arts, photography and optics, that is, "any embellishment, illustration, or picture unenclosed in a border, or having the edges shading off into the surrounding paper," or again, "a photographic portrait, showing only the head or head and shoulders, with the edges of the print shading off into the background" (*OED*). The salient feature of this technical definition, which I would generalize and apply both literally and metaphorically, is the undecidability of the relationship between inscription (image) and inscribed surface. I use vignette to mean any phenomenon where an image, representation, text, or simulacrum can be said to resolve into the material surface on which it is imprinted.

Levels of representation are at issue here, as they are with the veneer, but in this case it is not the issue of some "three-dimensional reality" (literally, spatial volume or, metaphorically, history, social relations, etc.) being flattened into two dimensions. Rather it is a matter of the hierarchy of representation contained entirely within the two dimensions of the surface, the hierarchy of image and medium. Vignettes problematize this relationship, set it in motion so to speak, by demonstrating simultaneously the materiality of the image as it merges with the material surface, and the signifying properties of that surface, which can be perceived as gradually drawing itself up to become the inscribed image. An important difference between the postmodern veneer and the vignette, then, is that the rhetorical strategy of the former type of surface entails mystification of its own materiality, while the vignette foregrounds that very materiality and locks one into the hermetic, self-sustaining play of its levels.

If veneer mystifies the materiality of surfaces, while vignette foregrounds that materiality in a way that keeps us from breaking free of those surfaces, vignette also foregrounds the materiality of texts. In book and magazine illustrations vignettes typically appear in marginal spaces, at the beginning or end of chapters for example. In that position they could be said to mediate between the page itself and the printed text inscribed upon it. They illustrate the text, which is to say, they reinscribe (re-cite) it imagistically and so are themselves textual, but they also merge at their edges with the inscribed surface, thus manifestly enacting their material substance.

To extend this conception of vignette as a technique of visual rhetoric beyond the realm of literal inscription, I would submit that the mill/gallery portion of the Brandywine River Museum accomplishes the effect of self-legitimization through the very practices I am associating with vignette effect. I would note first of all that several of the images hung there are vignettes in the technical, visual arts sense. As a form of visual representation, the vignette comes into its own under conditions that allow for the mechanical mass reproduction of images. It is especially associated with book illustration and photography. The so-called Brandywine Heritage of art that is the subject of this museum identifies its originating moment as the flowering of commercial illustration centering on Wilmington art teacher Howard Pyle and his many students. Some of Pyle's painted vignettes, purposely designed to be reproduced as book and magazine illustrations, hang in the gallery.

But the more relevant instance of vignette, the one analogous to the circulation core as veneer, has to do with the relationship between the images hung in the gallery and the surface of the gallery itself, the gallery as material support for those images. Viewed through one lens, the one we are probably best trained to use by our previous experience of art museums, the gallery surface is merely the neutral backdrop against which the framed images are highlighted. But by adjusting our frame slightly, drawing back to the middle distance suggested by the postcard view of the gallery interior, a kind of inversion occurs. The uneven white plaster of the walls, the heavy, rough-hewn pillars and beams, the braided rope strung to keep visitors from approaching the paintings too closely, even the dimensions of the rooms and management of the space—these things collectively take on their own signifying power. They themselves come to constitute a display in their own right. A hierarchical ambiguity comes into play. Is the gallery surface (in some extended sense that would include the material properties of the exterior as well as the interior) merely the supporting medium for the framed images, or does this material surface have its own, independent "image life"? Or, still more paradoxically, is there some sense in which it could be true that the framed images, the paintings, constitute the background for (excuse for, alibi for) the gallery's restored surface, which signifies old grist mill, which in turn signifies rural life, or perhaps simply the nebulous concept of traditionality? In any case, this ultimately undecidable play of figure and ground never breaks the plane of the gallery conceptualized as a surface. The two-dimensional space is sealed and entirely sufficient unto itself, and this capacity for complete self-legitimization is the key rhetorical property I associate with vignette.

If the framed cutaway upstairs at the Barns-Brinton House is an especially vivid realization of the logic of postmodern veneer, the restored panelling downstairs belongs in the domain of vignette. The restoration plan for this building seems to revolve around an ethic of truthfulness. Unlike the many historical restoration projects that strive for a completely smooth surface by fabricating replacement pieces to look as much like the original elements as possible, the Barns-Brinton reconstruction would let us in on the restoration process, though in a way that doesn't totally disrupt the overall impression of "original appearance." Hence the fabricated replacement panels precisely reproduce the form of the remaining original sections, but their wood is of a slightly different shade to clue us in that they are simulations.

One effect of this restoration practice, I assume unintentional, is to activate the figure/ground dialectic of vignette. The same ultimately undecidable question of hierarchy or priority—which is medium and which is text, which is image and which is inscribed surface—that I find in motion at the museum gallery is operating just as clearly here. We cannot finally say that the replacement pieces form a background against which to view the originals, for it seems equally plausible to argue that the original elements serve to make the restoration visible. At Barns-Brinton, as in the museum gallery, the activity of restoration itself becomes part of the display. This is quite the reverse of restoration projects that strive for a uniform look. These have as an implicit goal the complete invisibility of the restoration process and are, perhaps, of the veneer species. The rhetoric of the Barns-Brinton restoration is such that the question of original vs. reproduction is literally laid out for inspection as a surface effect. All attention is focused on this interplay and the result is the appearance of that closed material world characteristic of vignette, sufficient unto itself and oblivious to extrinsic determinations.

As with veneer, instances of vignette abound at Chadds Ford. Precisely analogous to the restored panelling, for example, is the front wall of the restored mill on the Wyeth property, the building which houses Andrew Wyeth's private art gallery and the business office through which his paintings and their reproduction are managed. As part of the restoration process the exterior stone surface was cleaned and repointed. It was Wyeth's wish, however, that one patch be left in its decayed, crumbling state. Is this patch the visible vestige of a surface that has had superimposed upon it a restoration, or is the cleaned, repointed restoration the canvas upon which the picturesque patch of weathered, crumbling stone has been inscribed as an image signifying the passage of time?

Related to these restoration phenomena is a principle of interior decoration that appears increasingly common in the domestic material culture of deep-suburban life. Magazines catering to the deep-suburban lifestyle typified by Chadds Ford showcase with some frequency homes in which paintings or prints of rustic rural life are juxtaposed to antiques or other three-dimensional objects that are related in some way to what is going on in the pictures. So, for example, the magazine *Early American Life*, which is targeted precisely to a clientele like the Chadds Ford suburbanites[4], displays home interiors in which a primitive still-life of fruit is hung above an antique table decorated with an actual fruit arrangement (Handler 1983:22), or an antique wooden sled is propped against the wall beneath an old print of ice-sledding (Hammond 1983:40).

We have seen much the same sort of image redundancy in Wyeth's commissions of hand-crafted reproductions of objects and whole tableaux drawn from his paintings. Although the dialectic here would seem to be between a two-dimensional image and a three-dimensional reality, I would argue that conceptually such phenomena operate within the closed surface space of vignette. The three-dimensional tableaux and miniaturizations are every bit as "textual" as the painted or reproduced images they correspond to, and the undecidable play of levels of reproduction is every bit as hermetically sealed in its self-referentiality as the restoration phenomena described above.

As a last instance I would include as a species of vignette the undecidability of scale that seems so characteristic of the Chadds Ford scene. I have pointed out that in its postmodern context the early eighteenth-century Barns-Brinton House is "cited" by the modern buildings that surround it. The effect of this environment, though, is to leave indeterminate the historicity of scale. Are the structures of Chadds Ford West enlargements or is in some sense the Barns-Brinton a miniaturization? The very fact of undecidability is the point, and this dialectic of miniature vs. enlargement, original vs. reproduction, background vs. image, epitomizes the closed space of vignette as a rhetorical structure.

In the next chapter I return to the community celebration Chadds Ford Days, now to view it as a specific text to be read. My argument will be that this event is perhaps the most concentrated and elaborated instance of vignette at the Site. It demonstrates how the rhetoric of vignette creates a self-sustaining space with the capacity to colonize everyday life and to extend new modes of consumption along every avenue of discourse. I will suggest that under the regime of postmodernity the rhetorical process of vignetting is most fully realized in these new modes of consumption. It is above all the postmodern consumer who enacts the rhetoric of vignette. In order to understand what is most postmodern about Chadds Ford Days we will need a new way to think about consumption, one that does not assume individual subjects driven by internal desires to purchase particular objects. Something like a notion of impersonal, dispersed consumption, analogous to the flattening of the object world and the dispersal of the individual consciousness, will be required, and, as we shall see, vignette is the rhetorical figure appropriate to this new mode of consumption. It above all creates the condition of a completely enclosed space within which a self-sustaining play and exchange of images can take place. The postmodern consumer, combining qualities of spectator, actor, participant, observer, producer, tourist, collector, and others, is the native creature of such spaces. Postmodern consumption *is* ceaseless vignetting, and consumers themselves become the medium through which this process operates. Which brings us back to television.

Vignette and Televisual Space: A Digression

I have limited my discussion of vignette to a few of its physical manifestations at our Site, instances pointing up its operation as a cultural technology that greatly influences how we experience the material world. The micro-climate of Chadds Ford represents, however, just one local manifestation or "dialectal" version of this largely unacknowledged rhetorical figure that, I would suggest, pervades our current conditions of postmodernity. In fact, the cultural scene most saturated with vignette effects is television, the signature medium of our age.

Mark Crispin Miller puts his finger on the same quality I have tried to evoke with the Chadds Ford examples in his discussion of what it means to say that television has "come into its own" or reached maturity as a medium. It's not that TV has realized its documentary or dramatic potential. Such a culmination would require it to point beyond itself, when in fact its real coming of age "consists precisely in TV's near perfect inability to make any such outward gesture. TV tends now to bring us nothing but TV (Miller 1986:192–193). It is a closed, self-referential, self-legitimizing world that recognizes no outside.

It has become a cliché in media studies that the internal boundaries of the medium, for example between news and entertainment programming or, paradigmatically, between TV ads and everything else, tend increasingly to blur. The same questions about the hierarchy of reality, about image and background, about inscription and inscribed surface, that I have associated with the rhetoric of vignette are dramatically highlighted in television and the televisual experience.

Technologically television is well supplied with the visual means to produce vignette effects. Increasingly common, for example, is the use of a technique where the digital quality of the television image is foregrounded. The seemingly analog or continuous picture our brains resolve out of the minute dots of light on the screen is broken into a field of discontinuous (digitalized) squares that enlarge to the point where the image becomes an abstract pattern of movement and color. The process then reverses and the pattern resolves into a new scene of recognizable shapes and actions. This sort of transition is quite different from the lap fade familiar in the discourse of film, a kind of segue we read as the "natural" indicator of a change of location or the passage of time. The movement from analog image to digital and back to analog visibly lays out the materiality of the electronic signal and the apparatus of its production and sets in motion an undecidable dialectic between image and medium that is not at all unlike the oscillation between original and simulation in the Barns-Brinton restoration. Typically this transition effect is used to move between "levels of reality" of the televised image, for example between the "real" Hulk Hogan and his cartoon reincarnation on a Saturday morning kids show (Sorkin 1986:169–170). Increasingly television uses techniques that, in one way or another, deploy the rhetoric of the vignette to lock the viewer into a hierarchical chain of simulations, a series of levels of representation (all of them equally projections on the televisual surface) across which there seem to be variations in the degree of reality, but which never entertains the possibility of a reality (historical, social, material) outside this self-contained, self-referential televisual space.

Although it may sound rather strange to say so, Chadds Ford is a postmodern Site to the degree that it is a space of such televisual experience. I propose this connection because it is one way to get at a crucial feature of Chadds Ford's postmodernity that I have only alluded to. So far I have been mainly concerned with the postmodern transformation of the object world, the change in the very nature of materiality itself that distinguishes the postmodern order and that is visible in the more or less physical veneers and vignettes collected at our Site. The other side of the postmodern transformation is of course the fundamental change in the nature of subjectivity, indeed, the very dispersal of the subject as previously constituted.

Television offers countless instances where the rhetoric of vignette operates to blur distinctions in the hierarchy of the reality of subjects.

One case already mentioned is the digitalized transition from "real life" figure to cartoon image, the veneering effect implicitly suggesting that the transition could go in either direction, thereby rendering undecidable the question of which is the higher "reality."

Many other examples come to mind if we think in terms of the theoretical distinction that is sometimes characterized as discourse space vs. story space, a distinction with wide currency in media and narrative studies. In this specialized terminology "discourse space" refers to that plane of expression in which the actual processes of production of a discourse (images, narrative, etc.) make themselves known and visible. "Story space" is the plane of those images or narratives in themselves. In terms of the postmodern surfaces I've been talking about it is basically the simple distinction between the medium or inscribed surface and the text or image inscribed upon that surface. Vignette refers to the constant movement between these "planes," to the point where it becomes difficult or impossible to determine which is which.

Unlike commercial film, which does everything it can to suppress audience awareness of discourse space so as to involve viewers more completely in the story, television grows increasingly sophisticated in its foregrounding of the plane of discourse and in its violations of the boundary between discourse and story. One form this takes is the more and more frequent phenomenon of the human subject (the TV actor) who moves freely between these spaces, thereby implicitly calling into question the very status of subjectivity itself.

Michael Sorkin points out, for instance (1986:172–175), that the announcer on the currently popular afternoon show *The People's Court*, which simulates the proceedings of small claims court, occupies through most of the show a position apparently outside the banal drama of litigation, outside the story space. But at the end he appears in the "courthouse hallway" to interview the litigants and even to act as a kind of court officer who directs them to the signing of papers that presumably legitimize what has just gone on in the courtroom. A seemingly unified subject has slipped across and thereby blurred some fundamental boundary and thus enacted a vignetting of subjectivity itself. As this phenomenon becomes more and more characteristic of the medium, the larger effect is to create a space of televisual experience which binds spectators neither into story nor into discourse, but into a ceaseless play between these levels that allows no exit to a position from which the process could be examined globally and, perhaps, critically.

I hope it is clear by now that these digressive remarks on television are not beside the point of this case study. I believe in fact that they shed light on some of the more interesting souvenirs collected in Chapter 1.

When Andrew Wyeth shaves and stains his head and tapes his eyes and nostrils to "become" Tom Clark, one could conclude this is just a reflection of the artist's empathetic feeling for his subject. But we have seen many ways in which Wyeth is deeply implicated in Chadds Ford's postmodernity. I think it justifiable to read this supposed personal identification as a kind of vignetting of subjectivity. Wyeth's physical self-transformation signifies the impingement of discourse space upon story space. Precisely the opposite movement occurs when Wyeth paints the Kuerner farm and a generation later that site spontaneously reproduces a simulacrum of the artist himself [Chapter 1, sec. XV]. Taken together these two movements constitute an especially compelling instance of vignetting staged on the very ground of Chadds Ford. Something characteristic of televisual experience has here escaped the screen to colonize the everyday of a postmodern Site. As I have suggested above, it is in the process of postmodern consumption that this vignette effect comes most into its own.

III. A MYTHOGRAPHY OF TRADITION

The rhetorical patterns I have been calling veneer and vignette are by no means unique to Chadds Ford. But by identifying them one has at least a minimal framework for talking about the specificities of this Site. They allow one to sort out and demonstrate connections between actual texts without reducing them to mere reinscriptions of some master Text of a totalized postmodernity. As rhetorical figures, veneer and vignette occupy a domain that falls somewhere "beneath" this global image but "above" the raw texts themselves. Only by occupying this domain, which I equate with a kind of ethnographic practice, can one begin to give an adequate account of particular stagings of advanced consumer culture. But the recognition of such rhetorical structures is not enough. To present even in broad outline the ideological apparatus of a particular postmodern Site requires as well the identification of the content that fills the rhetorical forms. We need to specify the Site's ideological themes, its distinctive "myths" in Barthes's terminology, and show how they are rhetorically realized in particular texts.

Even a cursory perusal of my souvenirs impresses one with the sense that the cultural production of Chadds Ford is concentrated in a few central themes, although these are subject to endless reproduction and variation. A key text, the orienting slide show at the Brandywine River Museum, offers a vividly redundant expression of Chadds Ford's mythological dominant:

> The Brandywine valley is filled with the echoes of the past. From the early
> forest Indians, who lived along the banks of the Brandywine River, to the

Quaker settlers, whose strong traditions remain rooted in the attitudes of the region today, the valley has shaped a special destiny. It played a role in history when, for a brief time, George Washington, in the midst of battle, moved his troops over these quiet hills. In his wake today there is a heritage of monuments and markers; solid stone houses of the valley which witnessed that battle still stand in testimony to the permanence of traditions. The continuing heritage of the Brandywine valley is thus strongly rooted in religious and historic circumstances....

Apart from inscribing yet again the received mythological past of Chadds Ford, this brief passage forces upon us the signature theme through which the Site recognizes itself. *"Strong traditions...rooted* in the attitudes of the region," *"heritage* of monuments and markers," "testimony to the *permanence of traditions," "continuing heritage* of the Brandywine valley," *"strongly rooted* in religious and historic circumstances": these are the markers of a thematic complex that might, for simplicity's sake, merely be called the concept of tradition. It is a concept of course that, like the rhetorical patterns, is hardly unique to this Site. What is distinctive, I think, is the single-mindedness with which Chadds Ford devotes itself to its elaboration and dissemination. A nebulous concept of "the traditional" is by far the most important ideological device for legitimizing the institutions of the Site.

In fact Chadds Ford participates in the "exportation" of this ideological product as a legitimizing agent for massive institutions far removed from the three middle Brandywine townships. The Wyeth "tradition" of art, of course, is the premier mediator of the product. A recent print ad for an international Wyeth exhibition demonstrates the point. Beneath three reproductions of Wyeth paintings, one from each of the three generations (N.C., Andrew, Jamie), the main caption reads: THE RUSSIANS ARE ABOUT TO EXPERIENCE THREE GENERATIONS OF AN AMERICAN TRADITION. The text elaborates:

> Three generations of America's most beloved family of artists will travel on canvas to Leningrad and Moscow in March, to be seen for the first time by the people of the Soviet Union.
> Made possible by AT&T, the exhibition, "An American Vision: Three Generations of Wyeth Art," will circle the globe for the next two years, bringing new understanding and appreciation of our special American way of life to thousands of viewers.
> AT&T has a century-old tradition of bringing people together. We at AT&T like to think that the quest for excellence in our products and services springs from the same spirit of excellence that shines from these canvases.

After circling the globe, the tour will end at the Brandywine River Museum. The efficacy and potential influence of the mythology that Chadds Ford makes its speciality can hardly be overestimated. Although the lines of connection may be obscure, the cultural work done at our small Site plays a part in much larger networks of power and legitimization.

This theme of tradition that is Chadds Ford's stock in trade seems to me important enough to examine more closely, at least closely enough to recognize that two of the institutions I have singled out in this study, the Brandywine River Museum and the Chadds Ford Historical Society, realize the theme in quite different versions and through different technologies. In the two following chapters I will offer close readings of the primary public texts generated by these institutions: the community celebration sponsored by the Historical Society, and the gallery display at the Brandywine River Museum. But first I need to lay out the difference between their two versions of the myth of tradition, which is basically a difference between historical sensibilities or modes of relating to the past.

Tradition, I think it safe to say, is one of the great mystified categories of Western thought. Current political deployment of such notions as "traditional values" is only a small chapter in the centuries-long history of the ideological operation of this concept. The most important architects of this mythological theme were the early Romantic philosophers and poets of the late eighteenth and early nineteenth centuries in Europe. It was they who disseminated the notion of tradition as quite literally a property of organic nature, a conception that served their philosophical polemic devoted to the transvaluation of Enlightenment categories. With "a particular attitude that again addresses itself to the truth of tradition and seeks to renew it" . . . , romanticism conceives tradition as the antithesis to freedom of reason and regards it as something historically given, like nature" (Gadamer 1975:249–250). This is a response to the Enlightenment understanding of tradition as the dead weight of the past artificially constraining rational thought. In the Enlightenment view, tradition, like superstition, taints the truth. The Romantic reaction is to remove tradition from history and locate it in nature. "Tradition in itself," Herder says, "is an excellent institution of Nature, indispensible to the human race" (1968[1784–1791]:164).[5]

This is not the cold, impersonal nature of universal physical forces; it is the tangible nature of visible landscapes and organic processes. Furthermore, it is a diverse nature with regional variations. The variety of tradition is part and parcel of the variety of natural environments. Thus, for example, to the Swiss participants in the proto-Romantic *Sturm und Drang*, native Swiss traditions were shaped by exactly the same natural energies as those that shaped the Alps (Cocchiara 1981[1952]:152–154).

Essentially the same conception of tradition as a function of natural rather than historical forces is deeply entrenched in American ideology,

for example, in the long unquestioned assumption that American institutions like democracy and individualism are a direct result of the encounter with a particular natural environment. This is essentially the
ideology the Brandywine River Conservancy subscribes to when it asserts
that the very landscape of the middle Brandywine valley has "grown" the
cultural patterns visible there, and most especially the art.

The ideological effect of this conception of tradition is to forge links
of continuity between past and present, links marked by the persistence
over time of a particular complex of cultural goods—a heritage. We have
seen any number of Chadds Ford texts operating to convey such notions
of natural inheritance and historical continuity. Contrary to this conception is the critical perspective which sees tradition as a reductive process
of radical selectivity (Williams 1977:115–120). The focus here is not upon
the inherited goods, but upon the process of "traditionalization" through
which forces in the present legitimize current institutions by obscuring
historical complexities and discontinuities. A heritage in this view is the
simplified set of images, objects and narratives that, though presented as
natural and inevitable, have been selected/constructed to serve particular
interests (for examples, Hobsbawm and Ranger 1983).

As we shall see, it is not difficult to demonstrate that through the
organization of its gallery display, the Brandywine River Museum is in
the business of traditionalization. The so-called Brandywine Heritage of
art is a selective narrative that establishes a single authoritative line of
artistic production, the centerpiece of which is the Wyeth dynasty, the
three male generations across which artistic talent is naturalized as a
biological inheritance. And as we have seen, the construction of this heritage as a powerful legitimizing discourse can be dated to the late 1960s.

An elaboration of the details of this traditionalizing process must wait
for a subsequent chapter. The important point here is that for the Brandywine River Museum the concept of tradition implies a particular and
definitive heritage, a continuous narrative comprising an uncomplicated
line of artists and artifacts generated by some natural force that inheres
in the very landscape of the middle Brandywine Valley.

In contrast, the Chadds Ford Historical Society is not much concerned
with producing the sort of narrative continuity between past and present,
so central to the discourse of the Brandywine River Museum. In fact, the
ideological strategy of the Historical Society could be read as the opposite
of the Museum's traditionalization. Rather than tracing a line of continuity, it installs an impenetrable barrier between past and present. Its
technique could be characterized as archaeological rather than narrative,
in the sense that it excavates an "absolute past,"[6] namely, the early eigh-

teenth century, or perhaps the late colonial period generally. This is the period in which the Chad and Barns-Brinton houses were built, and that the Society recreates in its restorations.

Rather than presenting the historical continuity of these structures, which would include their physical decay and use as tenant houses in a now vanished agricultural system, the Historical Society focuses on the social environment of their original production. It is impossible for Chadds Ford's deep-suburban residents, most of whom have no generational connection to the area, to construct a chain of continuity between themselves and this past. But once it is "dug up" and identified as the *definitive* past, it becomes a kind of indigenous historical otherness that affords many opportunities for participation and involvement. It is a past conceived as a clearly bounded, solid object, subject to various manipulations and appropriations.

Through the process of traditionalization the Brandywine River Museum reduces a diachronically complex history to a single-stranded, immediately comprehensible heritage. The Historical Society on the other hand reduces the synchronic richness of a past period, with all its complex social forces and relations, to an immediately comprehensible ensemble of a few key elements—a kind of tableau. To put it simply, this tableau is a living history image of rural colonial domestic economy. More specifically, the image consists of a few elements from the domestic sphere of the prosperous, though not overly wealthy, rural household of late colonial southeastern Pennsylvania. Politics, religion, trade, agricultural labor, transportation, warfare, and the like have no place in the image; nor do such everyday things as privation, hardship, disease, prejudice, and poverty. The most glaring instance of this reduction is the fact that in its public presentations the Historical Society is very little concerned with the Revolutionary War. This might seem odd, given that shot and ball of the Battle of the Brandywine quite literally flew over the roof of one of the Society's restored houses. In the increasingly specialized division of labor in Chadds Ford, the Commonwealth of Pennsylvania has assumed the task of preserving the history of the battle through the mediation of its Battlefield State Park just east of the village. The battle has largely disappeared from the discourse of the rest of the Site.

At the core of the Historical Society's living history image, I want to suggest, is again tradition, but tradition in a specialized sense, that is, as a form of "symbolic exchange." The Society's reproduction of colonial domestic economy focuses mainly on food and household artifacts (including the buildings themselves), and the processes of their production. The pre-industrial, artisanal mode of production is a controlling idea and the hand-crafted object is the dominant emblem. Constitutive of the Historical Society's living history image, then, is "a mode of social relations in which not only is the process of production controlled by the producer but in which the *collective process remains internal to the group*, and in which producers and consumers are the same people, above all defined through the reciprocity of the group" (Baudrillard 1975:97). Whether symbolic exchange accurately describes actual pre-capitalist social/economic formations is a vexed question. For immediate purposes it is enough to claim that an *image* of such formations does exist in the discourse of our Site.

What most characterizes this imagined social order is the inseparability of the objects, instruments, and processes of production from the concrete social relations through which they are enacted and deployed. In other words, the image is of a non-commodity or pre-commodity economy of symbolic exchange in which production, exchange and consumption are unalienated from the participants in these social activities. When I say that the Chadds Ford Historical Society participates in the reproduction of tradition as the dominant ideological theme of Chadds Ford's postmodern discourse, I am using tradition as a kind of generic name for this image of a social order characterized by symbolic exchange, the so-called traditional society. To justify this usage I need to explain more fully how tradition can be seen as a form of symbolic exchange.

Tradition as Symbolic Exchange: A Digression

A little folk parable embodies the basic principle of tradition conceived as symbolic exchange:

There was once a man whose prize possession was an ax. It was a good ax, above all because it had come down to him through generations of his family. It was already so old when his grandfather inherited it that the haft had to be replaced; when his father got it he found that it needed a new head; but the man was inspired every time he used it to think that it was the very ax that had been held by all his forebears.

The ax, completely replaced yet completely the same, exemplifies the ambivalence definitive of symbolic exchange, in which the object is not an autonomous entity existing independently of the social relations enacted through its transfer. "In symbolic exchange, of which the gift is our most proximate illustration, the object is not an object: it is inseparable from the concrete relation in which it is exchanged, the transferential pact that it seals between two persons: it is thus not independent as such" (Baudrillard 1981:64). Furthermore, "the symbolic is not a value (i.e., not positive, autonomisable, measurable or codifiable). It is the ambivalence (positive or negative) of personal exchange" (Ibid.:127; see also Gregory 1982).

Nothing is more taken for granted than that tradition involves passing something on or handing something down, but little thought is given to the exact nature of such transactions.[7] Another way to characterize tradition as a mode of symbolic exchange is to define it as the enactment of the social life of time, time not as mere duration, but as the unfolding and maintenance of social relationships.

Tradition in the sense I am suggesting here is but one region within the general realm of symbolic exchange, and the qualities peculiar to it can be brought out through comparison to the most familiar category of this general mode of exchange—gift giving. The gift in symbolic exchange is not an object to be appropriated, kept, and accumulated, as is the sort of gift which we are most used to in advanced consumer culture, that is, the gift as a commodity one receives and possesses. Rather, it is the object that only "assumes meaning through continual reciprocal exchange," thereby eluding the system of economic exchange value "in the ambivalence of an open relationship, and *never in a final relation of value*" (Baudrillard 1981:212). It is the gift that never sits still, that never can be taken and owned. To enjoy it, "it is necessary to be able to receive, to give, to return, to destroy—if possible, all at once" (Ibid.:207).

The classic ethnographic instance of gift giving as symbolic exchange is of course the Kula system of the Trobriand Islanders described by Malinowski (1961[1922]:81–104). Necklaces and armshells are given, received, and eventually passed on in the elaborate and endless cycle through which the Trobrianders enact a complex social network. Folk stories about gift exchange, it has been observed, mostly involve a minimum of three people. While dyadic exchange, gift and counter-gift, is the pattern typically associated with primitive gift exchange, in fact this is only the simplest form. Something like the Kula circuit requires that each man have at least two gift partners, someone from whom he receives and someone else to whom he gives (Hyde 1979:15–16; Mauss 1967[1925] for the classic statement). Such "circular" exchange is in fact paradigmatic for the symbolic order. When the gift "goes around a corner before it comes back" (perhaps transformed), it is not readily subject to personal control or accessible to the measurements by which it could be assigned a fixed value (Hyde 1979:16). In short, it remains ambivalent and resistent to commodification.

Tradition as symbolic exchange is also minimally triadic. It is an immediate act of delivery which contains within it both a prior reception from elsewhere and the promise of a subsequent transmission to yet a third place. "Tradition sei die Weitergabe von etwas Empfangen, damit es wiederum empfangen und weitergegeben werde" (Pieper 1970:39). (Tradition is the transmission of something received, so that it may again be grasped and given on.) Tradition is thus time experienced as immediate human relationship—the sort of relationship for which the succession of generations is the prevailing metaphor. Tradition is like gift giving but with the temporal dimension foregrounded. In both forms a present act of transfer "contains" all prior and all subsequent transactions, which is to say, these transactions are inseparable from the system of social relations enacted in the exchanges. The affinity of gift giving and tradition appears most vividly, perhaps, in the heirloom, which is often given as a gift but represents a link between generations.[8]

With this conception of tradition as a type of symbolic exchange in mind, it is possible to be more precise about the difference between the ideological apparatuses of our two institutions, the Museum and the Historical Society. The former presents its audience with the totalized image of an accomplished heritage, a specific saga of filiation and natural inheritance that is laid out in the gallery display.[9] It is designed to be consumed as a whole, largely through the mechanisms of spectatorship and touristic marking (guided tours, postcards, exhibition catalogs, prints, snapshots of the building and landscape, amateur artistic reproduction, etc.). The larger ideological work of legitimization accomplished through the consumption of this particular myth of tradition will be the subject of Chapter 5.

The Historical Society mythologizes not a particular tradition like the Brandywine Heritage of art, but trades rather in a myth we might call, in an ugly neologism, "traditioning." That is to say, it reproduces a global image of a social environment characterized by symbolic exchange. The Historical Society devotes itself to the image of a general mode of social relationship and social time in which objects, the processes of their production, maintenance, transfer, and consumption, and subjects, producers, and users, are not autonomous categories that can be isolated and assigned abstract values. The raw material of this image is the domestic sphere of late colonial life, including especially domestic crafts, foodways, costume, architecture and the artisan mode of production in general.

Two further differences between these two myths of tradition are worth mentioning. First, where the Brandywine River Museum's myth is geared to passive, spectatorial consumption, the Historical Society's image of symbolic exchange allows for, in fact depends upon, "participatory consumption." Because the Historical Society mythologizes tradition as a mode of social relationship linked to a mode of production, its consumers are implicitly invited to engage it more actively and to consume by doing (to join the Society, to take up a craft hobby, to attend the theme events, to decorate their own homes according to the image, etc.). Living history is one name for the mechanism that opens this more active space of consumption.

The second difference has to do with an ideological division of labor between these two institutions that is gender coded. The myth of tradition reproduced at the Museum is primarily male, while the Historical Society's is primarily female. The genealogy of the artistic heritage traditionalized at the Brandywine River Museum is traced through the male line. So, to anticipate a later discussion, the sanctioned pre-Howard Pyle Brandywine artists, mostly specialists in landscape and genre scenes, are primarily male, while the centerpiece of the heritage (Pyle—N.C. Wyeth—Andrew Wyeth—Jamie Wyeth) is exclusively so. As we shall see, a female principle is introduced in the gallery display just at the point where it serves to complete a family romance and "explain" the appearance of the male heir to the heritage.

The Historical Society myth, centering as it does on an image of the domestic sphere, is predominantly female. Although men are certainly involved in the activities of the Society, at the moment of its organization, and still at the time of my fieldwork, its activities and ideology were being shaped and guided primarly by women.

And there is one final difference between these two institutions and the myths they reproduce, namely, their different relationships to the postmodern order. As I have said, I read them both as vehicles of postmodernity. However I also believe that the Historical Society and its ideological apparatus is the more fundamentally postmodern of the two. As we shall see, the ideology of the Museum as conveyed in its gallery display serves the interests of what is perhaps the definitive postmodern class (if it can be called a class)—the mobile, largely anonymous experts and managers of information and display upon whom advanced consumer capitalism depends. However, the mechanism through which that ideology is reproduced is hardly peculiar to postmodernity. Traditionalization, the selective reduction of historical complexity and contradiction to a simple, continuous chain of connections, that is, to a sanctioned official tradition, can be detected in virtually any social/moral order, though some depend on the process more than others.

In contrast, through mechanisms that seem to be largely vernacular (i.e. unreflexive), the Historical Society has arrived at an ideological strategy that is postmodern through and through. This is what leads me to suggest that, although much more modest in its scope and in its influence beyond the immediate micro-climate of Chadds Ford, the Historical Society represents a more advanced postmodernity than the Brandywine River Museum/Conservancy.

One way to make this point in light of the foregoing discussion is to say that the discourses generated by the Historical Society are the most thoroughly televisual I collected at this Site. The ideological space of living history, especially as it is staged in Chadds Ford Days, is thoroughly turned in upon itself—self-sustained, self-inscribed, self-legitimized and self-perpetuated.

The basic mechanism of Historical Society ideology can be summarized thus: the myth or flattened image (i.e. simulacrum, textual reproduction) of an archaic mode of exchange (symbolic) is generated in a new, postmodern space where the economy is one defined precisely by the exchange and consumption of such images. In other words, the textualized image of one mode of exchange is appropriated for the purposes of—inscribed onto the surfaces of—an entirely new and distinctly postmodern system of exchange. And one kind of ambivalence, the inability to isolate objects from participants in symbolic exchange and assign fixed values to them, is itself reproduced as an image and put at the service of another, a postmodern ambivalence, that of image and medium, inscription and inscribed surface. If this characterization recalls the ideological/rhetorical figure I identify above as vignette, it is no accident. The space which the Historical Society opens for itself is above all a space pervaded with the rhetoric of vignette. And nowhere is this more true than in Chadds Ford Days, an event that, even more than the restored houses or colonial theme parties, lays out the Society's ideological content and rhetorical strategy. It is the purpose of the next chapter to make these explicit by way of a close critical reading of this event in its most developed form.

NOTES

1. Any number of studies and collections of essays exist which, although they may not identify themselves as analyses of postmodernity, nevertheless contribute directly to an understanding of advanced consumer culture. Most important of these for present purposes is Dean MacCannell's seminal study (1976) of modern tourism. See also Eco 1986; Gitlin, ed. 1986; Williamson 1986, 1979; and Hebdige 1979. The *locus classicus* of this analytical tradition is Barthes's *Mythologies* (1972[1957])).

2. One good example of a corrective to Jameson's grand abstractions is Mike Davis's work (1985, 1987) on the urban renaissance of the city of Los Angeles. By looking closely at economic forces, class relations, demographic shifts, political institutions, and commercial interests, he demonstrates the complexity of an urban transformation that Jameson's sort of analysis grossly oversimplifies. What Davis largely ignores, however, are precisely those cultural texts in which Jameson discovers meaningful patterns, though he does not deny that such patterns exist.

3. It will no doubt have become apparent to readers of Leo Marx's classic *The Machine in the Garden* (1964) that a long-standing and deeply entrenched American ideology of pastoral ideal and industrial threat has been taken up as a key theme of Chadds Ford's postmodern discourse. This Site seems almost a textbook demonstration of Marx's argument that what for centuries had been largely a literary convention in Europe was recast in the American context as a potential social reality and an achieveable landscape.

4. The June 1983 issue features a "Brandywine Manor House," which turns out to be the home of George "Frolic" Weymouth, Chairman of the Museum/Conservancy Board. The same issue contains an article on the Conservancy itself and recipes from the "Tavern Fare at the Barns-Brinton House."

5. He continues his sentence, however,

> but when it fetters the thinking faculty both in politics and education, and prevents all progress of intellect, and all the improvement that new times and circumstances demand, it is the true narcotic of the mind, as well to nations and sects, as to individuals.

Here in one sentence Herder demonstrates his transitional position, one foot in the Enlightenment and another in early Romanticism.

6. This concept of a completed past or absolute past derives ultimately from Goethe and Schiller ("Ueber epische und dramatische Dichtung"), but I take it second hand from M. M. Bakhtin (1981:13).

7. The *Oxford English Dictionary* defines tradition variously as "the act of handing over [something material] to another, delivery, transfer"; "the action of 'handing down,' or fact of being handed down from one to another"; and "that which is handed down." The original Latin noun *traditio* designates an action. In English the static sense—tradition as a thing—was present by the end of the fourteenth century (Williams 1983:318–320).

8. The chapter of Thomas Mann's *The Magic Mountain* entitled "Of the Christening Basin, and of Grandfather in His Two-Fold Guise" is, among other things, a meditation on the affective properties of the heirloom, of the sense it gives "of change in the midst of duration, of time as both flowing and persisting, of recurrence in continuity." Also, it suggests the important connection between tradition and the ritual or religious artifact. The investiture of priests in the Roman Catholic Church involves the ritual transmission into their hands of the chalice and paten. The technical term for this is "tradition of the instruments."

9. "Recurrence or identity through time is not as such the decisive criterion of traditional belief or action. It is not the intertemporal identity of beliefs or actions which constitutes a tradition, it is the intertemporal *filiation* of beliefs which is constitutive" (Shils 1971:127, and see Shils 1981 for the definitive mainstream sociological discussion of tradition).

4 | Chadds Ford Days: Living History and the Closed Space of Postmodern Consumption

"Gosh," said one wide-eyed young man who identified himself only as Jeffey, "this is better than television."

West Chester Daily
Local News, 9/12/77
(from a report on
the bicentennial
reenactment of the
Battle of the
Brandywine)

A central convention of what has become one of the grand traditions in anthropology, call it interpretive/symbolic, is to focus on "key" events, recurring nodes of standardized collective behavior—rituals, festivities and celebrations, games and competitions, and so on. These are read as symbolic codings of deep cultural meaning. They provide models for everyday behavior and belief, crystallize cultural identity, or help manage recurring cultural contradictions. Such events reflect a cultural self-consciousness not typical of mundane existence. In them a culture suspends its everyday operations and holds itself at arms length for brief inspection, foregrounding and reaffirming, perhaps in some cases adjusting, its sense of itself.

But again postmodernity intervenes, complicating this model of symbolic reflexivity. If it is true that the line is breaking down between what professional ethnographers traditionally do and what the forces and institutions of postmodernity do, it is also true that under the conditions of postmodernity the supposed moments of collective self-representation no longer stand out sharply from the rest of ongoing behavior. Since the definitive property of postmodernity is its self-referentiality, these moments of collective self-expression cease to appear so special. It grows increasingly difficult to see them as cultural models set somehow apart from the rest of cultural production. In a social order characterized by spectacle, display, and the exchange of signs, these events seem merely to be slightly more concentrated enactments of what is going on everywhere anyway.

As we have seen, Chadds Ford has had an annual community celebration since the late 1950s. It seems that in contemporary American culture almost "every community is attempting to develop a calendar event that will become that community's signature" (Abrahams 1981:313). Some of these are transformations of older forms, others, as in Chadds Ford, are newly minted. With its avowed purpose to commemorate the Battle of the Brandywine of September 11, 1777, Chadds Ford Days typically falls on the weekend closest to the 11th. As currently practiced it is primarily a crafts fair; its emblem is the crafted object; its controlling image is the artisan mode of production as realized in the domestic sphere of late colonial America. This event does not really suspend the everyday of Chadds Ford cultural production so as to hold it out symbolically for inspection; rather it establishes a temporarily concentrated space for enacting a mode of consumption that is quite typical of Chadds Ford's postmodernity generally. If its guiding image (myth) is a traditional social order characterized by symbolic exchange and domestic handcrafts, it presents this image largely through the rhetorical structure I have identified as the vignette. This formal device suffuses the living history ideology of the Chadds Ford Historical Society, sponsor of Chadds Ford Days, and is one of the indispensable conditions of possibility for the distinctly postmodern mode of dispersed consumption. But this is to get ahead of myself. First some simple description.

GENERAL PROPERTIES OF THE EVENT[1]

The crafts fair is a ubiquitous feature of our age and it comes in a great variety of forms. There are massive events, like the Renaissance Fair held annually north of San Francisco, that coordinate craft merchants, dramatic performances, food, games, and other activities. around a general theme. Like county fairs, these events are likely to have their own permanent fairgrounds.

Then there are the elite fairs, usually called craft "shows," that involve only the display of finely crafted objects, many of which sell for thousands of dollars. The model here is the fine art show, and the problem of art versus craft is actively at issue. Such events are juried, a panel of judges deciding whether an applicant's works are of sufficient quality to be included. Once accepted, the craftsperson may be required to pay a large entrance fee.

At the other end of the scale are the sort of crafts fairs one finds in mall courtyards. They are temporary malls within the mall that provide an outlet for merchants who stand somewhat outside the normal whole-sale/retail system. The objects sold in such environments run toward the gadget and gimmick: candles with different colored layers, spaghetti mea-surers (flat pieces of wood with holes of different sizes corresponding to the number of people who will be eating), orgy cups (can only be set down upside down, i.e., when empty), scarves so constructed that they can be tied many different ways, and the like. Sometimes the gimmick is a matter of how the object is produced, in which case a demonstration is part of the display. The most dramatic example of this I have seen is a man who sets up a more or less sound-proof plexi-glass booth, inside which he creates "realistic" animal sculptures using only a small chainsaw.

Another craft fair form, an important one in the present context, is that which occurs as part of regional folklife festivals. The Kutztown Folk Festival is the paradigm of such events in eastern Pennsylvania. Craft fairs of this sort are more concerned than the others with the issue of authen-ticity. They are intended to educate the public in how objects were pro-duced in "the old days," or perhaps are still produced in certain rural areas and by marginal cultures. Craft demonstration, therefore, is the main activity in such events, with economic transaction relegated to a subsid-iary role. Many of the demonstrations, in fact, (e.g., shaping of barn timbers or various agricultural activities) don't produce marketable objects at all, or perhaps only souvenir samples.

Chadds Ford Days falls somewhere in the middle of these types, having some qualities of each. It is, as I have said, organized around the regional theme of colonial domestic life, but the crafts that express this theme are not the only attraction. An old farm wagon is used as a bandstand from which a variety of "old time music" performances occur at scheduled times over the two days of the celebration. A number of special events are included: a "colonial" fashion show (1981), a fife and drum corps (1981), Morris dancers (1981–82), colonial militia maneuvers (1980), a "colonial" magician (1981–82), a children's play entitled "American Heroes, Tall Tales and Legends" (1982). A few rides—antique car, antique fire engine, coach-and-four, antique tractor and hay wagon—begin from one corner of the fair grounds. There is a "kids' corner," with games, "meadow" races and other amusements (e.g., one can have one's picture taken in the stocks for one dollar). Most importantly, an amateur art show occupies one sec-tion of the fair grounds and is a significant element of the projected image.[2]

Neither the crafts nor the art are formally juried, but a loose set of guidelines is applied in deciding what should be admitted for display. The crucial criterion is that the craft or artistic image fit the fair's theme. In other words, the crafts must be justifiable as appropriate to the image of colonial domestic life, and the art must somehow conform to the themes of agrarianism, rusticity, or generalized rurality. Considerable latitude is allowed in both the appropriateness and the quality of what is admitted. Decisions are based on the written applications of the craftspeople and photographs of their crafts. Also, their display set-ups figure importantly in the evaluation, since the overall "look" of the event is really the decisive issue. Along with this procedure of selection, the members of the crafts committee attend other crafts fairs in the region and actively solicit applications from craftspeople whom they find to be particularly appropriate for the Chadds Ford Days theme.

The size of Chadds Ford Days is indicated by the fact that in 1980 and 1981 about thirty-five separate crafts booths were included. In 1982 this number grew to forty-six.[3] There is a certain amount of continuity from one year to the next, both in the particular people who display and, especially, in the kinds of crafts included. The crafts people admitted to the fair are charged a relatively stiff fifty dollar fee, ten dollars non-refundable registration fee and twenty dollars per day to exhibit. Nevertheless, most exhibitors prefer this to the percentage-of-sales fee (as much as 25%) extracted at many crafts fairs. Economically, Chadds Ford Days belongs to the middle range of such events. Some of the objects sold (those of the spaghetti measurer, orgy cup ilk) would be at home in a mall courtyard. At the other extreme are the objects, especially furniture, that have required many hours of work and are quite expensive. Few if any, however, belong to the category of objects represented in the elite crafts shows. The great majority of crafts at Chadds Ford Days fall well between the two extremes of kitsch gimmickry and "fine" craftsmanship. It will be necessary to look more closely at the craft objects displayed at Chadds Ford Days, but for the moment I will only note that most of the items available for purchase are in the ten to one hundred fifty dollar range.

Chadds Ford Days shares with the more elaborate regional festivals a concern for the authentic, which manifests itself in the emphasis placed on the craft demonstration. It is a definite advantage to one's admission application if a demonstration of the production process is part of the craft display. Ideally the display set-up should evoke a sense of the "natural" workspace in which the craft is produced, including an appropriately costumed craftsperson engaged in some phase of production. In other words, the living history ideal of "doing history" or somehow actively participating in activities associated with the past informs the principles of selection that guide the Historical Society's crafts committee. Appropriateness and authenticity are the touchstones.

Most of the displays fail to achieve the ideal, of course, and some of them are not even close. The practical, economic motives of the event require that many deficiencies in appropriateness and authenticity be overlooked. The Historical Society itself "covers" these deficiencies, at least to a degree, by presenting its own "authentic" colonial crafts demonstrations. One prominent area is set aside as the center of gravity for living history authenticity. In this area Society members, some of their children, and the trained guides from the two restored houses, all of them in colonial costume, demonstrate such emblematic activities of colonial daily life as candle dipping, natural dye production, spinning, weaving, knitting, crewel work and lace making. Here, life-style clearly intersects with formal touristic display, for the crafts demonstrated, especially textile production and decoration, are in many cases the hobbies of the demonstrators.

Brief mention of a few other components completes this quick survey of the general properties of Chadds Ford Days. One corner of the grounds is given over to food concessions: hamburgers, hotdogs, fried chicken, corn-on-the-cob, soft pretzels, soda, iced tea (see Map 1). Also, in the corner of the grounds opposite the main food area is that ubiquitous emblem of folk foodways in southeastern Pennsylvania—funnel cakes—the deep-fried and sugared dough that seems to have regional versions all over the country. Just inside the entrance to the fairgrounds is the official Historical Society tent, where one can purchase items of regional historical interest: old maps of the Chadds Ford townships, pamphlet histories of the area and its institutions, cookbooks, folders containing menus and recipes for colonial meals, and so forth. Raffle tickets are also sold from this tent. The items raffled reflect the basic themes of the event. In 1980 the prizes were a "handmade Amish quilt," a painting of the Barns-Brinton House by Paul Scarborough (well-known local artist and organizer of the Chadds Ford Days art show) and, of all things, an oriental rug; in 1981 an Amish quilt and Rea Redifer's painting *Retreat at the Brandywine* (a rare reference to the battle supposedly being commemorated); and in 1982 the predictable Amish quilt ("Clay's Choice"), and an interesting example of image redundancy—a print of John McCoy's painting of the Chad House and "a primitive hand-hooked rug" with a design that reproduced the painting. These two items were raffled as a unit.

An important introductory element of the fair is the Chadds Ford friendship quilt (Figure 1), which is hung on a frame near the entrance. Its squares synopsize Chadds Ford's significant past (see Chapter 1, sec. XVII). Until 1981 the fair also included a mock-up tableau of an Indian

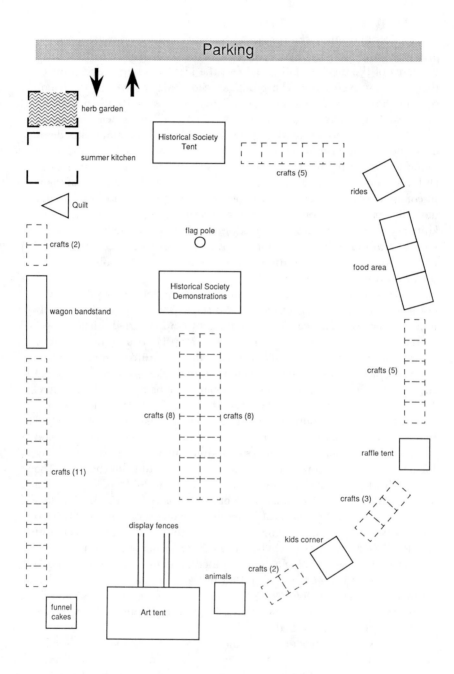

MAP 1.   Fairground layout—Chadds Ford Days 1982

FIGURE 1. Chadds Ford friendship quilt on its frame. Photograph by the author.

FIGURE 2. Summer Kitchen, exterior. Photograph by the author.

settlement, presumably meant to depict a Leni Lenape encampment along the Brandywine. As we have seen, undeveloped allusions to the Native American "pre-history" of the area crop up here and there in Chadds Ford cultural production (e.g., the menu history and the "Indian campground" areas of the housing developments). The encampment tableau is rather crudely constructed, without much attention to consistency of scale and having about it that distinctive look of the Boy Scout project, which in fact it was. Its disappearance from the 1981 celebration is part of a detectable streamlining that Chadds Ford Days seemed to be undergoing in the early 1980s. As a result, the American Indian allusion is now restricted to the kids corner, where the "children of the forest" metaphor is literalized in the paper headresses and face paint available to interested youngsters.

The other side of this streamlining, the introduction of a certain slickness to the proceedings, is visible in a significant innovation of the 1981 event. In that year a "Summer Kitchen" display was added, consisting of several free-standing facades decorated and arranged to suggest the enclosed space of a hearth room in a colonial house (Figures 2 and 3). This "kitchen," which has proved to be very popular, is stocked with appropriate food items (baked goods from the actual hearths and beehive oven of the restored houses, herbal jellies, herbed honeys, vinegars, etc.) available for purchase by fairgoers, who can actually enter the slightly less than life-size stage set. It constitutes, I believe, a miniaturized and reduced

FIGURE 3.   Summer Kitchen hearth. Photograph by the author.

emblem of the living history image, and hence a particularly vivid instance of the mythic theme of tradition (symbolic exchange) conveyed rhetorically in a vignette. This is an issue I will address more fully below.

THE LAYOUT: SPATIAL AND TEMPORAL

The current Chadds Ford Days is enacted annually in a meadow about one half mile north of the village intersection, at a point where the Brandywine River curves near to Route 100. The fairground itself, wedged into the narrowing end of the meadow, is more or less a rounded off rectangle with one of its corners sliced away. In its longest dimension the fairground extends about five hundred feet. The rest of the field, much the greater part, serves as a parking lot, as does the adjacent field when attendance is especially good. The John Chad House sits on the other side of Route 100 just a few yards below this second field, and many of the fairgoers visit it as well. A two dollar parking fee is charged, and this is a major source of the Society's income from the event.

The fair booths and attractions are laid out around the perimeter of the grounds and in a double line down the middle (Map 1). Temporary lines of snowfence mark the boundaries at either end of the grounds. With the entrance placed in the southeast corner, the general movement of the fairgoers is counter-clockwise, though this is by no means the only way people move through the grounds. There is much cutting back and forth between the center and periphery. At peak times however one does have the sense of being part of a continuous, moving line. One gets a good idea of how visitors proceed through the fairgrounds by imagining a combination of the characteristic movements of mall shoppers and museum goers.

Over the three years of my observation a number of changes were made in the arrangement of elements, although the components themselves stayed essentially the same. The Summer Kitchen added in 1981 is the only significant innovation. A notable reorganization occured between 1980 and 1981. The art show was moved to the end of the grounds opposite the entrance. Its former position was taken by a second Historical Society tent to house the used book sale, other money-making instruments (stenciled bags, dried flower arrangements, pressed flower pictures) and the raffle. The Historical Society demonstration area, located on the periphery in 1980, was moved to a prominent position in the middle of the grounds near the flag pole, and the number of demonstrations was increased. Although the number of craftspeople increased from about thirty-five in 1981 to forty-five in 1982, the general trend has been toward making the Historical Society's own activities, i.e., its living history images and reproductions, a more prominent component of the event. The tendency toward a general streamlining is a related development.

Chadds Ford Days usually occurs on the weekend closest to September 11, from 10:00 to 6:00 on Saturday and 11:00 to 5:00 on Sunday. The peak hours of attendance are early to mid-afternoon. No formal act marks the opening or closing of the event. At intervals of a quarter, half or full hour some sort of performance is given from the stage. The "old time" music runs to balladry, blue grass, dixieland and commercial folk.

Chadds Ford Days is not designed to occupy the visitor for a whole day. It seems unlikely that many people spend more than three hours there, this being plenty of time to watch a musical performance and one of the special events, view the craft displays and art show, have something to eat, and allow the children to play some games or take one of the rides.

Participants

Although I have no systematic data on the fair visitors, my observations suggest the following characteristics:[4] The audience is overwhelmingly, though not exclusively, white and predominantly middle class. Judging purely from outward appearances and from the kinds of automobiles driven, I am inclined to say that the majority of visitors are solidly middle, middle class but that a fairly large minority is upper middle. A great many of the cars come with more than two people and most of the visitors come in family groups. Many such groups include three generations, Chadds Ford Days obviously being a place one brings not only kids, but also grandparents. Presumably the old-timey aspect of the projected image is seen as appropriate for an older audience.

No accurate figures on Chadds Ford Days attendance are kept, but some sense of crowd size can be gathered from the fact that on the first day of the 1981 event approximately twenty-two hundred dollars came in from parking fees. A conservative estimate of three persons per car yields a crowd of thirty-three hundred for what I believe was a fairly representative day of the celebration. In more tangible terms, a crowd this size means a line of traffic stretching down Route 100 to the village intersection and around onto Route 1, and a meadow trampled to dust that blows in clouds across the parking area. In the afternoon heat, which can still be quite intense in early September, the mostly shadeless fairgrounds can become rather uncomfortable for the fairgoer.

The group that produces the fair includes a core of active Historical Society members and a number of their spouses and children, who serve as volunteer workers. A list of the fair committees and their sub-headings constitute a native taxonomy of the event:

Coordination	Food	Activities	Properties	Publicity
art show	funnel cakes	craftsmen	facilities	releases
raffle	hamburgers	demonstrations	layouts	posters
rides	hotdogs	features	parking	programs
games	pretzels	entertainment	signs	
plants	dinner			
books and prints				
kids corner				

The active Society members provide most of the energy with which Chadds Ford Days is produced and they are responsible for the image and ideology it embodies. For the most part they are women, of middle age or a bit older and upper-middle class, wives of successful professional people—upper level managers or technical experts; that class of people with the leisure time and the resources to have a boat on the Chesapeake or a summer home in the Southwest. Many of the husbands are connected, though not at the very highest levels, with the DuPont Corporation.

Younger women are also active in the Society and serve in various capacities at Chadds Ford Days, and a number of older women participate as well. In this last group are a few people whose connections to the Society go back to its beginning and who qualify as long-time Chadds Ford residents. A number of men, especially the husbands of the most active women in the Society, also get deeply involved in Chadds Ford Days. This is particularly true of those who are retired and have gotten caught up in the deep-suburban lifestyle of recreational farming and colonial imagery. Not a few of the Society's core members occupy the old farmhouses common along the middle Brandywine and cultivate the eighteenth-century image in their daily material surroundings and hobbies. This core of Society members does most of the costuming to be seen at the current Chadds Ford Days, using it to project the uniform image of eighteenth-century rural life that the event is meant to evoke.

According to Joseph Messersmith's account, in the early days of this event the craftspeople were mostly locals. Not so today. Now most of them come in from elsewhere, some from considerable distance (e.g., western Pennsylvania), and for many of them Chadds Ford Days is one stop on a regional circuit of annual craft fairs. These craftspeople form a diverse group, with a variety of motivations, differing degrees of expertise and a range of sophistication in marketing and display. The one thing they have in common is the profit motive, and they might best be categorized according to how they realize this motive.

Mr. Messersmith represents the upper end of a scale based on craft authenticity and craftsmanly expertise. His reproductions of tin lighting fixtures (lanterns, chandeliers, sconces, etc.) are completely appropriate to the colonial theme; he uses authentically archaic tools, enhances the sense of authenticity with finishes that give the tin a look of senescence, and gives demonstrations of his production technique (Breininger 1973, Robacker 1974). In the same category is the young basket maker who went to craft school and subscribes to crafts fair newsletters. His display consists of an appropriately rustic backdrop, in front of which he sits, in costume, at an antique drawing horse making oak splits or on a handmade chair weaving a basket (Figure 4). So as not to break the illusion created by the tableau, an assistant handles all the financial transactions and questions. Obviously, the craftspeople of this sort come closest to the living history ideal to which Chadds Ford Days aspires and which the Historical Society tries to introduce in its own craft demonstrations. At the same time, the amount of work that goes into the productions of such craftspeople tends to price them out of modest fairs like Chadds Ford Days.

Somewhat separate from this first type is what we might call the consummate craft professional, exemplified at Chadds Ford Days by a maker of briar pipes. His skill lies less in the production of the craft object than in its marketing. He travels the craft circuit with a truck and small camping trailer that he can pull right onto the fairgrounds and park behind his display space. His craft set-up is an appropriately rustic framework of raw wood contrived so that he can erect it alone in a matter of minutes. He sits in this framework behind a sheepskin covered table upon which are arranged (with calculated nonchalance) his large collection of pipes. One pipe, an especially elaborate and expensive example, he sets on a chrome frame that turns with the power of a small electric motor.

His pipes do not require particularly sophisticated skills to produce. Their interest is, so to speak, built into the raw material, the briarwood burls he imports from Europe. He drills these out, polishes some of the surfaces to create a contrast of rough and smooth, natural and man-made, and then affixes the ready-made stems that turn them into pipes. His greatest skill lies in fitting his production to the market. This means offering an effective range of styles and prices and recognizing the specific events where his kind of craft will be likely to sell well.[5] Another area of his expertise is knowledge about how to work the crowd, an issue I will return to presently. What really distinguishes this sort of craftsperson from those of the first category is their financial sophistication and success. The pipe maker talks about making as much as fifteen hundred dollars at some weekend crafts fairs. In 1980 a leather worker made in the neighborhood of one thousand dollars on just the first day of Chadds Ford Days.

Yet another kind of craftsperson quite prominent at Chadds Ford Days is the one trying to turn a hobby into a supplementary form of income. A

young woman who does small re-creations of Pennsylvania German fraktur and "primitive" painting (i.e., self-conscious re-creations of naive panel
paintings) is a good example. She began doing these crafts to produce
gifts for friends and relatives, but they became so much in demand that
she decided to try marketing them. Her husband developed his own craft,
comical "folk" carvings of animals, and together they began to attend
crafts fairs. Their productions rate rather low on the scale of authenticity,
the fraktur inscriptions, for example, being in English; but they at least
adhere to the image of rusticity and one-of-a-kind artisanal production.

Perhaps this category of craftsperson is the most fluid, requiring some
sort of development to make the crafts economically viable over the long
run. Such development might be in the direction of greater marketing
sophistication, or toward improved skill and autheniticty, or down-scale
toward the level of gimmickry and cheap souvenir. This latter category
of production is also represented at Chadds Ford Days (Figure 5), although
it is not particularly prominent. Examples are the potter who sells assembly line produced novelty items (standard shaped orgy cups in various
glazes) and the calligrapher who will, for a dollar or two, print your name
in ersatz fraktur script on a pennant. This sort of person can make out
quite well at Chadds Ford Days.

These examples cover the range of craftspeople at Chadds Ford Days,
but I should add that the categories might well be drawn differently. Even
the most serious and authentic artisans, if they want to survive at all in
this market, must offer a range of prices (and hence quality) in the items
they sell. In most cases this range includes a more or less standard, easily
produced, relatively cheap line of objects that can be purchased as souvenirs. But here we broach a separate issue, one especially crucial to
understanding Chadds Ford Days.

The Nature of the Craft Objects

In the 1982 event, forty-five craftspeople displayed a variety of thirty-one
separate crafts: windsor chairs, clocks, cabinetry (and country furniture),
wood carving (2), duck decoys, wood buttermolds, pipes, copperwork,
pewter, tin work (2), brass work, weathervanes, blacksmithing (2), bas-
ketry (2), leatherwork (3), spinning, weaving, quilts, applique, stencils,
dolls (2), pottery (3), scrimshaw, band boxes (2), dried flower arrangements
(3), spice wreaths, paper silhouettes (3), fraktur (3), folk art painting (2),
tole painting (on metal), reverse painting (on glass). At the 1980 and 1981
celebrations essentially the same crafts were displayed, though there was
slightly less repetition. Of the thirty-five people who exhibited in 1981, no
less than twenty-nine returned in 1982, a fact consistent with my sense
that at the time of this study Chadds Ford Days was in a phase that saw

FIGURE 4.   Basket maker. Photograph by the author.

FIGURE 5.   The low end of Chadds Ford Days crafts (spaghetti measurers in foreground). Photograph by the author.

it stabilized in a regular routine, one that could be expected to generate a consistent profit year to year. This stabilization turns out to be crucial to our understanding of Chadds Ford Days as a postmodern event.

One easily sees that almost all these crafts belong to the domestic sphere, both with regard to use and production: furniture, textiles, eating utensils, lighting fixtures, apparel, toys, and above all, decorative objects. The one thing that characterizes them all is their suitability for display. The "folk" art and decorative crafts (dried flowers, stencils, spice wreaths) are by nature display objects. The items that allude to spheres other than the domestic are reduced versions of the original forms and are designed for decorative purposes. The "weathervanes," for example, are mostly miniatures (Figure 6), small animal shapes cut from sheets of rusted metal and fixed to wooden bases. Likewise, the decoys are all high-gloss miniatures. Even the objects with real utility (e.g., some of the baskets, the furniture, the toys) seem intended for display, since most of them are too expensive to use unselfconsciously for purely practical purposes. Many of the hand-carved folk "toys," for example (Figure 7), are affixed to some sort of base.

The craft objects sold at Chadds Ford Days are mainly intended for display and, at bottom, *what* they display, what gets expressed through their physical presentation, are three basic properties: hand-madeness (which is to say, the artisanal order, the symbolic mode of exchange), age, either as archaism or as senescence (Lowenthal 1979: 108) (which is to say, tradition, the symbolic mode of exchange), and utility (which is to say, use value).

In identifying the properties that characterize the crafts as a whole, I do no more than support with ethnographic detail the contention that Chadds Ford Days is an operation performed upon the Historical Society's guiding image—the eighteenth-century rural household and the myth of tradition it embodies. But to understand just what that operation consists of requires that we examine how the craft objects differ from one another. The differences I am interested in are not the obvious ones of material, technique, form, and so forth, but the deeper ideological/structural differentiations that shape the transactions characteristic of the event.

Keeping for the moment to the ethnographic surface, I would note here that almost all the craftspeople include in their displays items that vary as to size, complexity of design, type of finish applied, variety of materials used and elaborateness of production techniques, all of these dimensions, of course, being interrelated. The presentation of difference is absolutely crucial to the effective marketing of objects at a crafts fair. The customer becomes involved with the craft through the process of comparison and selection, which in part means deciding among several

FIGURE 6. "Weathervanes." Photograph by the author.

price levels. Most of the craftspeople diversify their objects both vertically and horizontally, that is, they offer at least three price levels and within each level they offer a variety of objects (different forms, finishes, functions). Horizontal variation is especially characteristic of the middling price range. At the top of the scale the craftsperson might include only a few expensive, one-of-a-kind pieces, while at the bottom he or she will have many objects, but these will not vary greatly one from another. Often these latter items are produced in a quasi-assembly line process. Between these opposite ends of the scale the craftsperson is likely to provide the greatest possibility for choice.

At the bottom of the price range many of the craftspeople have what one of them, a buttermold carver and punster, refers to as his "bread-and-butter" item. For him it is a small rectangular mold suitable for use on stick butter; for Mr. Messersmith it is a candle snuffer; for a maker of colonial country furniture reproductions it is a simple wall box suitable for holding kitchen matches or a small plant; for one of the better fraktur artists it is a small, print-while-you-wait sample of fraktur calligraphy, this last example perhaps crossing the line into the realm of the throwaway souvenir. As a rule however, these items do not cross that line, since they might cost as much as ten or twelve dollars and are clearly continuous with the more expensive objects. But they do tend to rely on novelty as a source of interest and often have a quality of the gimmick about them.

The upper end of the price scale often extends beyond the crafts fair itself, especially for the more committed craftspeople. Many of them can

FIGURE 7. "Folk toys." Photograph by the author.

be commissioned to do unique pieces to suit a patron's specifications. Needless to say, these commissions are highly prized, since they are lucrative and give fuller opportunity for the exercise of craft expertise. For many of the craftspeople, then, events like Chadds Ford Days are as important for advertising and generating a future clientele as for direct marketing. Most of the exhibitors have printed cards to hand out and many of them include in their displays scrapbooks containing newspaper articles about themselves, background information about the crafts they practice and letters from satisfied customers.

If the production of differentiations characterizes each craft individually, it is also a property of Chadds Ford Days as a whole. I have already pointed out that the range of displays includes craftsmanship of varying quality and craftspeople who differ considerably in the relationships they bear to their productions. Far from being a deficiency of Chadds Ford Days, a failure of the crafts committee to present a uniform level of expertise, these differences are in the very nature of the event and are crucial to its success. Each craft display, its space numbered and marked off with stakes, is a clear unit of difference, an invitation to compare and choose. The fair goers mark or "enact" these differences simply by moving around the fairground, and this marking is at the very heart of the crafts fair as a postmodern form.

Difference of this sort is perhaps most visible in the considerable amount of craft redundancy one sees, of which fraktur is a good example. In a circuit of the 1981 fairgrounds one could see astonishingly authentic looking reproductions of large and elaborate fraktur pieces (Figure 8), accurate right down to the look of age in the paper (done by soaking in tea) and the ink (done by mixing with watercolor); small birth and marriage certificates in English, with none of the religious references typical of original fraktur and sometimes a blank left for the name (Figure 9); and paper pennants filled in on the spot with a kitsch-fraktur inscription of your name or the name of your school (Figure 10). Because the Chadds Ford fair is small, such graded redundancies are quite apparent to the visitor, even though the layout committee takes pains to make sure that displays of the same kind of craft are separated as much as possible.

It is not only multiple examples of particular crafts that promote comparison and constitute a closed set of contrasts. Since they are presented within the framework of a single, overriding image, *all* the crafts belong to one set of contrastive differentiations. Each is a unit of the same general thing but also a separate aspect of that thing; and so each is available for evaluative comparison with all the other aspects. Chadds Ford Days is itself a "system of differences." Even more than with the craft objects, this process of evaluative comparison is applied to the displays that contain them. Some displays consist of no more than a table or vertical panels with the objects arranged on them; others include an appropriate background, such as the weathered pieces of planking set behind the miniature weathervanes; still others, such as the basket maker's set-up mentioned above, create little tableaux of the work setting. One husband and wife team, she doing fraktur and he making the "antique" frames for them, set up a concave triptych of panels on which to hang their wares, put down a braided rug, and sit in antique chairs at either side. An old chest completes this tableau meant to give the customer a sense of experiencing fraktur in its native habitat—the country parlor.

These various categories of difference are, of course, part of the economic system appropriate to the unique market form of the contemporary crafts fair. To understand this system we need to look more closely at the nature of the transactions within it, which entails a consideration of the relationships among participants.

RELATIONS AMONG PARTICIPANTS AND TYPES OF TRANSACTION

Two kinds of interaction are important for understanding the discourse of this event: the relationship between fair-goers and the commercial craftspeople, and the relationship between the fair-goers and the Historical Society. The craftspeople and the fair organizers interact in ways that are more instrumental than ideological, and these do not concern us much here. Their relationship mainly amounts to a short-term rental contract through which the exhibitors secure temporary marketing outlets, although there is a minor "backstage" politics based on the belief of some craftspeople that where they are placed on the fairgrounds can affect sales. The organizing committee has to be sensitive to these issues and tries to take into consideration seniority (i.e., number of years a craftsperson has been displaying at the fair) when arranging the displays and assigning locations.

Much more complex is the relationship between the craftspeople and the fair audience. The real interest of this relationship lies in its uniquely postmodern combination of spectacle and marketplace. To the craftsperson, the fairgoing public is both an audience, or perhaps better, a spectatorship, and a clientele. Of course connection between the spheres of spectacle and market is not unique to contemporary culture. One need only think of medieval and Renaissance market fairs, where commerce and spectacle were closely intertwined (Boissonnade 1950:170–173, Bakhtin 1968:145–195). But what does seem unprecedented is the completeness with which advanced consumer culture conflates these spheres. So thorough is the mixing in fact that one begins to feel in need of entirely new

FIGURE 8. Fine reproduction of franktur. Photograph by the author.

FIGURE 9. Ersatz fraktur, with some attention to "authenticity." Photograph by the author.

FIGURE 10. Kitsch fraktur. Photograph by the author.

designations for the space in which transactions occur and for the transactions themselves. Some of the ethnographic details of the transactions conducted at Chadds Ford Days will give a sense of what is distinctive about this new space of consumption.

The exchanges between fairgoers and craftspeople are characterized by a strange passivity and reticence. For the most part the craft objects are not touched and most of the conversation goes on within already established groups of audience members (i.e., a family or a couple). With regard to intra-audience interactions, you might say that behaviorally the fairgoers generally "stay in their automobiles" as they peruse the craft displays. On the other side of the counter the craftspeople also maintain a distance and reserve. There is virtually no hawking of wares and the experienced merchant rarely initiates interaction with the audience. One gets the feeling that the fairgoers are most comfortable when the craftsperson completely ignores them, and one can gauge the craftsperson's sophistication by the amount of attention he or she pays to the audience. The novice reveals him- or herself by watching the crowd expectantly, eagerly waiting for an opportunity to answer a question or demonstrate a technique, in other words, to reveal knowledge.

The crucial issue in crafts fair transactions is the management of information. The distance maintained between buyer and seller in overt crafts fair behavior "stands for" the difference of skill and knowledge between artisan and layman/client. At its core the basic crafts fair transaction involves creating and sustaining the illusion that the craftsperson stands in relation to the fairgoer as the artisan to his community of production. In part this means managing information to foreground the impression of a knowledge differential. The experienced craftsperson reveals enough information to convey a sense of his or her expertise but not enough to demystify the craft or reduce the aura of artisanship.

That this is true may be seen in the various ways information flow is restricted at the crafts fair. Experienced exhibitors are laconic in response to questions. Typically, they occupy themselves with some aspect of their crafts, preferably the most picturesque and "craftsmanly" (the toy maker sits carving, the basket weaver shaves splits), and answer questions almost without looking up. One never hears from them a detailed account of the production process. When the craftsperson does give a formal demonstration it has the quality of a significant revelation, such as a master might vouchsafe his apprentice, and the fairgoer comes away with the sense of having had an authentic encounter with artisanship.

A successful crafts fair like Chadds Ford Days provides the visitor an opportunity to imagine himself or herself encountering the artisanal social order, though only passively. Indeed passivity is an essential quality of the participation, since the illusion is too thin to support an active engagement. Ideally the fiction created is one in which the fairgoer plays the part of a passerby happening upon the craftsman at work, or of someone peeping unseen into the workshop, or perhaps of a customer visiting the local artisan to place an order. If the fictional situation is not properly maintained, economic transactions are thwarted. As the fraktur and "folk art" painter astutely observed, the more the customer talks the less likely he or she is to buy. In other words, the more actively the fairgoer engages the craftsperson and the more he extracts information, the harder it is to maintain the delicate illusion that is the precondition of efficient crafts fair consumption.

The most complex of the participant relationships at Chadds Ford Days is the one that obtains between the fairgoer and the Historical Society. There are two clearly distinct sides to this relationship. In one respect the audience is a source of income pure and simple, so many cars parked, raffle tickets purchased and funnel cakes consumed. This is the side of the relationship that, along with the economic interaction between the Historical Society and the craftspeople, accounts for Chadds Ford Days' purely economic function.

The other side of the relationship belongs to the same sphere of image production and exchange as the interactions between fair-goers and craftspeople. Physically, the contact between the fair audience and the Historical Society is concentrated around the entrance to the fairground and thus comes first in the visitor's experience of the event. Three things in particular embody this form of interaction: the Summer Kitchen, the Society's own demonstration area, and the Chadds Ford Friendship quilt (see Map 1). The last of these, as we have already seen, is the emblem of Chadds Ford's significant past expressed in a medium that appropriately conditions the viewer's affective response to that past. The quilt serves to set the tone for the experience the visitor is about to have.

The Summer Kitchen and the Historical Society demonstrations are key emblems of the definitive living history image, representing respectively, colonial foodways and eighteenth-century household crafts, especially textile production. In these two things the very essence of the colonial domestic image is distilled. They represent the highest standard of authenticity Chadds Ford Days has to offer within the enclosed space of the fairgrounds, being, so to speak, transplanted pieces of the Society's two restored houses. The Summer Kitchen in fact is a kind of transplantation of the houses themselves, albeit in a miniaturized allusive form that comes close to caricature. Periodically over the two days of the event, the fairgoers are invited by loudspeaker to walk the short distance down Route 100 to visit the John Chad House, where they can see a *real* colonial hearth and beehive oven in action and spinning demonstrations in a truly authentic setting. This small tourist side trip at first might seem to anchor Chadds Ford Days outside its space of unstable, drifting authenticity on the firm ground of the definitive historical otherness. In fact it has the opposite effect of inscribing the seemingly final authenticity of the restored house onto the closed surface space established by the crafts fair, a space characterized by the endless play of levels of authenticity. The presumably ultimate authenticity of the houses, the presumed point of origin of the living history image, becomes just another position in the game.

The Society's demonstrations and its Summer Kitchen are attempts to bring the living history principle directly onto the fairgrounds. As in-

FIGURE 11. Outside the Summer Kitchen. Photograph by the author.

troductory elements they prepare the audience members to accept the thinner fiction of the artisanal mode of production they will encounter in the craftspeople's displays. Two things distinguish the Historical Society/audience interactions from the craftspeople/audience exchanges. First, the fair-goer is allowed a more active engagement with the Historical Society displays. Rather than being just spectatorial participants, here the visitors can actually cross the boundary that separates them from the display space of the craftspeople, or enter the tableau of the Summer Kitchen and move around. The latter is a fairly elaborate stage-set, with an outdoor area (Figure 11) consisting of potted vegetation, an "herb garden" (small plastic herb pots arranged in a square), hay bales, dried corn stalks and a suggestion of snake fence. Inside is a hearth with a fire actually burning in it, country furniture, cooking utensils and items of apparel (see Figure 3). Breads, jellies, preserves, vinegars, honeys, and so forth, are arranged on the tables and in cupboards. Most of the plants, herbs and food items are for sale and many of them were actually grown or made by eighteenth-century methods at the Society's restored houses.

Still farther up the scale of authenticity are the Society's craft demonstrations (Figure 12). They introduce to the fair the educational element so important to the Historical Society's self-image. Unlike the demonstrations and discourse of the craftspeople, there is no attempt to restrict information in the Historical Society's demonstrations, their purpose being precisely to convey as much as possible about the everyday productions of eighteenth-century domestic life. Spectators are frequently invited to step into the display and to try their hands at one or another of the crafts, especially the forms of textile production.

These sorts of interactions bespeak a different relationship between fairgoer and Historical Society than between fairgoer and craftsperson. Although the objects produced in the Historical Society demonstration area are not generally for sale, the demonstrations nevertheless contribute to the construction of an enclosed space of consumption. As tourists of historical otherness, the fair's audience helps to validate the authenticity of the Historical Society's living history productions, and in the process Chadds Ford Days becomes the mechanism through which the Historical Society instrumentalizes these productions to generate the income needed to maintain itself, its chosen image and its material embodiment in the two restored houses. The event transforms the avowed educational func-

FIGURE 12. Historical Society demonstration areas. Photograph by the author.

tion of the Historical Society into a temporary financial instrument by exploiting the authenticity that arises from the restored houses. Chadds Ford Days is part of a completely closed, endlessly cycling system in which images transform to dollars and dollars back to images, all of this achieved through the seamless, infinitely self-referential logic of postmodern discourse. To put it succinctly, Chadds Ford Days is a concentrated and self-sufficient space characterized by the semiotic play of authenticity. And the rhetoric through which this is achieved is predominantly the rhetoric of vignette.

MODES OF EXCHANGE AND VIGNETTE AS A VEHICLE OF CONSUMPTION

It has been observed that fairs are to be distinguished from festivities on the grounds that they subordinate play to the exchange of goods (Abrahams 1981:317). If we understand "play" in its normal anthropological sense, then it is true that play and festivity (e.g., the rides and children's games) are peripheral at Chadds Ford Days. Conceived more abstractly or metaphorically, however, play is quite central to this event. I am referring here to the ceaseless play of signs that characterizes the postmodern age. This play is itself a form of exchange, not of goods in the normal sense, but of images, texts, simulacra—of the very fact of difference. Under the regime of postmodernity the simple distinction between play and exchange completely breaks down. As I say, in the case of Chadds Ford Days the code primarily at play is the hierarchy of authenticity, and vignette is its main rhetorical vehicle.

The Summer Kitchen, I think, is the clearest instance of this figure. Its introduction in the 1981 fair signifies a kind of culmination of the event as a postmodern form, marking its "televisual" coming of age. It carries the self-referentiality of the fair to its logical conclusion, so that it now refers to nothing beyond the enclosed world of its living history imagery. The first thing to notice about the Summer Kitchen tableau is that physically it is quite literally a vignette, although a three-dimensional one. The tableau is by no means intended as a complete simulation of eighteenth-century domestic space. It is designed like a stage set, except that it is miniaturized and "incomplete." It consists of fragments that allude to the *image* of the country kitchen. One does not enter and exit by a door, there being no sharp distinction between inside and outside. The space is fluid and it is difficult to say when one has entered or left the imaginary world it evokes. Also, when one is in this space the fairground "outside" is always visible. So, for example, the hearth of the kitchen has a mantel, is surrounded by appropriate decorative and household objects, and has a pot on the fire. But the fireplace itself is merely a square hole in a free-standing wall through which one can see the ground beyond, the snowfence marking the edge the fairground, and even the portable water tank supplied by the National Guard for use at the fair. All of these qualities are three-dimensional analogues of the formal properties of two-dimensional pictorial vignettes, characterized as they are by the ghosting out of an inscribed image until it merges with the inscribed surface.

We might notice that the Summer Kitchen combines elements of the two main arenas of display at the fair—the Historical Society demonstrations and the craft exhibits—and thereby completes the logic implied by their juxtaposition on the fairgrounds. The Society's demonstration area is a permeable space. Visitors can actually enter it to try their hands at the craft activities being performed by Society volunteers. Interestingly, this demonstration area is marked off by a white tape that one has to duck under in order to enter. The sense of transgressing a boundary is thus foregrounded. One moves clearly from the role of spectator to the role of participant. The objects produced in this area are not, or at least not immediately, for sale (some of the results, like the wax candles, are transferred for sale to a separate booth), and the visitors never really have the chance to produce a craft object.

Though I mean to imply no priority by putting it this way, the exhibits of the craftspeople invert the structure of the Society demonstrations. For the most part the fair visitors cannot enter the space of these displays and no active participation in the image is allowed. As I have suggested above, however, the display tableaux and the general atmosphere of the fair work to create at least a minimal participatory space for visitors, in that they can imagine themselves, probably only fleetingly and below the threshhold of full awareness, in a spectator role consistent with the artisanal image—as passersby looking in on a workshop perhaps, or as potential clients happening upon the artisan at his work.

We need to distinguish this fictive spectatorial space or "participatory spectatorship" from the more familiar spectatorship of sporting events, stage performances, concerts, and so on. While the spectators in these situations may become emotionally involved in what they are watching, the performance space remains separate from the spectator space. It is a hallmark characteristic of postmodernity to merge these spaces. The new kind of space that results is realized with particular concreteness in the living history ideology that the Historical Society is committed to. Living history is virtually defined by the creation of a new discourse space that hovers on the boundary between spectatorship and participation, and it is precisely there that a dispersed, distinctively postmodern consumption arises.

If the fairgrounds and its displays provide the structural and material conditions for such consumption, the fair-goers constitute its efficient cause. It is their very movements and perceptions that enact the rhetorical process. As spectator/participants, occupying a postmodern role we have no good name for, they cross and recross the boundary between the levels that characterize the space of living history. Or more accurately, the fair suspends them in the distinctly postmodern space where final determinations of "image" and "reality," text and inscribed surface, inauthentic and authentic become impossible. Another way to characterize this situation is to say that fair-goers are themselves suspended between discourse space and story space; they themselves enact the dispersal of subjectivity that television only depicts. And this dispersal is virtually inseparable from a new mode of consumption which can no longer be understood in terms of buyers and sellers as centered subjects, or commodities as bounded objects or quantifiable values.

The Summer Kitchen is the most vivid example of all these properties, bringing together in a single place the participatory opportunities of the Historical Society demonstrations and the options for consumption of the craft exhibits. Its strategy, brilliant in its simplicity, is to contrive a space in keeping with the general theme of colonial domestic economy and in which consumption itself is the appropriate participatory activity. Colonial foodways, an element central to the interpretive activities at the Society's two restored houses, is the specific vehicle. This kitchen tableau, outfitted with antique cupboards and tables, is stocked with jars of herbed jellies, honey, herb vinegars, and breads baked in a beehive oven. "Outside" in the kitchen garden the herbs grow in small pots available for individual purchase. In the vignetted space created by the Summer Kitchen the role of consumer in the tourist economy, of which the purchase of souvenirs is the definitive activity, blends imperceptibly with the fictive participatory role of the eighteenth-century consumer of homegrown and home-processed foods. That the items one can reach down from the shelves and buy in the Summer Kitchen were all produced with colonial methods and/or using the authentic eighteenth-century ovens, utensils, and hearths at the restored houses establishes all the more firmly the vignetted space which is the primary condition of possibility for this new, distinctly postmodern, mode of consumption. The activity of consumption in this environment is itself the vignetting process, the ceaseless marking of difference between inscription and inscribed surface in which no position can be said to have priority. The rest of the fair tends toward this mode of consumption, but the Summer Kitchen realizes it most fully.

One observable property of this mode is that it renders almost invisible the actual exchange of money for goods. That sort of exchange is characteristic of a different mode of consumption. The sale/purchase transaction as a bounded exchange between individuals is in a sense residual to the new mode. Although of course such transactions go on at the crafts fair, they are subdued. There seems to be almost a tacit agreement between artisan and client that the actual exchange of money for craft object should be hidden as much as possible. To make it too visible would interfere with or point outside the self-sustaining, self-referential space of this postmodern event to a world where an abstract money economy prevails. The hermetic image of symbolic exchange upon which the success of the fair depends is quite the opposite of an abstract money economy. To let that system intrude too visibly would threaten the mythological foundation of the whole event.

There are, then, really three systems of exchange at work in Chadds Ford Days. By sorting them out we can arrive at a formula for this event as an advanced mechanism of Chadds Ford's postmodernity. First there is the system of symbolic exchange, which I have associated with artisan production, traditional objects, a social order based on tradition, and the pre-industrial environment of everyday domestic life in late colonial rural Pennsylvania. This system exists in the fair not as an operating mode of exchange, but as the dominant image or concept, the definitive past around which the Historical Society organizes its living history activities. In Barthes's terms it is the Society's primary mythological text.

Then there is the system of abstract economic exchange, the money economy, which is enacted at the fair in parking fees, purchase of non-souvenir food (e.g., a hamburger for lunch at the food stand), and the actual purchase of the craft objects. This is of course what we normally mean when we speak of economic exchange.

And the third system is the one I am identifying with Chadds Ford's postmodernity. Although I think we have no very good name for this system, it is what Jean Baudrillard means by an economy of sign exchange. The difficulty with Baudrillard's designation is that it seems strange to think of the operation of this system as an exchange process at all, conditioned as we are to see exchange in simple dyadic terms—money paid for goods and services rendered. Sign exchange is the more dispersed, unlocalized process I have been describing as manifest most vividly in Chadds Ford Days. Its definitive feature is the generalized movement across boundaries marking difference or along a hierarchical chain of discriminations. For example, the system Baudrillard calls sign exchange is represented in Chadds Ford Days by the general processes of comparison, judgement and choice between multiple alternatives allowed for by the coded system of differences in craft objects available for purchase. As we have seen, there are several dimensions of variation in these objects: in the fair as a whole a differentiation of craft types, within each type a vertical differentiation of price ranges, within each price range a horizontal differentiation of styles, finishes, models, and so on.

From the point of view of the producers of these objects such differentiations are part of a marketing strategy to maximize profits, and so are a function of the economic system. For the fair audience, however, the visible differentiations are a function of a hierarchy within the code of authenticity. By moving through the system of differences, comparing, judging, selecting or rejecting, what fairgoers primarily consume at Chadds Ford Days is this global system of authenticity. The individual act of purchase is really secondary to this larger process and serves mainly to insert the buyer into it at a particular point, to put, so to speak, the consumer's stamp of approval on the global system of differences, or better, to identify the consumer with the process of differentiation itself.

The interesting complication Chadds Ford Days creates in the relationship of these three modes of exchange is that its dominant system, sign exchange, appropriates the simulacra of one of the other systems, namely symbolic exchange, as its raw material. The myth of colonial domestic economy becomes the basis of the hierarchy of authenticity that is at the core of the Historical Society's ideology. Symbolic exchange becomes the text for a system of sign exchange.

I have suggested at several points that of all the texts addressed in this study, and by extension the institutions associated with these texts, Chadds Ford Days represents Chadds Ford's postmodernity in its most advanced form. We are now in a position to understand why this might be so. Even by craft fair standards, Chadds Ford Days is a relatively modest event. At the time of this research it was predictable that the fair would generate about $20,000 in profits anually. Given the overhead costs and operating expenses for the two restored houses and related Society activities, this is not a great sum. Although some of the craftspeople make out quite well, if we take a broad view it appears that the economic function of the event, in purely monetary terms, is not of paramount importance. As we have just seen, this fact is in keeping with the suppression, for ideological reasons, of money transactions at the fair. What the Historical Society has achieved through Chadds Ford Days and its other living history activities is a kind of equilibrium or steady-state. Since its flurry of economic activity in the late 1960s and early 1970s, when the two houses were purchased and restored, the Society has settled into a kind of routine. While we might view this as stagnation, I think another possibility is that this stasis reflects the operation of vernacular postmodernity at its most advanced.

I have argued that the rhetorical structure of the vignette is characteristic of postmodernity, and that the effect of this rhetorical figure is to create a self-sustaining, self-referential, self-legitimizing "televisual" space which acknowledges nothing outside itself. It is just such a hermetic space that Chadds Ford Days helps establish and legitimize. The accumulation of too much capital might well disrupt this space by forcing the Historical Society to "look outside" the living history image it has created. At least as of the early 1980s the Society had discovered a formula which would generate just enough revenue to maintain, internally elaborate, and carry to its logical conclusion its living history program, but not enough to cause large-scale changes. Presumably a system of pure sign exchange would entirely do without monetary transactions. Whether such a pure system can exist under current conditions seems doubtful. However the Historical Society, through the mechanism of its crafts fair, has arrived at something almost as good—a steady-state in which the dominant sign exchange system of its living history mythology can be deployed to generate just enough monetary revenue to allow that sign exchange system to keep running, but not enough to disrupt the image and ideology it depends upon.

It is perhaps such modest and vernacular modes of postmodernity, rather than its more self-conscious and cynical variants, that achieve the deepest penetration of this cultural dominant into the everyday of contemporary life. In the next chapter we will see that an institution with very large economic resources, the Brandywine River Museum, serves the ideological interests of a class—or at least a type of managerial expertise— upon which postmodernity depends. The economically much more modest Historical Society reproduces an ideology that legitimizes a whole social order, a deep-suburban way of life. And in that sense it is the more advanced postmodern apparatus.

I cannot conclude this examination of Chadds Ford Days without qualifying slightly my characterization of the event as a seamless postmodern text. Although it is extremely efficient in its operation and well shielded against intrusions that might disturb its postmodern surface, I need to record some minor blips on its otherwise smooth screen. In 1981, the same year that the Summer Kitchen was introduced at the fair, an unknown man in a beret, blue wool suit with a yellow rosebud in the lapel, black and which checked tie, and white bucks, set up an unofficial booth, really just a small folding table, in one corner of the fairgrounds. On the table he laid out a chess board. For a fee of one dollar you could challenge him, with a three dollar pay-back if you won. Now in many respects this figure was an anomaly at the fair. Not only did his display clash with the overall historical and handicraft image of the event, it foregrounded a competitive economic function quite inimical to the postmodern mechanism of sign exchange. The fair organizers tolerated his presence with good humor, though one suspects that had he made himself more obtrusive measures would have been taken.

And that same year an elderly black man, identifying himself only as Jaybird, a resident of West Chester, appeared at Chadds Ford Days. Wearing a flimsy felt tricorn and carrying a faded American flag, he set up shop under a corner flap of the art tent (Figure 13). His "display," which he

FIGURE 13.   Jaybird. Photograph by the author.

spread out in front of him on the ground, consisted of an odd, apparently unconnected collection of objects: a picture of a covered bridge, a horseshoe, a copy of *TV Guide*, a plastic pumpkin, a jackknife, and some toy musical instruments, among other things (Figure 14). It turned out that he had a story or recollection connected to each of these items. For example, the horseshoe was designed for use on ice and prompted an account of gathering ice for the ice house. Jaybird spent the day drinking Budweiser and playing harmonica and accordian for quarters.

We might be inclined to dismiss Jaybird merely as a derelict who saw the chance to make some change and who was too insignificant for the fair organizers and visitors to bother about. I choose instead to read him as a moment of rupture in the living history space of Chadds Ford Days. In him a radical otherness, an "outside," makes its presence felt, however trivially or evanescently. Although by no stretch of the imagination a threat to the smooth operation of the dominant ideological discourse, he is an instance of noise in the system, of dirt, in the sense of matter out of place. His sartorial allusions to the Revolution, his at least implicit connection (the horseshoe, the ice cutting story, the covered bridge picture)

FIGURE 14. Jaybird's display. Photograph by the author.

to an economic order that disappeared from Chadds Ford with the rise of its current social order, and of course his race, are all decidedly in conflict with the imagery of the event. Perhaps most significantly, his mysterious collection of seemingly unconnected objects scattered on the ground belong to an entirely different order of materiality from the craft objects on display in the other exhibits.

Jaybird can be taken as a small moment of unincorporated discourse, a tiny island immune to colonization by postmodern agencies. Elsewhere in Chadds Ford we find a somewhat more substantial, even institutionalized, instance of the same sort of otherness. The Chris Sanderson Museum is decidedly marginal to the postmodern context of our Site. Its presence is not in itself a critique of this dominant discourse, but it does at least raise the possibility of alternative discourses. Just how it does so is an issue for the next chapter.

NOTES

1. I observed and participated in Chadds Ford Days in three consecutive years, 1980–82. When I use the ethnographic present I am primarily referring to the period of these three celebrations.

2. I am leaving out of my account the art show, its exhibitors forming a separate group of participants. Chadds Ford Days has become a stop on the regional art show circuit, just as it is part of the crafts fair network. One might say it is constructed from the intersection of these two systems, which are brought together to express the two basic Chadds Ford themes, regional art and the colonial past. It goes without saying that Wyeth and the sanctioned artists of the Brandywine Heritage have nothing at all to do with contemporary Chadds Ford Days.

3. For comparison we might note that in 1983 the Kutztown Folk Festival had in the neighborhood of two hundred fifty craftspeople. A good sense of this event can be gathered from the annual summer supplements devoted to it in the journal *Pennsylvania Folklife*. The Kutztown festival serves as something of a model for Chadds Ford Days, and one result is the inclusion in the latter of many Pennsylvania German and nineteenth-century elements that are inconsistent both with the English Quaker heritage of Chadds Ford and the colonial theme to which the Historical Society is committed.

4. In 1981 I served as a volunteer worker at the event, some of my time being spent collecting parking fees. This is quite a good position from which to determine a general, if impressionistic, profile of the fair's audience.

5. Certain kinds of items seem to be particularly efficient money makers in the crafts fair market. They are the ones that are produceable with fairly mechanical techniques but that are manifestly the result of an encounter with the organic world. Also, they are likely to have some ongoing function other than display and be the sort of object someone might collect. We might compare here the influence of tourist markets on the objects produced by fourth world peoples (Bascom 1976:308–319, Graburn 1976:14–21, Ryerson 1976:129–135).

5 | An Allegory of Museums: A Comparative Reading of Two Gallery Displays

The museum, instead of being circumscribed in a geometrical location, is now everywhere, like a dimension of life itself.

Jean Baudrillard,
Simulations

I have sand gathered out of the Granicus; a fragment of Trajan's bridge over the Danube; some of the mortar which cemented the watercourse of Tarquin; a horseshoe broken on the Flaminian way; and a turf with five daisies dug from the field of Pharsalia.

from Quisquilius's
inventory of his personal
collection of curiosities
(Samuel Johnson, *The
Rambler* No.82, 1750)

Chris Sanderson (Figure 1) and Andy Wyeth (Figure 2) were friends. One thing they had in common was a reputation for eccentricity. Wyeth is, or at least is popularly perceived to be, an eccentric of the reclusive sort. This image is compounded, I think, of two clichés: the shy, simple man of country life, and the genius so consumed by his art that he shuns the practical business of the mundane world. Sanderson, even more than Wyeth, was a fully vested eccentric—a paragon of eccentricity in an area that has produced more than its share of characters and originals. Sanderson's eccentricity however was thoroughly extrovert. Endlessly garrulous, active, and inquisitive, from youth to age he was on the move—

FIGURE 1. *Chris Sanderson,* Barclay Rubincam. Christian C.
Sanderson Museum

meeting people, gathering information, disseminating it, performing,
seeing sites and, most important here, collecting things. He was a tireless
gatherer of what he called "relics." As a Scottish visitor to Chadds Ford
once observed, Sanderson seems to have been cast in an English mode of
eccentricity (Thompson 1973:400). The required image here I think is of
the country schoolmaster (Sanderson taught in the Chadds Ford area for
twenty-two years) who is also the local antiquarian and vernacular
historian.

More significant than the fact of their eccentricity, Sanderson and
Wyeth both embody, each in his own way, a pervasive phenomenon of
Chadds Ford cultural production: both have been the objects and the active
agents of *museumization*. Although Wyeth's works constitute a relatively
small percentage of the Brandywine River Museum's collection,[1] their
importance is out of proportion to their number. Wyeth's status in the
elite art world and, perhaps more to the point, in the current art market,[2]
invests him with an aura that extends to the institution where major

FIGURE 2. *Portrait of Andrew Wyeth*, James Wyeth. Private collection.

examples of his work are displayed. There is a kind of accuracy to the popular tourist perception that the Brandywine River Museum is the "Wyeth Museum." Furthermore, Wyeth represents the advanced guard of a general movement in which forms of museumization penetrate daily life. His Chadds Ford residence itself is a virtual museum, albeit a private one. He inhabits a representative display, one of his paintings made flesh; and if someday the property is opened to the public, very little will have to be done beyond the installation of a turnstyle.[3]

On the way from the Brandywine River Museum to Wyeth's museumized residence, just after you turn north on Route 100, there is a small sign on the right announcing the Christian C. Sanderson Museum. A second sign entices with the promise of "Wyeth art." The museum building, open only on weekends, turns out to be the small, mid-nineteenth-century house (the "little gray house") where Sanderson lived from 1937 until his death in 1966. Sanderson was a student of American history, especially of the Revolutionary and Civil Wars. Before the site of the Brandywine battle was itself subjected to official museumization in the form of a state park (1952), Sanderson had been its unofficial curator and the resident authority on the events of September 11, 1777. For seventeen years he and his mother lived in the house Washington used as headquarters for the battle, and during those years they received thousands of visits from tourists and historians. Sanderson conducted tours of the battle sites and lectured locally about the conflict. Eventually he set up the front room of his house on Route 100 as a little museum for the display of a few of his more important relics. Now, after his death, the whole house has been organized by friends and acquaintances as a museum display—and a very odd and interesting one it is.

What I want to conduct here is an exercise in comparative museum "reading." The specific texts I will read are the gallery displays at the two museums and the argument I will make is that the Brandywine River Museum is eminently and quite intentionally "legible," while the Sanderson Museum is not. Ultimately, my point will be that this difference in legibility reflects entirely different modes of social experience and fundamentally opposed relationships to the past. These contrasts suggest profound differences in the positions of these two institutions with regard to Chadds Ford's postmodernity.

The Brandywine River Museum is without question the primary legitimizer of an ideology geared to the reproduction of a hegemonic discourse. Specifically, it serves the interests of a class of professionals whose business is the control of cultural information. These are the managers of an official display and the mediators of a definitve imagery. I am not particularly interested here in identifiable individuals on the Chadds Ford scene, but rather in a much more general and anonymous apparatus, a kind of "style of expertise," a discourse that seems distinctly postmodern.

The Chris Sanderson Museum, in contrast, is perhaps the most institutionally visible instance of a counter-hegemonic moment in the general discourse of our Site. I will not be arguing that it is actively anti-hegemonic or oppositional in any way. In fact, it promotes its Wyeth connection and thereby feeds indirectly off the touristic prestige of the Brandywine River Museum. And purely in terms of its institutional importance, it could pose no threat to the dominant order even if it wanted to. But if there is a single, overriding quality of postmodern hegemony, it is that dominance becomes almost entirely a matter of texts or images, of the rhetorical deployment of discourse practices. One corollary of this fact is that postmodern hegemony has the potential of penetrating more deeply and colonizing more completely every sphere of experience than those orders of dominance that require visible forces of coercion and external control to sustain themselves. A second corollary, the flip side of the first, is that postmodernity is vulnerable not so much to external critical forces as to internal textual practices that are not entirely in keeping with its self-reflective discourse. The more polished the mirror surface of postmodernity becomes, the more visible and disturbing even minor disruptions of that surface appear to be. The Sanderson Museum is one such minor disruption in the increasingly smooth surface of Chadds Ford's postmodernity.

The Brandywine River Museum is a model of efficiency in the way it constructs and offers forth an *experience*. Meticulously arranged in all its parts, this institution resembles nothing so much as a small factory—a factory, that is, of ideological reproduction. Once, a precise sequence of wheels, cogs, pulleys, belts, and chutes moved grain through the calculated logic of flour production that organized the levels of the mill. Now these levels answer to an equally precise logic of image production, which is to say, ideological reproduction. The gallery is architecturally arranged to conduct the perceptions of visitors through a controlled sequence of stimulations that will produce the desired uniform result, namely, a complete and official picture of the "Brandywine Art Heritage." The spatial arrangement itself impels one in the appropriate direction through the gallery, but there are also guided tours that make the correct sequence explicit.

One is meant to experience the museum's images by following a spiral path upward through the four levels of the gallery. The glass-walled circulation core leads on each level from the head of the stairway around to the entrance of the gallery on that floor, providing in the process an open view out over the Brandywine River. One alternates experience of the art with experience of the landscape.

I will first describe the sequence of this gallery display as it existed up until 1985, at which time a new wing was added to the museum building (Figure 3). This addition not only transformed the overall configuration, but affected the organization of the internal display as well. In Chapter 3 I suggested that the external design of the museum addition made even more emphatic the building's postmodern discourse. Likewise, the internal redistribution of spaces and images carries through to a kind of logical conclusion the narrative discourse that already existed in the earlier, pre-1985 form. We have an opportunity, then, to compare not only two different texts, the displays at the Brandywine River and Sanderson Museums, but two "versions" of the same text, the second being a kind of clarifying "revision" of the first. It seems likely to me that as postmodernity develops, this process of clarifying revision, in which one text is replaced by another that reproduces the first but in such a way as to abolish all obscurities and make what was implicit explicit, will become increasingly prominent.

I begin then with the pre-1985 display at the Brandywine River Museum, adopting for the time being the convention of an ethnographic

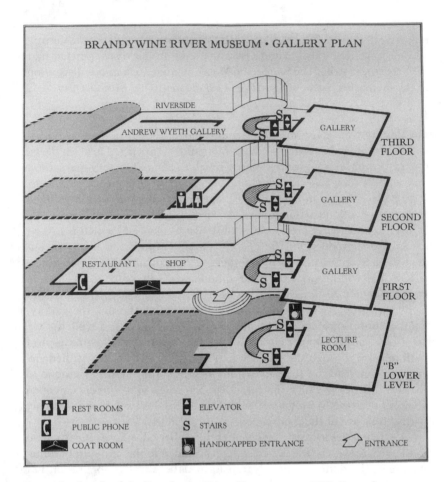

FIGURE 3. Levels of the Brandywine River Museum, post-1985. From the gallery guide brochure, Brandywine River Museum.

present. Most of the bottom floor of the museum, where formerly the mill-race entered the building, is off limits to the public. It contains offices of the curatorial staff and the infrastructure of museum bureaucracy. However, the museum auditorium is found on this level, and ideally one begins there by viewing an orienting slide show that synopsizes the Brandywine heritage and explicitly states the Conservancy ideology. The rest of the building recapitulates the slide show by moving the patron past a sequence of stable images rather than running images by the stationary viewer.

Entering properly into the first floor gallery, you see some enlarged photographs of the "old" Chadds Ford, of Howard Pyle's studio, and of his summer art class at work. A brief text on the wall introduces Pyle and his school, to which this gallery level is mainly devoted. Each floor is articulated by an irregular series of partitions that serve as syntactic markers for the experience as a whole, and the first section defined by such partitions contains images that constitute an introduction and "pre-history" of the Brandywine heritage. A set of three landscapes depicts the middle Brandywine through the seasons. "Notice the haze in the painting of summer," a guide says during one July tour. "You can go outside right now and actually see that haze in the air." The pre-Pyle phase of the Brandywine heritage, that is, the unconnected group of nineteenth-century genre and landscape painters who worked in the valley, is represented by the likes of Herman Herzog, Alexander Charles Stuart, Edward Moran and Bass Otis, whose painting from 1832 is one of the oldest in the gallery. These nineteenth century works include both landscapes of the valley itself and depictions of unrelated scenes by artists who made the Brandywine their home. This combination of works by artists personally associated with the Brandywine and paintings of the local landscape itself characterize the whole display. Two *trompe l'oeil* works by George Cope mark the end of the introductory section.

Works by F.O.C. Darley, a pre-Pyle illustrator associated with the valley (Pitz 1969:28–32), introduce the main theme of this gallery level: the Golden Age of Illustration, which consitutes the "archaic" phase of Brandywine art. A small display case containing emblems of the reproduction technology for turning paintings into book and magazine illustrations (photo-lithography) is immediately followed by examples of Pyle's own work. In this section of the guided gallery tours, the volunteer guides tend to dwell on the technical aspects of late ninteenth- and early twentieth-century commercial art and on Pyle's pedagogical technique, which emphasized working from costumed models and, when possible, gaining first-hand experience of one's subject (Pitz 1969:123–125, 129–135).

Pyle's paintings occupy a section of their own, and a diverse sampling of his student's mature work fills the remaining sections on this level. Harvey Dunn, Violet and Thornton Oakley, Maxfield Parrish, Clifford Ashley, Elizabeth Shippen Green, Frank Schoonover, and Jessie Wilcox Smith are some of Pyle's better known students. Judged on the depth of its collection and its research resources, the Brandywine River Museum should really be considered an institution specializing in nineteenth-century genre and landscape painting and late ninteenth- and early twentieth-century commercial art. According to the gallery display, however, this segment of the Brandywine heritage plays a subordinate and preliminary role in support of the "real" drama of artistic development yet to come. It signifies the "old dispensation" in what turns out to be a narrative about transformation and transcendence.

As a kind of coda to this level of the gallery, a painting (*Saying Prayers*) by Horace Pippin, a black primitive artist and sign painter from West Chester, hangs by the exit to the stairway. Chronologically, Pippin is somewhat out of order here, and in general he stands outside the main sequence of the Brandywine heritage. One tour guide, at first forgetting Pippin's name, said of the domestic scene he depicts in a 1943 painting that, "Of course the proportions here are impossible. Nobody that size could possibly fit through that doorway. But he painted his people as he saw them."

Pippin's presence as an implicitly sanctioned member of the Brandywine Heritage constitutes, I think, a small gesture toward incorporating a moment of Otherness. While obviously there is no tangible connection between his presence here and Jaybird's insinuation into the text of Chadds Ford Days, in broader terms of the general cultural discourse of our Site, perhaps it is not too far fetched to propose some analogy between them, an analogy we might expand and schematize thus—Jaybird : Chadds Ford Days :: Pippin : Brandywine River Museum :: Sanderson Museum : Chadds Ford as a postmodern Site. This analogy breaks down in one respect, however. Jaybird and the Sanderson Museum are for the most part dealt with in the dominant order by being ignored. Both constitute minor dirt in their respective contexts—a bit unsightly but not important enough to worry much about. Pippin, on the other hand, has developed a kind of autonomous standing as a twentieth-century primitive artist independent of the Pyle/Wyeth connection. As a significant moment of Otherness, he cannot merely be ignored and so is actively incorporated into the Brandywine Heritage by representation in the gallery.

One might say that the nineteenth-century genre and landscape painters constitute a pre-history of the Brandywine Heritage. The Golden Age of American Illustration, centrally represented by Pyle, counts then as its archaic phase. Fittingly enough, its Herioc Age corresponds to the founding of a dynasty, the Wyeth clan. N.C. Wyeth was its founder and he is the transitional figure in the crucial juncture of the Heritage—the move from commercial to Fine Art. This shift is emphatically marked in the syntax of the display by the movement from the second to the third gallery level. N. C. Wyeth was the best known and most successful of Pyle's students and the entrance to the third level opens into a large room devoted entirely to his paintings. These are mostly large, melodramatic oils depicting romantic scenes from the adventure stories he specialized in illustrating. While the technical/commercial/ pedogogical theme dominates the floor below, here the "artistic" aspect of commercial art presses forward. The guides begin to talk more of the use of light and the manipulation of perspective. The monumentality of Wyeth's oils, mainly the "originals" from which his book and magazine illustrations were photo-lithographed, lends itself to such aestheticizing. Predictably, the N.C. Wyeth segment of the display usually includes toward the end an example or two of this artist's self-conscious forays into the world of Fine Art. It is not surprising that the Brandywine River Museum has mounted a special show entitled "Not for Publication" to focus on this aspect of N.C. Wyeth's painting, which is reflected in such works as *April Rain* (impressionist influence), *The War Letter*, *Nightfall* (exercise in creating a mood), and *Island Funeral* (quasi-modernist use of impossible perspective).

The doorway to the next section of the third level gallery frames Jamie Wyeth's large and immensely popular painting of the pig Den-Den, the subject of much secondary elaboration in the local tourist industry. In this relatively small middle section of the third level one detects an intersection of the two organizing principles that control the display overall. The temporal sequence of artistic generations and Wyeth genealogy is crosscut by the official hierarchy of artistic merit.

As you move clockwise around this section, the "natural" direction, you first see examples of the work of the Wyeth sisters, Carolyn and Henriette, who belong to Andrew's generation. Sometimes works of the men who married into the Wyeth clan at this generation hang here as well (John McCoy married non-artist Ann, Southwestern artist Peter Hurd married Henriette). Isolated in their own sub-section by the doorways leading into and out of this middle area are works by Jamie Wyeth. He represents a step down in generations but an aesthetic advance, for artistically Jamie is the uncontested heir apparent to Andrew's crown.

On your right as you leave this section is the exit from the gallery, and beside it, in a position roughly corresponding to Pippin's painting on the level below, hangs a work by George Weymouth (*August*). Although nothing explains his presence at this point, you can learn from a guard that Weymouth is chairman of the Conservancy board. He is, in fact, the behind the scenes "boss" of the Conservancy/Museum and the man most responsible for its coming into existence. He owns an estate in a bend of the Brandywine just north of the Delaware border and represents the clearest link between du Pont wealth and Wyeth art (Rose 1982:75–83; Meyer 1975:37).

You turn left, away from the gallery exit, to enter the last section of the third level display. That this is a completely enclosed room from which you must retrace your steps in order to exit the gallery gives you the sense of being in the museum's *sanctum sanctorum*; and indeed you are, for this is the Andrew Wyeth section, climax of the display. In the deepest corner, which you come to after a series of works mostly depicting Chadds Ford subjects, you find the treasure of the collection: the series of four Siri paintings (*Siri*,

The Sauna, The Virgin, Indian Summer). Three of them—nudes that shocked Wyeth devotees when they first appeared—are considered among his greatest paintings. Here ends the story of the Brandywine Heritage, and you come away from the third level gallery with a satisfying sense of closure, having moved in clearly defined steps from nineteenth-century genre scenes and landscape, through commercial art, to the apotheosis of the Heritage in works by "America's greatest living artist."

The fourth level of the gallery, the last, constitutes an elaborating coda in the overall experience of the museum display. It is the space reserved for special shows wherein the expertise of the professional curatorial staff makes itself felt. Particular topics related in some way to the standing collection on the floors below (e.g. Wyeth pre-studies, small shows devoted to lesser Brandywine artists, a John McCoy retrospective, etc.) come in for close scrutiny according to the standards of scholarly research.

In Chapter 3 I characterized the Brandywine River Museum as a vehicle of traditionalization, the selective reduction of a complex history to a simple, readily comprehensible set of linkages that establish legitimizing connections between present institutions and an imagined past. We can now see that this particular traditionalization takes the form of a narrative with a familiar plot and conventional devices. By moving properly through the levels of the gallery one tracks a natural unfolding of art-historical epochs in the Brandywine valley. And at the climax of the narrative this apparently natural development merges with a family saga of biological inheritance across three generations. The climactic moment is, of course, the apotheosis of Brandywine painting—its transcendence of its regionalist and commercial roots as it passes into the timeless realm of Fine Art.

The three levels of the gallery display correspond to three significant phases. The flights of stairs leading from the second to third and third to fourth levels are the physical correlatives of significant transitions. As one mounts from the second to third level the narrative register shifts from rather abstract considerations of "precursor" figures, most notably Howard Pyle, and production processes to a discourse about taste and esthetic judgement. The narrative also becomes at this point a story about fathers and sons. One sees in this movement the progressive closing out of all allusions to external material and historical factors. I would argue that the gallery display as a whole is designed precisely to suppress all considerations of concrete historical determinations and the material process of production and reproduction. The commercial art, the genre scenes and *trompe l'oeil* illusions of three-dimensional reality, and even the romantic landscapes of the Brandywine Valley, foreground on the second level the materiality and regional specificity of the Brandywine Heritage. One realizes as he or she spirals up through the gallery that these images constitute the roots of the Brandywine Heritage, but also represent a phase of that Heritage which has been transcended. The images on this second level represent those factors which, though of some historical interest, have been purified out of the Heritage as it has matured.

The Wyeth family saga, the primary text on level three, is the signifier of this dehistoricizing transition. Here the Heritage ceases to be a broad stream of artists and images and gets channeled narrowly into a dynastic inheritance. Historical and material determinations, already reduced but still visible on the level below, are here replaced by the ahistorical, indisputably "natural" mechanisms of biology. This transition is most evident in the middle section of the third level gallery, which is devoted in part to the works of Andrew Wyeth's sisters Henriette and Carolyn and includes from time to time works by the male artists, Peter Hurd and John McCoy, who married into the Wyeth clan. In the same section, though subtly separated from the paintings of the previous generation, are works by Jamie Wyeth, Andrew's son and heir apparent to the Wyeth legacy.

The ideological subtext in this section of the gallery is about biological reproduction and the natural perpetuation of the Heritage in future generations, in short, about the production of heirs. Although well into his forties, James Wyeth is positioned in the popular mythology as the Prince Hal of the conventional dynastic scenario—somewhat rebellious inheritor of the full weight of Wyeth talent who promises to bring the Heritage to new heights.[4] The crucial point is that by arranging the images so as to signify the idea of the family romance and biological generation, the Brandywine Heritage of art here becomes completely naturalized and frees itself of history.

The climax of this movement is prepared for by the absence of the real Father, the reigning monarch of the dynasty, from the little primal scene of the middle gallery section. Andrew Wyeth, as represented by the images he produced, stands outside even the naturalized biological scenario. That the area containing his paintings is beyond the gallery exit and thus separated from the other sections on this level not only creates the climactic impression of entering the holy of holies, but lifts this artist out of the foregoing narrative sequence. His trace is present in that previous sequence, mainly in the son to whom he has bequeathed the artistic legacy, and perhaps in the (surrogate?) male artists who married his sisters. But his full presence is located elsewhere—in a realm that stands outside all temporal succession, historical or biological.

While this may seem an over-precious reading of the pre–1985 gallery display at the Brandywine River Museum, the changes that occured in its organization at mid-decade go some way toward bearing it out. For the most part the 1985 addition to the museum building did not significantly affect the gallery display. In broad outline its sequence and syntax remain the same. They have only been clarified by the expansion and more emphatic compartmentalization of some segments of the story (Maps 1 and 2). For example, the corners of walls as well as the partitions have become syntactic markers of the display (see Map 1). Complete walls are now devoted to the series of early Brandywine landscapes and and to *trompe l'oeil* works.[5]

There is however one glaring exception to this general stability of the gallery narrative. It is a change that serves to make even more explicit a movement that was already legible in the earlier version of the story. Andrew Wyeth's paintings are now completely separated from the rest of the display, having been installed in a new third floor gallery all of their own, the Andrew Wyeth Gallery (see Figure 3). The second floor display now literally ends with Jamie Wyeth, and it is at this point as well that the Brandywine Heritage as a continuous narrative ends.

But even more than this, the new gallery is part of the 1985 mirror-glass addition to the building. That Wyeth in some way stands apart from and above the Heritage, outside of its temporal ordering, is signified by his paintings being lifted up and out of the restored-mill section of the building and deposited in a space veneered with a reflective surface and physically connected to the offices out of which the Museum's imagery (in all senses of the word) is managed. Recall also that before 1985 the top level of the mill/gallery was reserved for special exhibits and so constituted the primary space for the display of knowledge and expertise by the Museum's professional staff. The function of this third floor gallery has remained the same. The movement of Wyeth's works onto the third floor and into a new gallery of their own places them conceptually in a context that is entirely appropriate to the unspoken, unacknowledged, "unintended" ideological project of the Museum. We can read the 1985 change in the gallery display, like the addition of the Summer Kitchen to Chadds Ford Days, as an ideology bringing itself to logical conclusion in a self-referential text—a revised version of itself. But we need to pin this ideology down, which in part means identifying the interests it serves.

To move appropriately through the galleries of the Brandywine River Museum is to move progressively out of history, or more generally, out of time and place. A subtle alchemy is worked by the discourse of this Mu-

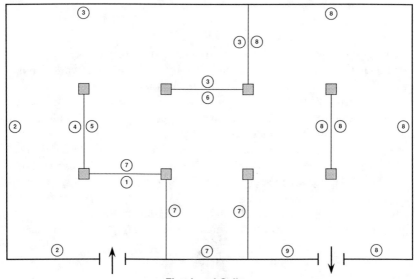

First Level Gallery

Key to schematic map of first level gallery—Brandywine River Museum

1. Introduction to the Brandywine Heritage (text, historical photos of Pyle, his summer art school and turn-of-the-century Chadds Ford)
2. Sequence of nine 19th century paintings of the Brandywine landscape (spanning the period 1825 to 1899 and depicting all the seasons)
3. 19th century still lifes and *tromp l'oeil* works
4. Five paintings by Jefferson David Chalfant, a late 19th-early 20th century artist of the region
5. Exhibits demonstrating the development of the photo-engraving process that made possible the "Golden Age of Illustration"
6. Three works by F.O.C. Darley, the most prominent pre-Pyle illustrator associated with the Brandywine Valley
7. Howard Pyle engravings and drawings
8. A sampling of the work of Howard Pyle's students (N.C. Wyeth absent)
9. A work by Horacce Pippin (black primitive artist who lived in West Chester)

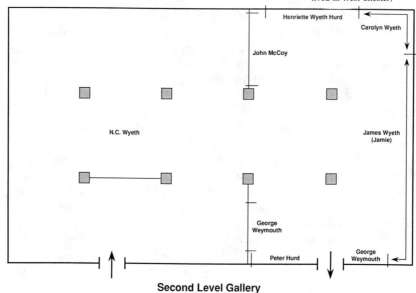

Second Level Gallery

Maps 1 & 2.   The Brandywine Art Heritage as a gallery narrative.

seum. As we have seen in numerous ways, the texts generated by this institution, and even more emphatically by the land conservancy that is its other face, return again and again to the theme of the distinctiveness and specificity of the local environment, natural, cultural, and historical. The basic premise that Chadds Ford is a special place is absolutely indispensible to the reproduction of the Site. This idea is acknowledged in the gallery display by the set of historical photographs of Chadds Ford and the Pyle art school and the series of Brandywine landscapes. These are the first images one sees upon beginning the gallery tour. The glass circulation core, of course, acknowledges the concrete specificity of the environment most convincingly. In order to enter the gallery at each level one passes by windows through which can be seen the "actual landscape" that generated the art.

These things, as well as the narrative encoded in the gallery display in so far as it is experienced as a particular story, are the signifiers of a Brandywine Heritage that appears to be a specific history situated in a specific place. But from a slightly different perspective the progression of the gallery display appears to encode a movement away from such specificities.

This is most apparent in the disjunction that occurs between the discourse of the third floor of the museum and the message that saturates the lower levels. The story of the Brandywine Heritage as a definitive tradition ends as one leaves the second floor. There is no question that the vast majority of visitors take away the satisfyingly finalized, legitimized and packaged experience of this tradition, marking it perhaps with postcards or reproductions of the paintings. The third floor, containing the special exhibit gallery and now the Andrew Wyeth Gallery, speaks with a different voice and to a rather different audience, what we might call the elite art world, the world inhabited by academics, sophisticated connoisseurs, specialists and serious collectors. This disjunction inscribed in the division of gallery space represents a conflict—a paradox that resonates with many others generated in Chadds Ford cultural production. The regional associations and sense of specificty in local tradition conveyed by the standing exhibit is fundamentally at odds with the aesthetic principles of the elite and professional art world. That world's ambivalence toward Wyeth's status as a fine artist is grounded precisely in his regional associations and his development out of, at least according to the implicit narrative encoded in the gallery display, a local tradition of landscape, genre painting and commercial art. His popularity with the general public confirms these associations in the view of many artworld professionals.

Yet the physical separation of Wyeth's paintings from the continuous narrative of the Brandywine Heritage, fairly weak before 1985 but quite emphatic since then, conveys the message that while Wyeth may in some sense be from a specific tradition, he is not entirely *of* that tradition. He has transcended it, and he has done so, of course, by passing into the unsullied realm of Fine Art, upon which specificities of time and place have no hold.

The Brandywine River Museum, then, orchestrates its ideological discourse so as to have it both ways. It suspends in a kind of unresolved dialectic the ideas of, on the one hand, historical and geographical specificity ("One can go outside right now and see that haze in the air") and, on the other, a timeless, placeless aesthetic order ("Wyeth is the greatest living American artist"). The Museum is double-voiced and its voices are in apparent conflict. But, and here recurs a characteristic quality of Chadds Ford's postmodernity, that conflict embarrasses no one, remaining hidden by the enchantment of image production. The two voices are audible together at various points. For example, the duality of the Museum's architecture—rustic restored mill/mirrored-glass tower—that I have made so much of in earlier chapters I would take here as a material expression of these two voices. Conservancy ideology would have us hear it as a "harmonious blend" of old and new, art and nature, inside and outside. The efficacy of this ideology can be gauged by the fact that it seems strange to no one that the crowning glory of the Museum's collection should be Wyeth's Siri paintings. The rhetorical alchemy of the Museum discourse overrides any jarring we might feel at the fact that these paintings have nothing to do with the middle Brandywine. Their subject belongs to Cushing, Maine, the other of Wyeth's "two worlds" and the site of his summer residence (Hoving 1978:120–185). The Brandywine valley and the Maine coast are interchangeable, or rather immaterial, as far as the judgments of Fine Art are concerned. Art in this sense by definition always transcends the specific associations of its content. And the gate keepers of this realm of Fine Art are, of course, the professional arbiters of taste, the image managers and brokers of cultural knowledge and information.

And there is another level at which essentially the same duality of voice—specificity/generality, concreteness/abstraction, in time and place/ atemporal and unlocalized—operates in the gallery display of the Brandywine River Museum. I have described at some length the narrative properties of the gallery's standing exhibit. While we can read it as a story with a specific content and structure, we might also recognize in it the mythic impoverishment of a narrative. The process of traditionalization generates not just an abridged, synopsized or outlined story, but the *emblem* of a story as well, a representative specimen of the narrative principle. Seen in its pieces it is a specific tale; swallowed whole so to speak it becomes the signifier of the generalized idea of continuity over time. One comes away from the Museum with a sense of its plot (nineteenth-century landscape and genre painting—the Pyle school of commercial art—N.C. Wyeth—the emergence of Fine Art in the Wyeth family—the family romance and the biological perpetuation of the legacy in Jamie—Andrew Wyeth as a modern master), and perhaps even a sense of minor digressive complications (e.g. Pippin, the male painter in-laws). But the very closure and clarity of the narrative scheme indicates its function as a vehicle of the global *idea* of Heritage, not a particular heritage but the nebulous mythological concept of traditionality itself, devoid of any specific content. This unconnected, abstracted concept, the idea of traditionality as opposed to a specific tradition, is, I believe, one of the Museum's most important ideological products.

The Brandywine River Museum is a meta-museum, homologous in this respect to the Chadds Ford friendship quilt, which is a kind of meta-quilt. Traditionality itself, not just the Brandywine Heritage, is on display there, and in this the Museum encapsulates a general movement of Chadds Ford cultural production. The restored-mill gallery is probably the most visible instance among a vast array of emblems that collectively "mean" traditionality. Chadds Ford, secure in its sense of the indisputable authenticity of its traditions, specializes in the reproduction of this detached, nebulous, notion of traditionality. The experience of traditionality available to the museum visitor is a generalized experience, empty of specific content and ahistorical. Its vagueness invites patrons to apply their own associations and to populate the vague generality with a concrete history of their own devising. Through the mechanism of the museum display, the ostensibly specific tradition of Brandywine art expands to embrace other worlds of association, floating free of the place and the history that legitimize it to begin with.

It appears, then, that both in the progression of the gallery display as a syntactic structure, and in the global image that the display as a whole conveys, the concrete specificities of time and place, of history and materiality, dissolve into nebulous, free floating, ahistorical concepts and images. The special magic of the Museum's alchemy, however, resides in the fact that the historical and material specificities are never entirely abolished. They are always available for strategic recall as legitimizing agents for the very concepts and images that have pushed them out of sight. The real question is, whose interests does this process serve in the particular micro-climate that is our Site.

One obvious answer is the legitimized painters of the Brandywine Heritage, Andrew Wyeth above all. He seems to occupy a position remarkably well suited to the enhancement of the dynastic coffers. On the one hand tourists flock to see Wyeth art in its "natural" setting and, if the travel magazines can be believed, seek out the actual scenes depicted in his work. On the other hand, he is the serious object of scholarly attention and has been validated by some of the major institutions of elite culture. One has the strong sense that debates about his status in the art world have significantly lessened even as the ranks of Wyeth tourists have swelled. In any case, it is now possible for AT&T to present Wyeth art to the Russians as a kind of definitive tradition of American excellence.

However, while the discourse of the Brandywine River Museum certainly does Wyeth no harm, he hardly needs whatever legitimation it might provide. And in any case, postmodernity renders such questions of individual validation moot. The "Wyeth phenomenon," which has mainly to do with the reproduction of images rather than with Wyeth as individual creator of art, is the appropriate level of analysis in the postmodern context. And this phenomenon is far too dispersed throughout our current culture to associate it with a single institution. It is more accurate to say, I think, that the idea of Wyeth legitimizes the Museum as a mechanism of postmodern hegemony.

When the images representing Wyeth are moved behind the mirror-glass of the museum addition, we see a rather overt expression of the real direction of ideological legitimation. The anonymous but increasingly powerful forces of image control and information management, the designers of postmodern surfaces, exist, one might say, as a pool of unconnected and mobile expertise. Concrete connections to particular historical situations or specific locations are of no moment, or indeed are positive impediments to the smooth deployment of the postmodern discourses these forces generate. The most immediate history obscured by the gallery display at the Brandywine River Museum is the quite recent process of radical selection and information control through which the display itself was constructed and a definitive tradition was codified and legitimized, all of which we can date more or less to the late 1960s. The postmodern institutions of detached expertise cannot afford to have revealed the material operations through which they achieve their ends. It is decidedly in the interest of these institutions that the Brandywine Heritage of art be perceived not as a rich history of connections, contradictions, suppressions and exclusions, but as Nature.

When the discourse of the gallery display lifts Wyeth out of the fallen world of time and local connection and places him in the purified realm of Fine Art it is serving these same ends. Wyeth's apotheosis places him in the same space, literally and figuratively, with the professional designers of the flattened world of postmodernity. It is a space sheathed in the mirror-glass that reduces all material substance to surface effect. By a kind of contagious magic the prestige of Wyeth's Fine Art transcendence of time and place automatically transfers to and helps legitimize the free-floating expertise that is an indispensable condition of possibility for the postmodern order. The Brandywine River Museum is a postmodern institution to the degree that it seals the ideological connection among a mythic concept of traditionality, an equally mythic notion of Fine Art, and a social formation dependent upon the effective control of images, texts and surfaces by a professional managerial class.

Since I have been treating the gallery display at the Brandywine River Museum as a significant text in Chadds Ford's postmodern discourse, it seems appropriate to conclude by locating its rhetorical structure in the typology I have laid out in Chapter 3. If vignette is the master trope of the Historical Society's living history discourse, the Brandywine River Museum enacts its ideology mainly through the rhetoric of veneer. Although I have identified the bifurcation of the Museum's architecture with the veneer/vignette distinction, the strategy of vignette does not figure prominently in the primary discourse of this institution. As its definitive text, the gallery display mainly exhibits the characteristic features of veneer. It does so, however, in a way that reveals veneer's underlying dialectic, a kind of movement or alternation that invests veneer with its rhetorical power.

The postmodern veneer entails the projection of some supposed prior reality—social, historical, material—onto a reproducing surface. The overall effect is the dispersal, replacement, or suppression of that reality by textual simulations of it. In its fullest development the postmodern veneer tends toward even the dissolution of its own material surface.

My reading of the gallery display identifies two ways in which it disperses or suppresses the concrete materiality of space and the temporal specificity of history. On the one hand the narrative progression through the gallery is a movement through stages of decreasing historicity and materiality, culminating in the timeless order of Fine Art and anonymous expertise. On the other hand, the gallery display viewed globally comes to signify abstract traditionality. Although its legitimizing alibi, always there to be invoked as needed, is the concrete historical and physical environment of the middle Brandywine valley, the gallery display is in the business of packaging and offering for consumption the nebulous, detached myth of traditionality.

It is precisely this process of flattening or suppressing a complex history and materiality in the interest of simplified, generalized images that Barthes identifies with mythological discourse. These images or myths are powerful tools of legitimation and hegemony, and I have attempted to identify the particular postmodern formation that most clearly benefits from the myth of traditionality reproduced by the Brandywine River Museum. I would only add that veneer as the rhetorical vehicle of this myth operates through a typical dialectic or alternation between perspectives. We have already seen that the efficacy of vignette depends upon a constant movement or oscillation, that is, between image and inscribed surface or between "levels" of surface. Veneer too depends on an alternating motion, but not the same one as in vignette.

It will be recalled that veneer differs from vignette in that it cannot be conceived without at least some trace notion of a prior reality that has been flattened. Veneer is a framed surface that depends upon at least a minimal sense that something lies outside or beyond the frame. Vignette on the other hand is a hermetic space which recognizes no such outside. Its play of alternation is completely contained on this absolutely self-referential surface. The characteristic alternation of veneer is between the surface and something that lies outside it—a concrete history, material processes of production, specificity of place, and so on. The real movement of postmodern veneer, then, is not simply the process of flattening and dispersal. It also entails the repeated alternation of such flattenings with legitimizing invocations of a supposed prior reality, some kind of depth. The metaphor of mirror-glass captures basic properties of postmodern veneer, but not this dialectic quality. Perhaps we need to combine it with Barthes's metaphor of viewing a landscape through an automobile window. Depending on how I choose to adjust my gaze, he says, "I can at will focus on the scenery or on the window-pane. At one moment I grasp the presence of the glass and the distance of the landscape; at another, on the contrary, the transparence of the glass and the depth of the landscape; but the result of this alternation is constant" (1972[1957]:123).

I have claimed that vignette is in some ways the more advanced of the two rhetorical structures, the more indigenously postmodern. This is the case precisely because vignette's dialectic process is hermetic, dependent upon no notion of prior reality discontinuous with the space in which it operates. Hence it is largely immune to potential disruptions from extraneous discourses. Otherness is recognized at all only to the degree that it has already been integrated into the play of the vignetted surface. Whether a prior reality exists or not, veneer depends upon a sense that it does. Its dialectic is between heterogeneous positions—an inside and an outside, image and reality. Although the purpose of the dialectic is precisely to suppress all outside realms, all concrete histories and specificities of time and place, the very possibility of an outside remains. And this means there is still the possibility, however remote, of disruption by some radical otherness. The strongest voice of such otherness at the Site of Chadds Ford, or at least the most institutionally visible instance of it, is the discourse of the Chris Sanderson Museum.

At present Andrew Wyeth has no rival as the premier figure in Chadds Ford's cultural discourse. We have seen how his image incorporates a number of phenomena characteristic of the postmodern order. One such phenomenon, the increasing difficulty of distinguishing between production and consumption, has a version that applies both to Wyeth and to Chadds Ford generally, namely, the merging of touristic consumption and tourist-site production. Though suppressed in gallery discourse, the Brandywine Heritage is among other things a tradition of tourism. The early Brandywine artists were tourists of scenic experience; Pyle preached an aesthetic emphasizing the search for "authentic experience," the *sine qua non* of tourism (MacCannell 1976:4–5); and Wyeth himself espouses a transcendentalized version of Pyle's pedagogical philosophy. The result of all this today is that Wyeth simultaneously occupies a tourist site, produces the occasion for others' tourism, and in his vocation practices a form of tourism himself.

In Chadds Ford generally, as in its most illustrious resident, touristic production and consumption transform endlessly into one another. The resident of Spring Meadows creates for himself the site of which he becomes the tourist; the Chadds Ford Historical Society restores early eighteenth-century houses as sites both for the evanescent visitations we normally associate with tourism and for the Society members' own participation in the authenticity of a definitive historical otherness.

Christian C. Sanderson seems to have anticipated this phenomenon of touristic circularity, yet he stands in a thoroughly ambivalent relation to Chadds Ford's postmodern hegemony. Depending on how we choose to view him, he can appear as either a bellwether of the emerging postmodern order, or as a residual force pulling against it. He was, without question, an indefatigable tourist. He bought one of the first models of the Brownie camera and photographed sites, events and monuments throughout his long life. We might recall the comment of a friend that Sanderson's own funeral procession in 1966 seemed incomplete without "Chris standing on the curb taking a picture." Although his life was never financially secure, Sanderson travelled a great deal, constantly in pursuit of touristic experience, and he often guided others in the hunt. His specialty was American history: the Revolutionary and Civil Wars.

To call Sanderson a tourist, however, is misleading, if we take that to mean he had a purely superficial relation to the sites he visited. To a remarkable degree he incorporated his tourism into his daily life, but in a way strikingly different from the touristic appropriation at work in such things as the Brandywine River Museum, the deep-suburban developments, the Historical Society's living history, and the Wyeth phenomenon. The contrast can be felt in the difference between the utter simplicity and clarity of the Brandywine River Museum display and the utter "illegibility" of the Christian C. Sanderson Museum just around the corner on Route 100.

Sanderson was a truly prodigious collector of "relics," a vague category in which he included just about anything that held some association with past events. Especially important to him were objects connected in some way to the Battle of the Brandywine, of which he became the unrivaled, if unofficial, expert. His tours of the battle sites that lie scattered for several miles north from Chadds Ford along the river and his collection of relics attracted an astonishing number of guests to his home—9,257 visitors in 1921 alone.

Forced to move at the end of that year, Sanderson set up one room of his new home in West Chester as a museum for some of his more important relics. He called it the Brandywine Museum. When he moved back to Chadds Ford in 1937,[6] he did the same with the front room of the "Little Gray House," his home for the rest of his life and now the museum completely given over to the display of his "collection."

Nothing could be farther from the galleries at the Brandywine River Museum. If they offer an eminently controlled, uniform, and comprehensible experience, the Sanderson Museum is opaque and "unreadable." This is not to say it has no organization, but practical rather than ideological concerns dictate the display. First of all, where the Brandywine River Museum evokes and exploits the image of the former mill while remaining largely unconstrained by the internal structure of the milling process, the Sanderson Museum is quite simply a house used as a display space. The original rooms constitute the divisions of the display and the logic by which we move through them is the bottom to top/front to back logic of the house. It has nothing to do with any discursive sequence of the display, with the exception that the "public" areas of the house (entry hall and parlor to the right) are devoted to the objects of "general historical interest," while the inner and upper rooms contain things of more personal association—but even this is not a strictly observed division. One moves from room to room as from one theme to another in Sanderson's life, with no particular orientation other than, fittingly, the one Sanderson himself lived with while at home. This museum tells no story, at least not in the way the Brandywine River Museum does.

Briefly, the divisions of the Sanderson Museum are as follows:

downstairs

- The parlor contains mainly war memorabilia, including relics related to his special interests (the Battle of the Brandywine and the Battle of Gettysburg, where both his grandfathers fought) and objects from other American wars (e.g., an airplane propeller from WWI). Here also hangs the large portrait of Chris done by a young Andrew Wyeth (Figure 1).

- The entry hall contains some of Sanderson's "formal" collections, as opposed to less ordered conglomerations of memorabilia. Prominent here are his commemorative plates and his glass bottle collection.

- The inner room on the first floor contains the objects most associated with Sanderson's public persona. A central display case contains his Indian clubs, which he was still swinging in his 80s, the large leather briefcase he carried everywhere, a sweater from West Chester Normal, the calendar page of June 1901 (his graduation year), and his fiddle (he was a member of the Pocopson Valley Boys and a square dance caller). His bedsheet map of the Battle of the Brandywine is in this room, as is the third edition of the Encyclopedia Brittanica (1797), with the appropriate volume open to the entry on the Battle of the Brandywine and a note added by Sanderson pointing out errors. Another display case contains material related to Bayard Taylor and his romance *The Story of Kennett*, set in the Brandywine area. Sanderson was first attracted to Chadds Ford and its history through this novel. He was so taken by it that he even appropriated the nickname "Sandy" from one of its characters.

upstairs

- A music room containing Sanderson's collection of fiddles. The prize among these is a violin that once belonged to Ole Bull, the Norwegian concert violinist.

- A room devoted to art, including works by the Wyeths, John McCoy, and Peter Hurd. Most of the Wyeth works are from Andrew's childhood or that early phase of his career when he was still doing illustration. Sanderson was involved with some of Wyeth's productions at this time. The collection includes no major works.

- A room devoted to Sanderson's career as a rural school teacher (1905–1929), including photographs of his classes.

- A room for his collection of china, fancy valentine cards, etc.

- A room of keepsakes with which Sanderson commemorated specific personal experiences and associations.

Such order as has been brought to Sanderson's accumulations really has little to do with the experience his museum offers. What one mainly feels there is the sheer density of commemorative objects. Unlike the spare, coherent narrative displayed against large expanses of white-plastered wall at the Brandywine River Museum, the Sanderson display hardly leaves a single bare surface. It is the full volume of Sanderson's life laid out for public inspection. The three dimensional clutter of his daily reality is conveyed in photographs of the rooms as they appeared at the time of his death, which is to say, literally stacked full of his accumulations. After his mother's death in 1943, her room was slowly sealed off by the ever-growing pile of material Sanderson began to store in the hallway. His biographer recalls literally shoveling Sanderson's random notes into a box for later sorting.

What we have in the Sanderson Museum, I want to suggest, is the polar opposite of the Brandywine River Museum, or perhaps the return of its repressed side. The Sanderson collection is the fullness of an actual life experience insofar as that can be captured in a gallery display. Sanderson made this possible through his compulsion to mark and document any experience that seemed meaningful to him. He spent a long lifetime collecting himself and he never threw anything away. A representative inventory, only a small fraction of the whole display, gives some sense of the museum.

Along with the cannonballs, weapons, insignia, uniform paraphernalia, and other military equipment from various American Wars, Sanderson's biographer lists among the objects related to military and political history,

> a leaf from the wreath placed by President Wilson on Lafayette's grave following the end of World War I; a piece of the Kaiser's private telephone line to the front; a rock from within ten feet of the famous flag raising at Iwo Jima; melted ice from the South Pole; a piece of bandage placed on Lincoln at the time he was shot; a Nazi flag secured by a member of General Patton's army after they crossed the Rhine.
>
> (Thompson 1973:375).

Other fragments of general historic interest are a piece of the dirigible Los Angeles, a piece of a zeppelin bomb, hair from the tail of Thunderhead the movie horse (marked as "rare"), a piece of tile from Eva Braun's bathroom, a piece of Plymouth Rock, a pulley from the Hearst building, where the Great Baltimore Fire began, a personal Christmas card and snapshot sent to Chris by Eva-Marie Saint (whom he once had occasion to teach squaredancing), a piece of the gas tank from the Spirit of St. Louis, a bullet fired by one of Pancho Villa's men at the Columbus, New Mexico raid, an iron finial from the fence around the National Gallery in London (unscrewed by a British soldier on V.E. Day and given to an American G.I.), sand from the Panama Canal, sawdust from Billy Sunday's sawdust trail, sawdust from a Ringling Bros. circus, a fragment of brick from Independence Hall, a shred of upholstery from Pretty Boy Floyd's getaway car (blood stains visible), a bullrush from the Nile, an old blackjack (with no explanation), Jordan water, and on, and on.

Sanderson also made more or less formal collections of certain things: commemorative plates, first day covers, and, in great profusion, autographs and handwriting samples. His collection of the latter includes the autographs of Sonja Henie, Shirley Temple (as a child), Harry Lauder, Buffalo Bill, Sitting Bull, Orville Wright, Tom Mix, Jim Thorpe, Roger Staubach, Eddie Cantor, Bill Robinson, Anthony Eden, Daniel Webster, Daniel M. Casey (Casey at the bat), D.W. Griffith, Ernest Tubb, Churchill, Carnegie, Lowell Thomas, Oliver Wendel Holmes, Babe Ruth, Basil Rathbone, and so on. The walls of the second floor hallway are covered with these autographs.

There is, then, another class of objects (Figure 4), which for present purposes is perhaps the most significant of all. It includes the flowers Sanderson carried when he saw Haile Selassie, a carnation carried when he saw Queen Elizabeth, cherry blossoms from Arlington the day Roosevelt died, a shoestring worn at Truman's inauguration, a piece of the plastic raincoat Sanderson wore at Eisenhower's inauguration, a piece of Sanderson's 1941 Christmas tree, the used flashbulb from the photograph taken at the Civil War site where his grandfather was killed one hundred years earlier, a counting exercise being done by his school class just at the moment they rang the school bell to mark Wilson's funeral, a Hershey bar wrapper from Sanderson's last purchase at Doc Green's Drug Store before it closed, a piece of bread from the loaf bought when he tramped to Kennett in a big snowstorm, flowers he wore the day Edison died, and so on and so on.

Although Sanderson's collection has been arranged for viewing, in overall effect the objects swarm together to make an uninterpretable or "unreadable" text; or perhaps it is better to say, an *infinitely* readable text. What this museum conveys is precisely the sort of dense historicity that the Brandywine River Museum effectively suppresses to produce its myth of traditionality. Sanderson seems to have been a person for whom virtually any event had some sort of historical connectedness, no matter how attenuated or artificially constructed. Because of his compulsion to mark these connections with physical objects—either collected or manufactured by his own hand—he has left a remarkably full record of historical meaning. It is meaning not in the sense that applies to "objective" history, but rather to the web of historical connections that constituted Sanderson's own life experience. It is this density of meaning that resists the insinuations of the mythological process and the postmodern reduction

FIGURE 4. Display case of some Sanderson mementos. Photograph by the author.

to surface effect. By carrying touristic activity to a level that approaches sublimity, he has generated a discourse that debilitates the rhetoric of postmodern dispersal and reduction. Certainly without intending to do so, and at a time before the complete installation of postmodernity as the hegemonic dominant, Sanderson put together a text that comes close to accomplishing the seemingly impossible task of parodying postmodernity.

The mythological process of course has multiple strategies at its disposal. When meaning is too solid and rich to be reduced and metabolized from the inside, as the discourse of the Sanderson Museum seems to be, myth can always unhinge its jaw and swallow the object whole. I suspect that many visitors to the Sanderson Museum have come away not with a sense of the thick historical connectedness of Sanderson's life experience, but rather with a nebulously totalizing mythological concept that we might call "eccentricity." In other words, the Sanderson Museum can easily be consumed as a myth of eccentricity. In this view Sanderson becomes the emblematic representative of all those odd characters inhabiting the newspaper filler columns: the compulsive collectors who die with houses full of twine, ceramic figurines, paper bags, or what have you. I prefer, however, to view the Sanderson Museum in a light that emphasizes its capacity for resistance to myth—a capacity that constitutes an implicit critique of the processes so much in evidence at the Brandywine River Museum and in contemporary Chadds Ford generally. In other words, I choose to read the Sanderson Museum as a moment of potential counter-hegemony.

The contrast between the two museums can be conceived in terms of their differing motivations and procedures for relating past and present. The myth of traditionality at the Brandywine River Museum requires as its raw material a particular traditionalization, a drastic selection that reduces the lines between past and present in a way that serves the interests of those groups with access to the means of traditionalization. As the recognized tradition of Brandywine art, the official Brandywine Heritage was produced by a subtractive process in which vast areas of cultural production were excluded. The outcome of this reduction was a coherent, single-stranded and causal progression from past to present that could be declared *the* tradition, an uncontestable inheritance of the middle Brandywine valley and as naturally given as the scenery or the river itself.

The myth of traditionality, then, begins with the already naturalized reduction that is the Brandywine heritage and reduces it to a still greater abstraction, one which can float free of the place and its history altogether. All the contending and interwoven "plots" that we might find connecting past to present are first reduced to an official, single-stranded story, and then the postmodern agencies of myth production, most notably museumization, makes this *particular* story the emblematic representative of all such stories. It becomes the metonymic signifier of the mythic concept of traditionality itself, tradition as veneer.

The Sanderson Museum represents an entirely different way of relating past and present. As the institutional expression of Sanderson's life experience, it is myth-resistant; but it is also resistant to the process of traditionalization. Far from reducing the connections between present and past to a single, official line of succession, Sanderson expended huge amounts of energy to complicate, ramify and extend connections, regardless of where they might lead. No global, totalizing story could encompass the profusion of plots Sanderson processed, some of them "found" and collected, others fabricated through his innumerable rituals of commemoration.

Sanderson was the past's *devotee* in the religious sense of the term. His use of the word "relic" for the objects he accumulated is entirely appropriate. Just as a pilgrim seeks immediate contact with the patron saint through the physical reality of the sacred relic, so Sanderson "participated" in history through the fragments he collected. Using another language, we can say that Sanderson related himself to the past *indexically*.[7] He participated in it not so much through the imaginative re-creation of events or of a past way of life, as in the living history model, nor did he seem given to viewing his present reality as the natural unfolding from some definitively significant past, as in the traditionalization of the Brandywine River Museum. Rather he appropriated to himself the tangible reality of the past through fragments chipped directly from it, in some cases quite literally.

Where the discourse of the Brandywine River Museum is geared entirely toward the suppression of temporal and spatial specificity and concrete materiality, Sanderson was almost obsessively devoted to their reproduction and preservation. And it was not the images of past things he was interested in, but the things themselves. Recall for example the photograph of his mother on the couch (Chapter 1, sec. XX). It is not at all inappropriate to consider it a ritual image, in the sense that rituals do not merely symbolize sacred things but conjure up sacredness itself. This quality clings to the objects in the museum display and it explains why Sanderson was such a stickler for accurate commemoration. No matter that it was convenient to hold the early Chadds Ford Day celebration on the weekend nearest September 11; Sanderson invariably observed the anniversary of the battle on the correct day.

Of course this quality of quasi-religious participation, this consubstantiality through the appropriation of relic/souvenirs of some sort, is a component of tourism generally. Yet Sanderson stands apart from the typical postmodern mode of tourism as we know it today. He is, as I have suggested, an ambivalent figure—combining residual and emergent tendencies. He is an example of what we might call the unalienated tourist, a designation that no doubt will strike some as an oxymoron. While modern tourism seems to involve the reduction of experience to a dispersed form of consumption (or sign exchange) and a weakening of the capacity for sustaining human connectedness, Sanderson represents virtually the opposite case. His drive to accumulate indexical contacts with the past was entirely at the service of a seemingly infinite capacity for forming human connections. Indeed, his relation to the past appears to have been entirely continuous with his contemporary social experience. Many of his relics came to him from friends. The object, the historical moment it indexes, and the personal connections of friendship or simple acquaintance seem to have formed a sort of unity for Sanderson. The objects that commemorate events from his daily experience (the candy wrapper, the piece of bread, the spent flashbulb) are continuous with the relics of regional, national, and world history.

Sanderson created for himself a richness of social experience through just those forms that in postmodern tourism seem to impoverish social relations. Perhaps we can partially explain this paradox by noting the absence from his collecting activity of a well-developed commodity structure. Of course he purchased some items for his collection, but the significance of the object was not exhausted in the moment of consumption. The act of purchase is entirely tangential to the indexical import of the relic. In fact Sanderson commonly engaged in a practice which transformed the abstract medium of exchange into an indexical sign, thereby disrupting the smooth circulation of monetary value. While visiting tourist sites he would often take coins from the receptacles set out for donations, replacing them with an equal amount from his own pocket. The collected coins he would then preserve and mark as souvenirs of this or that site. The final twist in this "indexical economy" occured when the museum was being set up after Sanderson's death. It turned out that several of the coins Sanderson gathered through the years were rather valuable. By selling some the organizers of the museum were able to defray expenses.

The Christian C. Sanderson Museum represents a cultural current that runs obliquely to, if not oppositionally against, the dominant Chadds Ford order. It represents on one hand the anticipation of that order, in the sense that Sanderson organized his daily experience in a fashion we can legitimately consider touristic. Throughout this study I have documented ways in which Chadds Ford displays that advanced form of postmodernity where tourism has ceased to be a separate leisure-time activity or specialized sphere of experience and comes to inhabit the private domain of the everyday (deep-suburban residence, forms of visual experience, living history, etc.). Yet Sanderson took touristic experience in a direction that has become increasingly alien to the postmodern order. One might say that where the deep-suburban resident incorporates the tourist mode into his or her daily life, Sanderson made his daily life over entirely *into* blatant tourism. This is an important distinction. The discourse of his museum violates postmodern trends precisely because it exaggerates them to the point of caricature. The display is a comic text, and that in itself is out of keeping with the general tone of Chadds Ford's brand of postmodernity.

The characteristic modes of deep-suburban tourism arise from a postmodern practice that suppresses all awareness of site and souvenir production. The smooth surfaces of authenticity generally prevail. The Sanderson collection, resistant to totalization, blatant in its pastiche, irreducible to narrative coherence, is the concentrated expression of a discourse/practice that runs against the hegemonic order. Read in the context of this Site, it becomes a moment of critical reflexivity. This is perhaps most obvious in the case of Sanderson's personally manufactured souvenirs. The faded flowers, burnt flashbulbs, fragments of clothing, are souvenirs only as the result of Sanderson's own obvious artifice. In them collection and production are virtually the same act, an act which asserts openly the historicity and material production of the collection. But this is just what most collections serve to mystify (Stewart 1984:151–154). The Sanderson Museum can be read as a collage of the anti-souvenir, a text which the hegemonic order in Chadds Ford would have a hard time incorporating, were it ever forced to acknowledge this alien discourse. But under current conditions the Sanderson Museum is not nearly disruptive enough to discomfit the prevailing hegemony.

One result of these conditions for Sanderson personally was his subjection to rather cruel displacement and marginalization as postmodernity became hegemonic in Chadds Ford. Throughout his years in the area he had expended much energy in trying to get the Brandywine Battlefield officially recognized as a national shrine, that is, to museumize it. When the Commonwealth of Pennsylvania finally created the Battlefield Park in 1952, Sanderson's contribution was largely ignored (Thompson 1973:347–348). As unofficial, vernacular custodian of local history, he was of little interest to the forces of professional culture management entrusted with the job of authenticating the tourist site that now "stands for" the Battle of the Brandywine in Chadds Ford—the same forces, broadly speaking, that are responsible for institutionalizing the myth of traditionality at the Brandywine River Museum.

The Sanderson Museum is decidedly peripheral to current Chadds Ford tourism. The little gray house is a tourist site devoted to a life organized around a touristic sensibility, but that sensibility was employed to produce a thick web of social connectedness, a form of experience that seems quite out of place in an environment of advanced postmodernity. Of all the souvenirs I have gathered in these pages, it is the Chris Sanderson Museum, itself a souvenir collection, that provides the best opportunity to disrupt the smooth surface of Chadd Ford's discourse. In that the purpose of this case study has been to conduct a critical reading of the Site, the Sanderson Museum is the Chadds Ford text that comes closest to offering an indigenous model for an effective ethnographic practice under the conditions of postmodernity.

By way of closing out my reading of Chadds Ford as a micro-climate of advanced consumer culture, I offer a schematic summary of the discursive properties of the three key texts (Chadds Ford Days, Brandywine River gallery display, Sanderson gallery display) from the three institutions I have focused upon (Chadds Ford Historical Society, Brandywine River Museum, Chris Sanderson Museum)

	Chadds Ford Days	**Brandywine River Museum**	**Chris Sanderson Museum**
rhetorical mode	vignette	veneer	? (caricature)
ideological mode	archaeological	narrative	quasi-sacral
ideological mechanism	absolute past	selective tradition	ritualistic commemoration
ideological vehicle	simplified tableau	simple sequence	dense network of connections
primary text	colonial domestic economy	Brandywine Heritage of Art	souvenir collection
myth concept	"traditioning" (symbolic exchange)	"traditionality"	— (non-mythic)
mode of consumption	dispersed (participatory spectatorship)	passive/touristic (simple spectatorship)	— (non-consumer)
vehicle of consumption	living history participation	standardized movement through gallery	—
rhetorical/ ideological effect	validation of deep-suburban life-style (hegemonic)	validation of postmodern expertise and image control (hegemonic)	quasi-parodic exaggeration of postmodern touristic discourse (potentially counter-hegemonic)

NOTES

1. As of 1981 only eleven paintings and some drawings were actually owned by the museum.

2. Wyeth's private gallery on the third floor of his restored mill contained, according to caretaker George Heebner's 1981 estimate, between three and four million dollars worth of art. The Siri paintings, which constitute the Brandywine River Museum's major Wyeth acquisition, were purchased for 1.3 million.

3. Wyeth's Chadds Ford residence is an especially interesting and complicated manifestation of postmodern cultural production in the way it quite literally fuses image and reality. Add to this Wyeth's apparent fascination for miniature replications (of his own images and related objects), costuming, and dramatization, and

the "Wyeth phenomenon" begins to appear as something of a postmodern archetype. See Sanford 1972, which reports the opening to the public of the Olsen house that figures so prominently in Wyeth's Maine paintings. This property is the analogue of the Kuerner farm and its public display as a kind of museum makes explicit some underlying trends pervasive in Chadds Ford.

4. It is perhaps significant that Jamie Wyeth has recently distanced himself from the minority status implicated by the nickname and now prefers to be identified as James Wyeth on museum labels.

5. The new prominence of the latter type of painting is an interesting development. *Trompe l'oeil* is of course a style which creates at least a brief impression of three-dimensional reality. The images depicted often contain printed material and even mechanically reproduced images. In other words, they are often paintings about illusion and mechanical reproduction.

6. Eager to have his friend (and later tutor of his children) back in Chadds Ford, N. C. Wyeth assured the landlord that he would pay the rent if Sanderson, who by this time had no steady income, could not (Thompson 1973:294).

7. "Index" is, I believe, the semiotic category needed to account for Sanderson's collection. It refers to those sorts of things that stand for other things by virtue of a physical connection. An index points to, touches, or, most relevant here, is taken directly from the thing it represents. Indices, in short, are signs causally connected to their referents, but see Eco 1976:115–121.

Conclusion:
Self-Estrangements

At the beginning of this book I used the word "post-ethnographic," taking care to cage it in quotation marks. My simple contention is that the historical conditions of advanced consumer capitalism have occupied the ground upon which ethnography as a special enterprise has traditionally been based. In its everyday practice postmodernity absorbs the ethnographic game, dissolving the boundary between the site of ethnographic experience and the site of ethnographic writing. One of the most "disturbing" effects of this historical condition is the inevitable appearance of the ethnographer-as-already-written. In so far as I have taken up a stance that is somehow post-ethnographic, I find my position already occupied; a version of "myself" has already been preinscribed at the Site.

It is increasingly common to hear from ethnographers anecdotes about textual ambush at the field site, for example, the anthropologist whose key informant checks his cultural facts by producing from the hut a previously published ethnography, the very one the fieldworker has relied on to formulate his own questions (Clifford 1986:116). Under the regime of postmodernity this defamiliarizing shock becomes the constant and pervasive condition. It is not just that one can increasingly expect one's subjects to have access to the same texts one draws upon. In post-ethnographic practice one can expect one's Site to "include" figures already spontaneously positioned in the very role one has consciously adopted in theory. The effect of such encounters is a flash of sudden self-estrangement; a *frisson* that operates in an entirely different register than the slow process of reducing the difference between Self and Other that is typical of participant observation fieldwork and that often goes by the name of "establishing rapport."

The critical potential of traditional ethnography resides of course in its capacity to make the Self appear strange and the Other seem familiar. A post-ethnographic practice will strive to suspend the Self/Other dialectic altogether through a sustained recognition that the centered Subject is an historical production. The post-ethnographer's goal ought to be the strategic, critical appropriation of the potential energy of those flashes of radical self-estrangement, moments of epiphany, or *jouissance*, or vertigo in which one glimpses the dissolution of one's own ostensibly stable subjectivity *as* ethnographer.

As I implied at the end of Chapter 5, Chadds Ford's post-ethnographer *avant la lettre* is Chris Sanderson. I have presented him, or at least his projection in the institutional texts through which he now exists, as something like a hero in the self-consciously allegorical comparison of gallery displays. He represents an unincorporated region within the general text of Chadds Ford. Paradoxically, this region remains marginal because of its excessive, even fanatic staging of the very social formation in which the Site arises. Sanderson is above all the consummate souvenir hound, the hyper-tourist and quintessential antiquarian collector of fragments. His museum is the extended collage of these fragments brought quite literally out of the attic. It is the obsessive intensity of this practice that positions it as a potential moment of critical estrangement of the suburban/tourist social order so firmly set in place at Chadds Ford. Left to itself, this Sanderson-as-counterhegemonic text does not seriously disrupt the entrenched ideology of the Site. It is by no means actively oppositional. The present study can be seen as a kind of rewriting—a revision of the Sanderson text that foregrounds and elaborates its implicit critique of the reigning hegemony.

The radically de-centered condition of advanced consumer culture might incline one simply to throw up one's hands and admit the superfluity of the ethnographer's role. Or alternatively, one could continue on with business as usual. The justification here might be that the proven methods of rigorous, self-conscious ethnography are bound to produce more adequate studies than the "spontaneous" texts generated by the institutions of postmodernity itself. Good work can be done, and is being done, without paying much attention to the specific historical conditions within which all work in the west now occurs. The obvious problem with this position is that it leaves these current conditions themselves inaccessible to ethnographic recording, interpretation and, above all, critique.

If one would document postmodernity *as* postmodernity, some sort of shift is unavoidable. Whether we characterize this shift as a move to post-colonial ethnography, or meta-ethnography, or merely post-ethnography, it must occur if one wants to give an account of what is most distinctive about cultural production in the advanced capitalist order. That ethnography must shift its ground does not, however, diminish the importance of the general ethnographic impulse to concretize, to specify, to go and look, to record and gather, to mark the Site. Most crucially, in the absence of the close critical focus sustained by these impulses, moments of contradiction and potential forms of resistance, such as those reflected in Sanderson and, more evanescently, in Jaybird, will go unnoticed. My goal in this study has been to realize the ethnographic impulse in a way that constitutes one kind of response to the conditions of advanced consumer culture. Perhaps it is appropriate in this conclusion to be a little more specific about the conceptual position from which my writing proceeds.

As I suggested in Chapter 3, we are relatively well supplied with accounts of postmodernity that totalize it or reveal its characteristic operation in the broad movements of mass and elite culture. However, advanced consumer culture has hardly been accounted for at all in its local specificities. At least one opportunity open to the displaced ethnographer, then, is to locate himself/herself as a reader of the immediate institutional citations through which a specific Site is constituted in a particular historical context. The post-ethnographer positioned thus begins to look very much like Barthes's mythographer of ideological micro-climates. This is the position I have attempted to occupy in relation to Chadds Ford.

I have treated a Site "out there" as a kind of library, or better, an apparatus that exists for and through the management of texts; and I have imagined my task as two-fold: first, the formation of a collection—selecting and arranging; and then reading, or more specifically, reading critically as a rhetorician, looking for the "motivations" of the texts, reading them as historically situated. The post-ethnography I have tried to practice is a combination of these two positions: a position of collector/transcriber/collageist, and a position of rhetorician/reader—in other words, the dual role of re-citer/re-siter, one who "tells over again" and thereby "relocates" the already inscribed citations by inserting them into a new context, in effect rewriting them (cf. Tyler 1986:127).

The Site literally constituted in the process of auto-ethnography generates an apparently endless supply of indigenous ethnographic texts. Obviously part of the professional post-ethnographer's job is to cut out, gather up and "paste in" these texts. Of course ethnography in any form can be thought of as the activity of culture collecting (Clifford 1988:230–

236). But as a self-conscious ethnographic methodology, collecting has largely been compartmentalized as those particular operations best characterized as folkloric/antiquarian—the gathering of native texts and artifacts. Conceptually, this gathering of native texts, rethought as auto-ethnographic fragments, now becomes the main activity, not just one source of "data" among many. The post-ethnographer becomes the collector of (re)citations.

The presentation of such fragments needs to make visible the artifice of their production and the arbitrariness of their selection and arrangement. It is the nature of collections that they may be diminished, supplemented, rearranged, subjected to various taxonomic schemes, and so forth, though their artificiality is often suppressed. Post-ethnographic practice needs to remain aware that collection never results in the complete series or the irrefutable sequence, and the post-ethnographic text will need to leave visible the signs of the labor by which it was produced, taking care not to hide its seams too completely. In other words, the collage of auto-ethnographic fragments is one way to foreground the historicity or "writtenness" of the post-ethnographic text.

The second function of the post-ethnographic role is that of critical reader. Without it the activity of collection degenerates into merely the self-indulgent delectation of Sites and the post-ethnographer becomes indistinguishable from the tourist, a figure already closely connected in any case. That Sites like Chadds Ford are identifiable (identify themselves) *as* Sites suggests that the auto-ethnographies which constitute them collectively express and sustain particular ideologies. Although endlessly and circularly self-referential, the discourse of a Site like Chadds Ford effects specific legitimations. It serves to reproduce a hegemonic order through an identifiable rhetoric. The other task of the post-ethnographer, then, is to unpack the rhetorical strategies, to read critically the auto-ethnographic souvenirs and identify the suppressed mechanisms through which they produce their effects.

It is the typical fate of the souvenir to be lost in the attic, making room for the next attempt to recover and mark the moment of full presence that is always receding into the past (Stewart 1984:132–151). My goal in this study has been to counter the natural tendency of the souvenir by assembling an array of them into some kind of collage, thereby recovering them from the attic and turning them out for inspection, cross-referencing, critical reading. Perhaps my collection of fragments and my reading of their rhetorical strategies together constitute an extended example of the anti-souvenir. And here again Sanderson, or rather the gallery display at the Sanderson Museum, appears as a pre-inscription—my text as already written at the Site. In any case, my intention has been to counter the souvenir's inclination to restore "a conservative idealization of the past" (Ibid.:150), so as to make visible the moment of the souvenir's own ideological production.

Perhaps this is the place to dissociate the task taken up here from the task usually designated as "interpretive" (Marcus and Fischer 1986:25–40). When I say I have intended in this study to conduct critical "readings," I do not mean my goal is the discovery of meaning. The fragments in Chapter 1 can in no sense be taken as key symbols, with mysteries waiting to be unlocked to reveal the fundamental principles by which Chadds Ford culture operates. I hope it is clear that their selection and order of presentation are highly arbitrary. At every point one must imagine the possibility of infinite substitution. However sophisticated and compellingly executed, the interpretive mode operates in the service of more efficient consumption—consumption of books, of cultures, of scholarly reputations, and so on. The goal here, rather, has been to reveal the conditions of production of a Site, the conditions within which a certain order of meaning and truth arises.

In this same regard, I hope it is also clear that in identifying Chris Sanderson as a moment of potential disruption amid the otherwise smooth surfaces of the Site, I do not mean to imply that he occupies a position of authenticity, while all around him evaporates into insubstantiality. That would be to reintroduce a version of the very mystification Chadds Ford depends upon. What Sanderson represents is every bit as textual as anything else at the Site. The textual practice I associate with his name is decidedly out of keeping with the dominant discourse, but that fact is entirely situational and contingent upon the local conditions of cultural production. Only in the particular context of *this* postmodern microclimate does Sanderson show up as a potential counterforce. And it is only through some sort of ethnographic practice that his critical potential can be identified and deployed.

Some methodological implications follow from the foregoing discussion. In a post-ethnography two of anthropology's privileged field techniques for gathering information, participant observation and informant interview, will be conceptually demoted. These activities cease to be the indespensible criteria of ethnographic authority, since postmodernity undercuts the empirical premises of traditional western social science, most fundamental of which is the common sense assumption that experience equals knowledge. It should be apparent that I have not been particularly concerned with the lives of people who inhabit Chadds Ford, nor with the social relations and categories of specific subjects. I confess my goal here to be unashamedly anti-humanistic. I have been primarily concerned with "authorless" texts, that is to say, texts for which it is trivial to identify their immediate producers. I am interested in texts generated institutionally, texts in which hegemonic discourses are most obviously inscribed. If what I have done here is in some sense post-ethnographic, it of necessity dispenses with informants as centered subjects who "speak for themselves." In so far as I present informants, they should be taken as parables, as foci of textuality, as things spoken rather than speaking. If it is true that postmodernity entails the final triumph of the commodity through its effective invasion of the everyday, the Unconscious, the Primitive, indeed all spheres that heretofore seemed to have escaped its corrosion, then a post-ethnography must be aware of the commodification of subjectivity in the informant.

Although I did not consciously set out to write this case study of Chadds Ford with a particular intonation, in retrospect it appears to have one. Its tone, especially evident in the gathering of Chadds Ford souvenirs, seems to be in a register compounded of vague perplexity, that kind of "blank irony" (Jameson 1984:65) that presumes no authoritative position that is not itself susceptible to ironization, and, I suppose, a bit of perverse delight in the very weirdness of the Chadds Ford scene.[1] I also detect, I think, overtones of uneasiness, which arise perhaps from a sense that the texts of this Site seem themselves utterly innocent of perplexity, ironic detachment or the least glimmering that there is anything weird going on. Perhaps it is appropriate to conclude with a personal narrative that is dramatically flat but at the same time has a certain weirdness about it, a distinctly postmodern combination.

On one of many random tours of the Chadds Ford back roads, I headed my decaying Datsun two-door up the entrance lane to Spring Meadows. When new in 1968 the car had been blue, but by this time one of the doors was a green replacement, a back quarter-panel was mostly reddish putty, and rust patches had broken out here and there. The whole ensemble had a quality of pastiche. The day was fine and the development seemed deserted—no children cavorting in the open space, no workmen putting in sod or putting down shingles on the new homes, no photographer by the roadside. I was driving slowly, just meandering and getting the feel of the place. For someone who grew up in a suburban landscape, albeit a much more modest version than this one, it felt quite comfortable and familiar.

The way the roads curved, the spacing of homes, the rural prospect, all made it seem oddly like home.

To glance up and find my rearview mirror filled with the windshield and light assembly of a state patrol car seemed, after the first shock, like a special affront—even like some kind of betrayal. I continued on at reduced speed and the cruiser kept right there on my bumper. What had I done? How did the police get there so suddenly, as if from nowhere, and so far off the beaten path? Who had called in a report? Who had been watching me? After what seemed a very long time, I decided to force the issue and pulled onto the shoulder. The patrol car drew around without stopping and disappeared over the next knoll. That's the last I saw of it.

Of course this "encounter" is easy to explain and shouldn't be surprising. The state of my car, the unusual pace of my driving, even my presence there in the middle of a weekday made me a suspicious character. Yet the scene keeps coming back to me pregnant with textual possibilities, so I offer it here as the last of my souvenirs. I choose to read it with exaggerated portentousness as the moment in which my Site had me most clearly in *its* sights. It is the strongest indication I had that the suburbs are capable of turning on one of their own, or at least capable of returning my gaze, reading me in the process of reading it.

Though this encounter with forces of social control came to naught, evaporating into a non-event, Chadds Ford had in a sense long since issued me a citation. It is in the nature of the postmodern Site that it presents itself to be read. One might even say that is its reason for being. It addresses itself with "frank adhomination" to an audience of readers. More than that, its discourse is a distinctly "interpellant speech" that positions, which is to say constructs (or "writes") its readership (Barthes 1972[1957]:124–125). In this case study I have tried to read critically a deep suburb. Perhaps post-ethnography as a critical practice means no more than to resist the Site's inclination to inscribe its readership in particular ways. A patrol car briefly dogging my heels I take as the sign that I was not reading Chadds Ford exactly according to acceptable conventions of reception. At least I hope that is so.

NOTES

1. Dana Polan (1986:181–183) suggests that a "fundamental weirdness" is a constitutive feature of postmodern mass cultural sensibility. For a similar characterization, in this case with regard to contemporary trends in film, see J. Hoberman 1987. It may be that an effective post-ethnography will entail taking seriously as analytical categories such things as this fundamental weirdness.

References

Abrahams, Roger
1981   "Shouting Match at the Border." In *"And Other Neighborly Names": Social Process and Cultural Image in Texas Folklore*, ed. Richard Bauman and Roger Abrahams, 303–321. Austin: University of Texas Press.

Alloway, Lawrence
1967   "Critique: The Other Andy." *Arts Magazine* 61 (April): 20–21.

Anderson, Jay
1984   *Time Machines: The World of Living History*. Nashville, TN: The American Association for State and Local History.

Arac, Jonathan
1986   "Introduction." In *Postmodernism and Politics*, ed. Jonathan Arac, ix–xliii. Theory and History of Literature Series, vol. 28. Minneapolis: University of Minnesota Press.

Bakhtin, Mikhail
1968   *Rabelais and His World*. Trans. Hélène Iswolsky. Cambridge, MA: MIT Press.
1981   "Epic and Novel." In *The Dialogic Imagination: Four Essays by M. M. Bakhtin*, ed. Michael Holquist, 3–40. Austin: University of Texas Press.

Barthes, Roland.
1972   *Mythologies*. Trans. Annette Lavers. New York: Hill and
[1957] Wang.

Bascom, William
1976   "Changing African Art." In *Ethnic and Tourist Arts: Cultural Expressions from the Fourth World*, ed. Nelson H. H. Graburn, 303–319. Berkeley: University of California Press.

Baudrillard, Jean
1975   *The Mirror of Production*. Trans. Mark Poster. St. Louis: Telos Press.
1981   *For a Critique of the Political Economy of the Sign*. St. Louis: Telos Press.

Bell, Daniel
1976   *The Coming of Post-Industrial Society: A Venture in Social Forecasting*. New York: Basic Books.

Bernstein, Charles
1987   "Centering the Postmodern." *Socialist Review* 96:45–56.

Best, Steven
1987/88   "The Chicago Experience—The City as Hyperreal." *Social Text* 18:79–82.

Boggs, Carl
1976   *Gramsci's Marxism*. London: Pluto Press.

Boissonnade, P.
1950   *Life and Work in Medieval Europe*. Trans. Eileen Power. New York: Alfred A. Knopf.

Boyd, Gloria
1979/80   "Gas-Stingy Weekends—Wyeth's White World Near Philadelphia." *Discovery, Allstate Motor Club Magazine* (Winter):28–30.

Breininger, Lester
1973   "The Lure of Tinsmithing." *Pennsylvania Folklife* 22 (festival supplement):36–37.

Bruno, Giuliana
1987   "Ramble City: Postmodernism and *Blade Runner*." *October* 41:61–74.

Canby, Henry Seidel
1941   *The Brandywine*. Exton, PA: Schiffer Limited.

Clifford, James
1986   "On Ethnographic Allegory." In *Writing Culture: The Poetics and Politics of Ethnography*, ed. James Clifford and George Marcus, 98–121. Berkeley: University of California Press.
1988   *The Predicament of Culture: Twentieth Century Ethnography, Literature, and Art*. Cambridge, MA: Harvard University Press.

Clifford, James, and George Marcus, eds.
1986   *Writing Culture: The Poetics and Politics of Ethnography*. Berkeley: University of California Press.

Cocchiara, Giuseppe
1981   *The History of Folklore in Europe*. Trans. John N. McDaniel. Phil-
[1952]   adelphia: Institute for the Study of Human Issues.

Corn, Wanda
1973   *The Art of Andrew Wyeth*. Boston: New York Graphic Society.

Crimp, Douglas
1983   "On the Museum's Ruins." In *The Anti-Aesthetic: Essays on Postmodern Culture*, ed. Hal Foster, 43–56. Port Townsend, WA: Bay Press.

Danielson, Larry
1972   "The Ethnic Festival and Cultural Revivalism in a Small Midwestern Town." Ph.D. dissertation, Indiana University.

Davis, Mike
1985   "Urban Renaissance and the Spirit of Postmodernism." *New Left Review* 151:106–113.
1987   *"Chinatown*, Part Two? The 'Internationalization' of Downtown Los Angeles." *New Left Review* 164:65–86.
Debord, Guy
1970   *The Society of the Spectacle.* Chicago: University of Chicago Press.
Dierolf, Claude E.
1953   "The Pageant Drama and American Pageantry." Ph.D. dissertation, University of Pennsylvania.
Eagleton, Terry
1986   "Capitalism, Modernism and Postmodernism." In *Against the Grain: Selected Essays,* 131–147. London: Verso.
Eco, Umberto
1976   *The Theory of Semiotics.* Bloomington: Indiana University Press.
1986   *Travels in Hyperreality.* Trans. William Weaver. San Diego: Harcourt, Brace, Jovanovich.
Eisenstadt, S. N.
1972   "Post-Traditional Societies and the Continuity and Reconstruction of Tradition." In *Post-Traditional Societies,* ed. S. N. Eisenstadt, 1–27. New York: W. W. Norton & Company.
Gadamer, Hans-Georg
1975   *Truth and Method.* New York: Continuum Press.
Gitlin, Todd
1986   "We Build Excitement." In *Watching Television,* ed. Todd Gitlin, 136–161. New York: Pantheon Books.
Gitlin, Todd, ed.
1986   *Watching Television.* New York: Pantheon Books.
Glassie, Henry
1968   *Patterns in the Material Culture of the Eastern United States.* Philadelphia: University of Pennsylvania Press.
Graburn, Nelson H. H.
1976   "Introduction: Arts of the Fourth World." In *Ethnic and Tourist Arts: Cultural Expressions from the Fourth World,* ed. Nelson H. H. Graburn, 1–32. Berkeley: University of California Press.
Gregory, C. A.
1982   *Gifts and Commodities.* New York: Academic Press.
Gutowski, John
1977   "American Folklore and Modern American Community Festival: A Case Study of 'Turtle Days' in Churubusco, Indiana." Ph.D. dissertation, Indiana University.
Hammond, Catherine
1983   "A Restored Pennsylvania Farmhouse." *Early American Life* (April):37–42.
Handler, Mimi
1983   "American Design at Home." *Early American Life* (April):20–25.
Heathcote, C. W.
1932   *A History of Chester County, Pennsylvania.* Harrisburg, PA: National Historical Association.

Hebdige, Dick
1979   *Subculture: The Meaning of Style.* London: Methuen.
Herder, Johann Gottfried von
1968   *Reflections on the Philosophy of the History of Mankind.* Abridged
[1784–   and trans. Frank E. Manuel. Chicago: University of Chicago
91]   Press.
Herron, Jerry
1987/88   "Detroit: Postmodernism Ground Zero." *Social Text* 18:61– 77.
Hobsbawm, Eric and Terence Ranger, eds.
1983   *The Invention of Tradition.* Cambridge: Cambridge University
            Press.
Hosmer, Charles B., Jr.
1965   *Presence of the Past: A History of the Preservation Movement in
            the United States Before Williamsburg.* New York: Putnam's.
Hoving, Thomas
1978   *Two Worlds of Andrew Wyeth.* Boston: Houghton Mifflin.
Hughes, M. L. Chandler and Freida W. McMullan
1982   *Ye West Side of the Brandywine.* Kennett Square, PA: KNA Press.
Huyssen, Andreas
1986   *After the Great Divide: Modernism, Mass Culture, Postmodernism.*
            Bloomington: Indiana University Press.
Hyde, Lewis
1979   *The Gift: Imagination and the Erotic Life of Property.* New York:
            Vintage Books.
Jacobs, Jay
1967   "Andrew Wyeth—An Unsentimental Reappraisal." *Art in Amer-
            ica* 55 (Jan./Feb.): 24–31.
Jacobs, Jerry
1984   *The Mall: An Attempted Escape from Everyday Life.* Prospect
            Heights, IL: Waveland Press.
Jakobson, Cathryn
1987   "Wyeth Country." *Signature* (April):102–109, 118.
Jameson, Frederic
1984a   "The Cultural Logic of Late Capitalism." *New Left Review* 144:
            53–92.
1984b   "Periodizing the 60s." In *The 60s Without Apology,* ed. Sohnya
            Sayres, Anders Stephanson, Stanley Aronowitz, Frederic Jame-
            son, 178–209. Minneapolis: University of Minnesota Press.
Jencks, Charles
1986   *What Is Post-Modernism?* London: St. Martin's Press.
Jones, Michael Owen
1975   *The Hand Made Object and Its Maker.* Berkeley: University of
            California Press.
Kuh, Katherine
1986   "Why Wyeth?" *The Saturday Review* 51 (Oct. 26): 26–29.
Kumar, Krishan
1978   *Prophecy and Progress: The Sociology of Industrial and Post-In-
            dustrial Society.* London: Penguin.
Lemon, James T.
1972   *The Best Poor Man's Country: A Geographical Study of South-
            eastern Pennsylvania.* New York: W. W. Norton.

Logsden, Gene
1971　　*Wyeth People*. Garden City, NY: Doubleday & Company, Inc.
Lowenthal, David
1979　　"Age and Artifact: Dilemmas of Appreciation." In *The Interpretation of Ordinary Landscapes*, ed. D. W. Meinig, 103–128. New York: Oxford University Press.
Lynch, Kevin
1972　　*What Time Is This Place?* Cambridge, MA: MIT Press.
MacCannell, Dean
1976　　*The Tourist: A New Theory of the Leisure Class*. New York: Schocken Books.
1979　　"Ethnosemiotics." *Semiotica* 27:149–171.
MacKaye, Percy
1912　　*The Civic Theater in Its Relation to the Redemption of Leisure*. New York: Mitchell Kennerly.
McMullan, Mary
1980　　*School Days by the Brandywine*. n.p.
Mainardi, Patricia
1987　　"Postmodern History at Musée d'Orsay." *October* 41:31–52.
Malinowski, Bronislaw
1961　　*Argonauts of the Western Pacific*. New York: E. P. Dutton.
[1922]
Marcus, George and Michael M. J. Fischer
1986　　*Anthropology as Cultural Critique*. Chicago: University of Chicago Press.
Marx, Leo
1964　　*The Machine in the Garden: Technology and the Pastoral Ideal in America*. London: Oxford University Press.
Mauss, Marcel
1976　　*The Gift: Forms and Functions of Exchange in Archaic Societies*.
[1925]　 Trans. Ian Cunnison. New York: W. W. Norton & Company.
Meryman, Richard
1973　　"Andrew Wyeth: An Interview." In *The Art of Andrew Wyeth*, ed. Wanda Corn, 45–79. Boston: New York Graphic Society.
Meyer, Susan
1975　　*American Artist* (February, Special Issue on Wyeth family).
Miller, Mark Crispin
1986　　"Deride and Conquer." In *Watching Television*, ed. Todd Gitlin, 183–228. New York: Pantheon Books.
Morse, Margaret
1985　　"Talk, Talk, Talk." *Screen* 26:2–17.
Muller, Peter O.
1982　　"Everyday Life in Suburbia: A Review of Changing Social and Economic Forces That Shape Daily Rhythms Within the Outer City." *American Quarterly* 34:262–277.
O'Doherty, Brian
1973　　"A Visit to Wyeth Country." In *The Art of Andrew Wyeth*, ed. Wanda Corn, 14–43. Boston: New York Graphic Society.
Pfeil, Fred
1986　　"Postmodernism and Our Discontents." *Socialist Review* 87/88:125–134.

Pieper, Josef
1970   *Ueberlieferung: Begriff und Anspruch.* Munich: Kosel-Verlag.

Pitz, Henry C.
1969   *The Brandywine Tradition.* Boston: Houghton Mifflin.

Polan, Dana
1986   "Brief Encounters: Mass Culture and the Evacuation of Sense."
        In *Studies in Entertainment: Critical Approaches to Mass Culture*,
        ed. Tania Modleski, 167–187. Bloomington: Indiana University
        Press.

Rabinow, Paul
1986   "Representations Are Social Facts: Modernity and Post-
        Modernity in Anthropology." In *Writing Culture*, ed. James Clif-
        ford and George Marcus, 234–261. Berkeley: University of Cal-
        ifornia Press.

Riesman, David
1958   "Leisure and Work in Post-Industrial Society." In *Mass Leisure*,
        ed. Eric Larrabee and Rolf Meyersohn, 363–385. Glencoe, IL:
        The Free Press.

Robacker, Earl F. and Ada F.
1974   "Metalcrafting at the Folklife Festival." *Pennsylvania Folklife* 23
        (festival supplement):48–56.

Rose, Dan
1982   "The Brandywine: A Case Study of an Ecological Strategy."
        VIA:75–83.

Ryerson, Scott H.
1976   "Seri Ironwood Carving: An Economic View." In *Ethnic and
        Tourist Arts*, ed. Nelson H. H. Graburn, 119–136. Berkeley: Uni-
        versity of California Press.

Sanford, Jean
1972   "And the House Wyeth Painted, Too." *New York Times*, 6
        August: 7,13.

Schjeldahl, Peter
1986   "Welcome to Helgaland." *Art in America* (Oct.):11, 13.

Shils, Edward
1971   "Tradition." *Comparative Studies in Language and Literature*
        13:122–159.
1981   *Tradition.* Chicago: University of Chicago Press.

Sorkin, Michael
1986   "Faking It." In *Watching Television*, ed. Todd Gitlin, 162–182.
        New York: Pantheon Books.

Stephanson, Anders
1987   "Regarding Postmodernism—A Conversation with Frederic
        Jameson." *Social Text* 17:29–54.

Stewart, Susan
1984   *On Longing: Narratives of the Miniature, the Gigantic, the Sou-
        venir, the Collection.* Baltimore: The Johns Hopkins University
        Press.

Taylor, Bayard
1866   *The Story of Kennett.* New York: Putnam's.

Thompson, Thomas R.
1973   *Chris: A Biography of Christian C. Sanderson*. Philadelphia: Dorrance and Company.
Tyler, Stephen A.
1986   "Post-Modern Ethnography: From Document of the Occult to Occult Document." In *Writing Culture*, ed. James Clifford and George Marcus, 122–140. Berkeley: University of California Press.
Ulmer, Gregory
1984   "The Object of Post-Criticism." In *The Anti-Aesthetic: Essays on Postmodern Culture*, ed. Hal Foster, 83–110. Port Townsend, WA: Bay Press.
Varenne, Hervé
1986   "Doing Anthropology in America." In *Symbolizing America*, ed. Hervé Varenne, 341–345. Lincoln: University of Nebraska Press.
Wainwright, Loudon
1967   "The Mass Sport of Wyeth Watching." *Life* 62 (March 10):27.
Wallace, Michael
1981   "Visiting the Past: History Museums in the United States." *Radical History Review* 25:62–96.
Warner, W. Lloyd
1959   *The Living and the Dead: A Study of Symbolic Life in America*. New Haven: Yale University Press.
Williams, Raymond
1977   *Marxism and Literature*. London: Oxford University Press.
1983   *Key Words*. Revised edition. London: Oxford University Press.
Williamson, Judith
1979   *Decoding Advertisements: Ideology and Meaning in Advertising*. London: Marion Boyars.
1986   *Consuming Passions: The Dynamics of Popular Culture*. London: Marion Boyars.
Wyeth, Betsy
1976   *Wyeth at Kuerners*. Boston: Houghton Mifflin.
1979   *The Stray*. New York: Farrar, Strauss, Giroux.

Index